PSYCHIATRY
AND MENTAL HEALTH

By

JOHN RATHBONE OLIVER

M.D., PH.D.

*Associate in the History of Medicine at the
Johns Hopkins University, Baltimore
Author of "Foursquare," "Victim and Victor," and "Fear"*

To ALL
PARISH PRIESTS, SEMINARIANS
MINISTERS AND SOCIAL WORKERS
WHO ARE LABORING
TO HELP THE BROKEN IN HEART
AND TO FIND
A MEDICINE TO HEAL
THEIR SICKNESS

PREFACE

The material of this book, which contains the Hale Lectures for 1932 delivered at the Western Theological Seminary in Evanston, has been carefully prepared for the press. Although each chapter represents a lecture, nevertheless each chapter contains more material than could possibly have been presented during the single period allowed for a lecture at the Seminary. This is especially true of the Clinical Material printed at the end of every chapter.

This book is addressed to clergymen, seminary students, and social workers—in fact to any persons without definite medical training and experience whose work brings them in touch with the mental illnesses and maladjustments of their fellow men. Fortunately, medical science has made great advances during recent years in its attitude towards and its knowledge of the subject. My readers obviously cannot assume the regular practice of psychiatry, but it is hoped that this book will help them to recognize some of the more common ailments, and will give some assistance in knowing how such cases should be (and should not be) handled. The physician cannot readily seek out his patients—they must come to him; whereas the true pastor or social worker is able to do much in the way of prevention. This very fact makes a knowledge of mental illness a proper part of his equipment. Some of a pastor's most important work is done in personal conference in his study. These lectures were delivered and this book was published with a view to making such conferences more effective.

My thanks are due to Doctor W. R. Reynell, a member of the Royal Society of Medicine in London, who graciously gave me permission to quote from one of his valuable articles. I am grateful to Doctor William A. White of St. Elizabeth's Hospital, Washington, who permitted me to quote extensively from his *Outlines of Psychiatry* and who has been willing to read the proof of several chapters.

To the publishers I am deeply indebted for the care and the interest that has been unstintingly given to the preparation of this book for the press. Finally I wish to thank my secretary, Miss Sara Katherine Caulk, for her patience and zeal in the copying of my manuscript which was a long and often disheartening task.

I realize only too deeply that my presentation of Pastoral Psychiatry is often inadequate. Some people will find it too simple and will feel that I have diluted objective science with an emotional popular appeal. Others may think that I have written in too technical and too difficult a manner. Between these two groups however I trust that there will be people who will find the book helpful and who will not hesitate to send me any suggestions or corrections that may occur to them. After all, my only desire is to be of use to others and to place at their disposal my own knowledge and experience.

J. R. O.

CONTENTS

FOREWORD

To be numbered among the Hale Lecturers of the Western Theological Seminary—to take however humble a place in the list of distinguished men who have brought so much glory to this ancient foundation—is an honor that the writer finds rather heavy for his slender shoulders. He realizes only too well that he is neither a theologian nor a learned student of Christian morality; that he is not a profound nor even a well-trained psychologist. But he has dared to undertake the burden of the task set before him, not because of any innate ability to achieve it, but because it so happens that through no achievement of his own, he chances to be both physician and priest, a practicing psychiatrist with a certain amount of experience, a medical historian and at the same time an unworthy representative of the Catholic priesthood. In no one of these three fields can he claim to have attained to distinction. But the chance combination in one personality of three forms of human activity, that are usually separated, makes him a logical, if not a particularly able source of information on certain problems that have become deeply interesting to men and women of to-day.

It is in this spirit that these lectures have been prepared and the book written. It makes no pretense of being a scientific treatise on mental disease and mental difficulties in general; but it is hoped that it may form a sort of introduction to such scientific sources. If it has any value at all, this value must lie in the personal experience in dealing with human personalities that came to the writer during many years of psychiatric practice. Moreover, it is intended to fill a gap between the scientific text-books on mental illness, and the ordinary standard works on moral and pastoral theology.

To-day, the seminarian or clergyman who is anxious to become a really sage physician of souls finds little help in the accepted treatises on Moral Theology when forced to deal with various types of individuals who are suffering in different ways either from mental disease or from imperfect adjustments to the duties of their every-day lives. On the other hand, the seminarian, the parish priest—the social case worker too—are not properly equipped to understand and to absorb the details of psychiatric treatises written in medical language and intended for medical men. Often they fall between these two stools and in falling, they make one or another of two mistakes. They either imagine that the dealing with difficult individualities is merely a matter of sanctified common sense, requiring no study and no experience, or else they get imperfect knowledge and very faulty understanding from books that are written "for the general public"—books about "What every young man should know" or "What the married woman should be told."

If these lectures succeed in giving the puzzled pastor some fairly definite knowledge of his "difficult parishioners"—of his patients with sick souls and fear-infected minds—the writer will be more than content.

A great portion of the material on which the content of this book is based has stood the test of use. Some of it has been employed as a foundation for numerous short conferences with the clergy of various dioceses on "What the parish priest should know about mental illnesses." It has also been presented to larger groups of men and women, of priests and laymen, during several summer conferences. It has been moulded and altered, arranged and rearranged to meet varying needs, until unnecessary and uninteresting material has been excluded and only such material retained as may really illustrate the points under discussion. But a greater amount of the material is fresh; and at least the manner of presentation is new altogether.

At the end of each chapter the reader will find Clinical Material—descriptions of cases that will, it is hoped, help to illustrate clearly the matters discussed in the lecture itself. This clinical material might be greatly extended. But the writer feels that the cases he has given will afford the reader fair pictures of the varying types of human beings who will most often seek out his aid as their parish priest or spiritual director.

The writer is deeply grateful to the Hale committee, not only for the honor of the lectureship, but also for giving him—for making for him an opportunity of putting into print a great deal of material that has been worked over and over again in his mind during the past ten years, but that he has never had time to reduce to writing.

Finally, the writer desires to end this Foreword in the same way that he has ended many conferences on the subjects which this book attempts to treat. He hopes that any one who hears these lectures, or reads them in print, will always consider the writer as a permanent lecturer, a lasting advisor, a persistent friend. If, in days to come, in their parishes, in their social work or even in their own homes, any case should come up on which they feel the need of help and advice the writer trusts that they will not hesitate to consult him. If he is still in this world, he promises to answer their letters to the best of his ability. He wants them to feel that the relationship, begun here during the short period of these lectures, is to be a lasting relationship. If there is ever anything that he can do for any one of them, he hopes that they will not hesitate to let him know. For every letter that he receives from readers of this book will not be, as one might think, an additional burden; it will be, on the other hand, a happy renewal of pleasant memories, memories of Evanston and of all the kindness and friendship that this name must always connote to any man who has once stood before you as one of the lecturers on the Hale Foundation.

Whatever the writer has written here, he submits, without

any reservation, to the criticism of wiser and abler psychiatrists
and physicians than himself. Above all, he submits it to the
judgment of the great Mother Church of the English-speaking
peoples, to whom he owes so deep, so lasting a debt, as one of
the least worthy of her many sons.

J. R. O.

PSYCHIATRY
AND MENTAL HEALTH

CHAPTER I

THE GENERAL FIELD AND ITS POSSIBILITIES

LIMITATIONS OF OUR FIELD OF INTEREST. CHRISTIAN BEHAVIOR AND MORAL THEOLOGY. CLINICAL MATERIAL, CASE HISTORIES, SUGGESTIONS FOR RECORD-KEEPING AND OUTLINES FOR THE EXAMINATION OF PATIENTS

OUR age is vividly interested in the whole question of behavior. Just as a repressed object or chain of thought tends to turn into a tormenting obsession, so those types of behavior, which were so rigidly repressed for the sake of a social ideal by our Victorian grandparents, have become to-day the obsessions of our younger generation. Obsessions of freedom, of self-expression, of sex, of speech and thought. We are obsessed by the determination to be behavioristically free; we are constantly calling attention to the fact of our freedom by doing all kinds of noticeable things; we feel impelled to prove our freedom to ourselves, because, in our heart of hearts, we are afraid that we may not be entirely free after all. We are like a woman who fears that she is losing her husband's love, and who is obsessed by a desire to hurt him in little ways, merely in order to prove to herself that he still loves her, because she still has the power to hurt and to annoy. For it is only those we love who can hurt us and who know exactly how to do it.

We are not greatly interested in what people *believe,* or in what they *think.* We are, on the other hand, greatly impressed by what they *do*—by their behavior. The anxious parents of to-day are not much upset by what sons and daughters think; their offspring might cherish the extremest of radical philosophies without causing much anxiety at home. But protesting hands go up in the air when thought is translated into action.

The public smoking of a cigarette or the use of a lipstick or a pocket-flask are infinitely more appalling than the most perverse habits of thought. Behavior—good or bad—is what we are interested in.

The type of so-called philosophy which is nowadays most popular among young people, which appeals most strongly to the undergraduate, the young business man, the active modern young woman, no matter how severely the system may be criticized by erudite professors, is called Behaviorism.[1]

It may seem that no two systems of human thought could lie further apart than Behaviorism, as we know it to-day, and that other system of behavior that we call Moral Theology, which has its roots far back in the Christian past and may almost be said to have had its beginnings in the writings of the early Fathers.[2] And yet both systems are primarily interested in behavior. Behaviorism regards the activities of human bodies and of human minds as the objective results of the reactions of heredity and environment upon the entity that we call the human individual. These results are said to be as assured and as inevitable as the electric current created by the action of certain chemicals on zinc; as inevitable as the fact that given the number four and the number six, the sum of the two will be ten and the product twenty-four. Moral Theology is also a science of human behavior, but a type of behavior that is outlawed by the Behaviorist; namely, behavior that is based upon a postulated freedom of choice which makes it possible for the individual to direct his or her actions towards a certain end.

[1]Like most philosophical systems it is to a great degree hall-marked by the human personality that first developed it; just as the Kantian system was the expression of Kant's own mental reactions to life. But one-man systems of thought are seldom broadly based enough to become applicable or helpful to masses of varied individuals. Behaviorism is popular to-day among young people because it appeals to their present obsession of moral irresponsibility.

[2]See *Tertullien et Saint Cyprien* by L. Bayard, in the very useful collection entitled *Les Moralistes Chretiens*. (For additional bibliographical details of books mentioned in the footnotes see the Bibliography.)

It is difficult to see why our modern age, with its obsession of freedom, its impatience of restraint, should find any attraction or help in Behaviorism, which in itself is the negation of freedom of action and is merely a newfangled way of evading moral responsibility by covering with a few flowers of psychological experiment the old hard chains of deterministic slavery. Our freedom-obsessed age might find a much more congenial atmosphere in a system of thought based on the possibility of free choice, even though this freedom may have been made to seem illusory by the preceding acts of an agent once free, but which has gradually enslaved itself in the machinery of habit formation.

If then theology be the science of the knowledge of God, and if morals be the study of a behavior that is the result of a more or less free choice, then moral theology must have for its object the study of human behavior, in so far as that behavior is directed to the attainment of a supernatural end—God— and is regulated by standards that have themselves a supernatural origin.

These chapters, however, do not dwell on the broad or the detailed domains of moral theology, as that term is generally understood, for we are interested only in a single, rather restricted field of human behavior. We are attempting to fill in a gap, to deal with types of behavior that were not properly understood in the past, that are seldom dealt with in books on moral theology, but that may become the causes of endless unhappiness and tragedy unless the modern pastor and social worker, as well as the modern physician, will take the trouble to study and to recognize these types whenever he meets them in the course of his daily life.

Therefore we shall not busy ourselves with the foundations of morals or of moral theology, or even of psychology; that is, with the nature of integrated personality, with concepts of consciousness or of the subconscious mind and its activities, with conscience and the existence of a moral law. You should know, of course, where to find modern explanations of such weighy matters, and so in the Appendix to this book I refer you to important works listed under several general classifications.[3] This brief survey of recommended reading is more than a bibliography as that word is usually understood. It will acquaint you with important contributions which the student of moral behavior must be somewhat familiar with, and I cannot begin my task without informing you, in rather a sketchy way, concerning these works. In all or most of these the writers tend to assume an imaginary norm of human behavior, a type of reaction that may fairly be demanded of "normal personalities." In this book, however, we are not intending to study any such imaginary norm of Christian behavior. We are not interested in what everybody ought to do because it is normal and right; but we are interested in what many people do in spite of their knowledge of right and wrong, in spite of themselves, in spite of their heredity, their environment, their training. In other words we are to deal with human behavior, not as the result of a perfectly conscious choice of action, but with behavior that is influenced by processes and conditions over which the individual has little or, at best, only partial control. Such types of human activity that lie between the extremes of clear free consciousness of choice and complete irresponsible mechanical reaction, really make up the greater part of our daily lives; yet they are often so camouflaged by our own sense of mental freedom that we ourselves do not recognize them for what they are. Moreover, the misunderstanding of them is often the cause of many human tragedies; the fear of them torments thousands of human minds; and the effort to deal with them by pretending that they do not exist often keeps men and women tense, unhappy, imperfectly adjusted to the work of their daily lives, unable to develop the best elements in their personali-

[3]See pp. 303 ff. for these classifications, the works listed thereunder, and full comment concerning the books mentioned.

ties and to do their utmost in a world that needs so keenly the finest efforts, the widest usefulness, even the greatest happiness of every one of its inhabitants.

The parish minister, if he is to be a true pastor, a real spiritual guide, a lover and a physician of souls, must have a knowledge of these types of behavior and some technique attained by study, experience, or personal gifts that will make it possible for him to deal with them. So should the social worker. These two groups more perhaps than any others could help thousands of distressed people to a deeper understanding of themselves, and so to the gradual acquisition of a more perfect adjustment, of a more adequate self-control. There need be no conflict between the pastor and the psychiatrist. Indeed, if the pastor did but realize his opportunities, it would be the psychiatrist who would envy the pastor and not *vice versa;* for the pastor comes into contact with his people in an easy intimate way that is seldom possible for the practicing psychiatrist. We physicians, as a general rule, never see a man or woman, who is battling with mental difficulties until those difficulties have become so great that normal habits of reticence are broken down, and the man or woman in question has made up his or her mind to be merely man or woman no longer and to become "a patient." Many people even to-day are afraid of physicians, afraid to enter a doctor's office, no matter how great their physical discomfort may be. They are afraid of what "the doctor may say"; afraid that this dull ache in their chest may really be an organic disease of the heart; that this constant sense of oppression after eating may be a sure symptom of gastric carcinoma. Of course, there are other people who have "the doctor habit"—a very bad habit indeed—and who are constantly rushing from one physician's office to another; but they are a minority. The average man or woman is still afraid that he or she may enter a physician's office with an uncomfortable pain in the back, and come out again with Bright's disease or diabetes. And if this fear is present in physical matters, how acute must it be in mental conditions, when it is not the digestion or the heart that is giving trouble, but the mind—the personality itself. Where one person is afraid of a surgeon or an internist, there are thousands who are terrified at the mere thought of a psychiatrist—a mind doctor—an alienist—a specialist in craziness and insanity.

Therefore we psychiatrists usually never see a mental patient until the mental difficulty has developed to such a degree that it can no longer be borne, or else interferes so definitely with the patient's daily life that he or she can no longer function at all. But the parish pastor—the spiritual guide—and the social worker have opportunities that to the physician are completely denied. The pastor who knows his people ought to be such a well-trained physician of the soul that he could recognize at once some mental maladjustment, some permanent source of anxiety, some obsession or tormenting phobia, as well as appreciate any unusual mental reaction that may be the forerunner of some definite mental illness. This would apply in a large degree to the social worker. Of course neither of them could attempt to treat mental disease—that is not their province; but they should be able to recognize the impending symptoms and send the patient to a psychiatrist or a mental clinic, and so not only prevent some tragedy but give the patient himself a greater chance of recovery. In the domain of what we call mental maladjustments, however, among the obsessions and inhibitions and phobias, the pastor and social worker should often be able to check the development of such mental habits before they reach a stage that demands specialized advice and help. There is a wide field for them here, a field of work and of achievement.

I count among my friends one priest who is neither a physician nor a psychiatrist, but who has spent several years working in a great mental hospital and following lectures on psychology at a famous university. He describes himself very humbly as a "young priest who is interested in mental difficulties." Often I have sent to him patients of mine who were either recovering from some mental illness or tormented by some mental difficulty, and he has been wonderfully successful with many such cases. My medical colleagues criticize me severely because I am encouraging a layman to practice medicine. I am doing nothing of the kind. I am sending certain types of unhappy, anxious or mentally ill people to a man who is a better psychologist than I am, who loves souls and who, as a priest, has something to give distracted and tormented people that the most distinguished psychiatrist does not possess. Because even the most distinguished psychiatrist is not a priest. I mention this fact, merely to show you how good a physician of souls a modern priest may become.

But the ordinary seminarian who is trying to train himself along these lines constantly complains that although books are all very well, you cannot learn from them alone how to deal with the intimate mental machinery of modern men and women. I have heard with the greatest satisfaction that at least one large state hospital takes into its wards, as student orderlies, a certain number of theological students and gives them, during the months of each summer, an opportunity to study mental cases at first hand. As a rule, however, such opportunities are rare. The seminarian must, to some degree, depend on books. But these books must try to do something more than give the student a mass of classifications and symptoms. The best way to afford a seminarian some idea of mental illness would be to shut him up for three hours each day in the history room of a mental hospital and to let him study there the case records of various types of mental patients. However, history rooms are usually most jealously guarded penetralia. We must, therefore, bring our history rooms into our books. We must make the student see, not cases of manic-depressive psychoses, not cases of schizophrenia, but men and women—individuals like himself—who

have had attacks of depression or who are at present developing schizophrenic symptoms. So I shall try to create a case
history room of our own. I cannot treat you as if you were
attending a mental clinic and present to you in the flesh various types of patients; but I can attempt to set before you the
mental histories of some cases: histories that may make it
easier for you to understand the type of illness or maladjustment with which we are dealing at the moment.

Above all, let me impress upon you the necessity of individ-
ualizing our moral theology in practice. You must not take the
rules and regulations of the Christian life—the laws and the
obligations of morals—and then apply them indifferently to
every penitent, to every person who seeks your guidance.
That, to my mind, has been the great weakness of Roman
moral theology. Its whole tone is too objectively legalistic, too
general. Each law, each rule, is split up into thousands of subheads. There is more than enough particularizing of the law
itself; but as a general rule there is no relative application to
the immense variations of human personalities, habits and
peculiarities.

Two boys are brought to you by their parents. Both have
been dishonest and stolen money from their employers. John
has never done such a thing before—dishonesty has been
absolutely foreign to his nature. And because this is his "first
offense" you are tempted to judge him more leniently than
you judge James, who has been a pilferer from childhood,
whose family have always had to cover up his petty thefts
and whom you are tempted to classify as an habitual offender.
As a matter of fact, John's offense is by far the more serious.
He has had no well-formed habit of thieving to fight against.
In order to steal he has had to break down all the resistances
to dishonesty that have been built up by the practice of years
of honesty. If the temptation offered to both James and
John were the same, then James is to be more softly dealt
with than John. For James it is almost impossible to resist tak-

ing any money that may be lying around. You do not hear
of the many times that he has resisted, but only of his fall.
Yet, if you individualize the case still further you may find
that the temptation was *not* the same. That James merely
wanted money to buy candy; while John needed it to cover
up the difficulties of some friend to whom he was emotionally
devoted. But, as a general thing, stealing is no real temptation
to John. To James it has become such a habit that he steals
almost automatically. The same law against dishonesty has to
be applied to these two individuals in quite different ways.

The same thing is especially true in the realm of sexual
reactions. The woman who from early adolescence has acquired habits of yielding to sexual desire and who later begins to make a definite fight against this habitual satisfaction,
has to face resistance to an urge that, humanly speaking, is
almost unconquerable. When she does fall, her fault is ethi-
cally unimportant in comparison with the fall of another girl
who has been brought up in a very guarded atmosphere and
who can only reach the act of indulgence by breaking down
the continent habits of many years. To one of these girls the
sexual act presents itself with such physical domination, the
result of many habitual lapses, that she has scarcely time in
which to realize what she is doing and has no power to
hold herself back when once the first steps toward satisfaction
have been taken.

You cannot judge these and similar cases justly unless you
know the past lives of your penitents; unless you know them
as individuals; unless you are familiar with the reactions, the
mental habits, the trains of thought that have made your
penitent or your parishioner what he or she now is, and
that make him or her different from the other members of
your congregation.

We have come to recognize this need in medicine. Not so
very long ago the average physician was a pure materialist;
he was not interested in anything that he could not taste or

touch or see or hear. The mind was not approachable by way of the senses, hence he paid little or no attention to the mind. He shut it up in a water-tight compartment and turned it over to a small group of his colleagues whom he called "alienists," and who were not considered to be on quite the same level as practicing physicians. If you read medical books of the early Victorian period, you will find almost nothing in them about the influence on bodily symptoms of what these writers used to call "the Mind." The result was quite what might have been expected; and modern medicine is occasionally inheriting the sins of its forefathers in the shape of Christian Science.

Christian Science, like the early heresies of Christendom, developed as a protest against a neglect of the mental elements in disease and as an emphasis, an extreme illogical emphasis no doubt, upon the influence of "mind over matter." But modern medicine is learning its lesson. Not so many years ago patients were classified and dealt with roughly in the following way. In some large out-patient department, for instance, routine examinations would be made and each patient ticketed with a definite classification. All the T. B. patients would be put in one group, the cardiac patients in another, the patients with kidney diseases in still another group, and so on *ad infinitum*. Then, after this group arrangement had been made, all the T. B. patients would be treated according to the rules for treating tuberculosis; the cardiac patients would be dealt with according to the accepted methods of treating "heart disease." It was only gradually that physicians began to understand how unscientific such a method was; for if *you* have tuberculosis and I am suffering from the same thing, then *your* tuberculosis reactions are not the same as mine, nor can they be treated absolutely in the same way. I am not you; neither are you exactly another copy of myself. We are two very divergent personalities, with different strains of heredity, brought up in different environments, trained according to varying habit-formations, and exposed to different sources of mental and physical stress. Your *locus minoris resistentiae* is not mine. Where you have a "spot of lessened resistance," I have an unbroken wall of defense; and so you and I react to our tuberculosis in entirely different ways, both mentally and physically. Therefore, until I *know* you as a personality, until I have a detailed knowledge of your heredity, your family history, your childhood, adolescence, manhood or womanhood, until I can get inside your mind and can reach some general idea of just how and why you have become what you are, I cannot treat your tuberculosis intelligently and with any sure hope of permanent results.

Why do two patients with the same intestinal trouble, *e. g.*, chronic appendicitis, react to the very same statement in such entirely different ways. To one patient you say, "You must enter the hospital at once for an operation." He or she nods quietly, looks at his watch or pocket calendar and announces that he is ready to enter the hospital at such and such a time. To another patient with exactly the same illness, you make the same statement; immediately his hands begin to tremble, he perspires profusely, becomes mentally agitated, confused and may even start to cry. Back of these two varying reactions lie two varying personalities. Until you understand each personality, you are not going to be able to get your two patients satisfactorily through their operations and on their feet again.

Nowadays there are groups or clinical associations of physicians who are specialized diagnosticians. Every patient who consults them is examined meticulously with every possible aid of modern science. Each patient, besides the general routine tests, is sent to the heart specialist, to the dental surgeon, to the ophthalmologist, to the endocrinologist, and to the psychiatrist. They go to the psychiatrist, not because the examining physicians suspect that they are mentally ill, but because a final diagnosis and adequate recommendations for treatment are not usually possible without what is commonly called "a personality analysis"—not a psychoanalysis, but a general picture of the man or woman's mental anatomy and pathology. The general diagnostician wants the psychiatrist to tell him, in as few words as possible, not only what kind of a man or woman the patient is, but also how he and she came to be what they are now, and why they have become habituated to react to the ordinary stimuli of every-day life in certain definite ways.

In order to illustrate this new attitude of physician to patient, I can do nothing better than to quote from a recent paper by Dr. Thomas Ordway, Dean of Albany Medical College.[4] "Such cases illustrate clearly the vital importance of the personal relationship between physician and patient in the practice of medicine. The whole problem of diagnosis and treatment [5] depends on your insight into the patient's character and personal life, and in every case of organic disease there are complex interactions between the pathological process and the intellectual process which you must appreciate and consider. Disease in man is never exactly the same as disease in an experimental animal, for in man the disease at once affects and is affected by what we call the emotional life. Thus, the physician who attempts to take care of a patient, while he neglects this factor, is as unscientific as the investigator who neglects to control all the conditions that may affect his experiment."

Dr. Ordway's paper ends with two sentences that apply to the parish priest as well as to the physician. I commend them most especially. "Time, sympathy and *understanding* must be lavishly dispensed, but the reward is to be found in that personal bond, which forms the greatest satisfaction of the practice of medicine. One of the essential qualities of the clinician (and of the parish priest also) is interest in humanity, for the *secret of the care of the patient is caring for the patient.*"

[4]"The Similarity of the Aims and Ideals of Physicians Today and Those of Seventy-five or More Years Ago, with Particular Reference to Conservative Therapeutics," in *The Clifton Medical Bulletin*, Vol. 17, no. 2, pp. 77–85.

[5]In cases of functional origin.

Time, sympathy and understanding! And an understanding that demands, in the parish priest, not only the study of books, but the study of individuals also. It demands his time—a very great deal of his time. And he must be willing to give of his time, not only during his years of academic preparation in the seminary, but also during the often over-crowded hours of his parochial life. That such a willingness exists is evident. The trend of modern life proves even more definitely still that people are beginning to demand of their pastors, as well as of their physicians, not only a willingness to help them in their individual difficulties, but also the power and the knowledge that will make such willingness something more than a mere benign mental attitude of sympathy.

Life-adjustment clinics are being created in some of the Protestant congregations.[6] The daily presence of a priest is arranged for in such churches as Old Trinity in New York— a priest not to hear confessions, but to listen to any one who cares to ask him for any kind of help. Such practices, as well as the readiness with which some people hurry off to the office of the newest psychoanalyst, are now mere commonplaces of daily life that could not possibly have happened twenty years ago.[7] Protestants talk about "restoring the confessional" and lament "the Reformation outlawing of confession" because they suppose that the Tribunal of Penitence, if properly Protestantized, might offer to their young people a safer means of sublimating sex or of solving emotional conflicts than the office of an unbelieving psychoanalyst. What they really want is, not the Sacrament of Penance—which they could not regain unless those among their clergy who wanted to hear confessions would be willing to receive the Sacrament of Holy

[6]Washington Congregational Church, Rev. Moses Lovell, pastor.

[7]See "D.D. versus M.D.," a paper by John Hyde Preston in *Scribner's Magazine* for May, 1930. Also "Psychology and the Confessional," by John Rathbone Oliver in the July number of the same magazine. See *Magazine Article Readings*, by Ernest Brennecke and D. L. Clark (Macmillan, 1931), pp. 523–531 and 532–541.

Orders at the hands of a bishop—but an easy means of mental or spiritual direction, with what I call "a protected approach," making it possible for the disturbed individual to seek and to find help, understanding and wisdom from some authoritative human being, without having to give his or her name, without the necessity of "making a definite appointment" and the danger of establishing with the person consulted a confidential contact that might later on prove unpleasant or mortifying.

Such a protected approach may quite possibly be arranged in some other way than through the Confessional itself. At any rate, every pastor should make such an approach possible for those people who want to see him, without his seeing or knowing them. After all, the Confessional is not a very satisfactory place for a mental consultation, or for the giving of lengthy and detailed advice on mental difficulties; that is not its real reason for existence, which is merely the fulfilling of the requirements necessary for receiving absolution. But the physician's office is often quite as unsuited for certain kinds of mental consultations as the "box" itself. Perhaps a pastor-psychiatrist will some day invent a more satisfactory arrangement. At present each parish priest must depend on his own ingenuity in arranging such hours and such places as may give to those who seek him a protected approach. But the hour once arranged, the place once determined on, nothing must keep him from being there at that certain time. Often some tormented soul gets up just enough courage to come as far as the open door and the protected approach, only to find that the door leads into an empty room or box. Wait? Not for a minute. Here is a good excuse to escape. And perhaps that same soul never gets up enough courage to try that approach again.

This leads us logically to another important matter. The whole question of what is commonly called spiritual counsel. Of course, it is often possible for the parish priest to give important help and advice in mental difficulties after he has heard a confession and before he pronounces absolution; but my own short experience in such matters has proven to me that, in the confessional itself, the priest hears very little about a penitent's important mental difficulties. What the penitent has to say is all said from the legalistic standpoint of self-examination according to the "shalt nots"—according to "sins." "I have done thus and so." Yet, in order to give permanent help, the priest must know not only what has been done, but *why* it has been done. The man accused of crime before a court and who pleads "not guilty," is forced to prove not only that he did not commit the act, but why, he being what he is, he could not possibly have committed it. If on the other hand, he pleads "guilty," there is no immediate opportunity for the court to discover why he committed the crime, since it is only interested in what he has confessed. The penitent, in the confessional, is in the same position. He pleads "guilty" to everything that he mentions. It is almost impossible for the priest to get very far into the question of motive, of environment, of past habits and conditionings. On the other hand, if during a confession the priest does come across suggestive traces of some emotional conflict, symptoms of some maladjustment involving tragic consequences, he is unable to follow up this line of investigation outside of the confessional. Without the penitent's permission, he may not refer to it in some later conversation. The whole situation involves many difficulties, for at any cost the seal of the confessional must be preserved intact.

One may divide people or patients into those who are willing to come to us for help and those to whom we must go ourselves. The first class is easy to help, as they will come to their duties. They will come, outside the confessional, to talk over their difficulties. But for the other class, there is nothing more satisfactory, nothing more generally helpful than the much maligned and often difficult "parochial or pastoral visit." If we psychiatrists could only go out and call on our patients at any time during the day, what opportunities we should have. The pastor can do this. He holds a key that opens the door of every house in his parish. Unfortunately, he often uses the wrong key; that is, to make a "social call," to sit down and gossip in a friendly way, to smoke a cigarette, or even accept a drink of legal home-brew or pre-war "stuff." Under such circumstances he may make himself very popular, but he will not get at many of the real troubles of his people. If, however, he comes in *propria persona,* as the parish priest, the lover and physician of souls, if he adopts the same sympathetic attitude that the physician in his office tries to adopt towards his patient, an attitude of evident willingness to listen, to sympathize and to help, then he may have to waste more than an hour on a single visit, he may have to possess a greater patience than Job's; but in the end he will establish a *rapport* of confidence that may lead at once to real knowledge of actual difficulties, or that may pave the way for the securing of that knowledge when he makes his next pastoral visit in that same house.

Almost every Manual for Confessors has a section on the mental and spiritual characteristics that are required of a good physician of souls.[8] Many of these manuals omit the virtue of patience. Uccello says that the confessor must not only *benigne et caute excipere, prudenter interrogare, causas medice perscrutari,* but also he must *patienter et dicrete auscultare.*[9] He must "be patient in hearing them *out."* He must not break into a penitent's stream of words with some impatient exclamation. If this be true of the confessional itself, it is ten times true of our efforts, outside the tribunal, to get at faulty mental habits, to smooth out anxieties, to analyse phobias, obsessions and inhibitions.

Pastoral visits require an endless patience. You must be ready to make them no matter how tired and rushed your

[8]See Uccello, *op. cit.,* pp. 33-199.   [9]Pp. 208-324.

life may be; and patience you must be willing to have, or, if you do not possess it, then develop it as part of your mental technique as a good physician of souls. But the *motive*, the only really satisfactory motive for both the visits and the patience, must be a true love of human beings. "The secret of the care of the patient is caring for the patient." And by love one does not mean a milk-and-water emotionally produced feeling of good-will. The love that is not inherently impelled to *do* something for the loved person, to give and to give without even the thought of reward or of love returned, is not worthy of the name. God so loved the world that he *gave*. If your parishioners, your penitents, your social groups, your patients recognize in you a persistent, open-hearted desire to help, they will very soon throw down the bars of reticence, which, as they know well enough, are things that make it impossible for you to translate your desire to help into words and actions.

To these three things, personal contacts, patience, love, you must of course join more concrete matters—study, constant reading, experience, wherever you can get it. Then, if at the same time you are doing your best to live on the spiritual plane of a priestly life; if before setting out on your visits you visit Our Lord in the Blessed Sacrament—if you supply your finite human patience by meditating on His patience with your own imperfections—if morning after morning at the altar you raise to a white heat the fervor of your own love for Him, so that he dwells in you and you in Him—then, all unconsciously for the most part, you will begin to develop a "technique," if I may venture to call it so, a method of dealing with individuals—a kind of mental atmosphere that you will carry with you wherever you go. And you will be helping people all the time, without knowing it yourself. After awhile you will hear some one tell you of the new courage you once gave him in the midst of difficulties, of the fresh gleam that you lighted for her in the midst of hopeless darkness, of the new life that you brought to one who so hated life that he was in love with death itself. You will hear these things, and you will say: "You must be wrong. I did nothing. I don't even remember what you told me, or what I said to you. If I did help you, I am glad, of course. But it could not have been I." And yet it *was* you. Or rather, it was God using you in His own way for the help of some soul in agony. Using you, because in making yourself a friend of human beings, in developing your patience, in giving because you loved, you have made yourself an instrument that He could use. "Not I. But Christ that liveth in me."

Doctor Harvey Cushing, one of the greatest of American surgeons, published not long ago a collection of papers that he called *Consecratio Medici.* Unless you have had some close contacts with medical men, especially with the younger ones, you will not realize the intense sense of personal consecration that many of them bring to their daily work, frequently on seven days of every week. Oftentimes in their self-forgetful service of human beings, they put us pastors to shame. In dealing with *your* "patients" then, in their mental and spiritual illnesses, you cannot go far astray if you imitate the devotion of these physicians of the body.

The parallels between the physician and the priest have always been prominent enough. They begin with St. Luke, evangelist and beloved physician. The ancient Fathers love to draw out the similarities between medicine and the gospel. Let me end this first chapter then with a quotation from St. Gregory Nazianzen. He is comparing the physician of the body with the physician of the soul.[10] "People," he says, "differ more widely from each other in their desires and passions than in their physical characteristics. Therefore to regulate these is no easy task. And since the same medicine and the

[10]Migne, *Pat. Graeca,* Vol. 35, p. 437, sec. 29–30. Also Eng. trans. in *The Nicene and Post-Nicene Fathers* (Scribners, New York), Second Series, Vol. 7, p. 211, sec. 29–30.

same food are not in every case administered to man's bodies, but a difference is made according to their degree of health or sickness, so *also are souls to be treated with varying instruction and guidance.*" But the pastor is dealing with immortal souls, not with mortal bodies. The material with which he works is infinitely precious; therefore, in comparing the physician with the priest, St. Gregory adds,[11] "But we priests, upon whose efforts is staked the salvation of a soul, what a struggle ours ought to be, and what great skill do we require in doing well our work as physicians of the soul."[12]

CLINICAL MATERIAL AND SUGGESTIONS FOR RECORD-KEEPING

Although most of the cases described at the end of these chapters are not taken from actual case records, they are, however, typical pictures of routine experience.

John Jones, aged seven, goes to a children's party. On his return his mother asks the nurse: "Did John behave?" The nurse answers, "No, madam, he ate his ice cream with both elbows on the table." The mother rebukes John. But John is not impressed; he cannot see why ice cream should be eaten in any one particular posture.

A few months later John gives a party of his own. When the guests have gone, John's mother asks his nurse; "Did Master John behave himself?" "No, madam," the nurse answers, "one of the other little boys was playing with Master John's tin soldiers and Master John snatched them from him and made him cry." John is again rebuked. Again he is not impressed with any sense of dereliction. Willie Smith has no real appreciation of tin soldiers; he was just ready to break off the magnificent tin sword of one of John's most precious captains, when John rescued his belongings from Willie's clumsy fingers. "Besides," thinks John, "those are *my* soldiers."

[11]Migne, *op. cit.,* Vol. 35, p. 437, sec. 28. Also *The Nicene and Post-Nicene Fathers, loc. cit.*

[12]This is a free translation of the sense implied in the Greek word *iatreusai,* "to do the work of a physician."

That same year, toward the end of the school term, John's mother happens to pass the school house. As she is rather a friend of
John's teacher, she stops for a moment at the door of John's class
room, during an intermission. The teacher, standing by her desk,
is a little embarrassed as she greets John's mother, who is looking
around the room, as she has already scanned the playground and
the halls, hoping for a glimpse of her son. "I hope," she says to the
teacher, "that this term John has been a good boy." At that moment John appears. "Where have you been, my dear," asks his
mother, as John edges away from her, fearing a maternal kiss in
the presence of his school mates. "Teacher," replies John, burning
with a sense of injustice, "just sent me to the principal for throwing a spit-ball." John's mother is distressed. She feels that the
teacher has probably been grossly unfair to her offspring; but she
knows that discipline must be maintained. She rebukes John. Why
has he not been a good boy? John is not impressed; his conscience
does not trouble him in the least. He threw a spit-ball at Louisa
Brown because she stuck out her tongue at him.

But John has a dog, a devoted little wire-haired terrier. John
teaches him tricks back of the barn. John does not realize how he
often torments the dog beyond the endurance of even a faithful
wire-haired terrier. It does not occur to him that the dog has
nerves; that he can feel pain. He simply belongs to John just as the
tin soldiers do. One hot summer afternoon John is teaching his
dog a new trick. The dog is tired. John is cross and hot. John tries
the new trick once more. The dog refuses to obey; or else he does
not understand. John loses his temper. Something that belongs to
him will not obey him. And, with his heavy hob-nailed shoe, he
kicks the dog in the mouth. The dog's mouth begins to bleed. He
licks the blood away with his tongue. He looks up at John with a
puzzled expression in his brown eyes. John is a little frightened.
What will his father, who gave him the dog, say, if the dog is
badly hurt? And the dog starts toward John. He limps, for John's
kick has hurt his shoulder too. But he manages to stand on his
hind legs. He looks into John's eyes, and, with the same tongue
that is still bloody from the blow his master gave him, he licks his
master's hand. Suddenly, John, who can take a licking without
whimpering from a boy bigger than himself, finds that he cannot

take another kind of licking from a helpless little dog. And John begins to cry. Stumbling blindly, he dashes into the house and runs to his astonished mother. He is blurting out something between his sobs, some sort of a confession, a form of words that his mother has never heard from his lips before. "I've been a bad boy—I did something bad—I did something bad."

When his mother learns, to her astonishment, that this mood of utter self-abasement is the result of her son's having kicked his dog, that wretched bothersome little terrier that yaps at passing automobiles, she is absolutely puzzled. Why did not John react in this same way to other more "serious" matters; to putting his elbows on the table, to snatching toys from his visitors, even to throwing spit-balls at Louisa Brown, who is really quite a well-brought up little girl? But John has learned from the look in a dog's eyes and from the touch on his hand of a dog's wounded mouth, what "being bad" really means. Deliberately to hurt some one who loves us, some one who cannot or who will not hurt us in return; some one who in spite of our hurting him, will go on loving us still and giving us another chance to hurt him again! Ah, that is so different from putting our elbows on the table and from throwing spit-balls. John Jones, and you and I and the whole world know that much when we really think about it. To outrage love—the love of God, or the love of a little wire-haired dog, this forces upon us a sense of personal guilt, which only those who delight in inflicting pain or who have hardened their own hearts may hope to escape.

There are so many ways of "misbehaving," of "misbehaving ourselves" or of "being bad boys and girls" which are imposed upon us by some exterior authority and which do not, as a usual thing, arouse in us any keen sense of guilt or sin. And in dealing with human personalities, we must be careful to distinguish the varying types of reaction.

Moral theology, for the most part, is written from the legalistic standpoint; it is filled with the rules for not putting elbows on the table, for not snatching, for not throwing spit-balls. Of course, such "behavior" must be regulated. But even in dealing with such matters as these, we must be careful to apply the general rules to the variations of individual cases. The casuistical material, case histories, that one finds in most books on moral theology, deals exclusively with *what* the penitent has done. Not with *why* he has done it? Or with *how* he came to be a person able or anxious or tempted to do such a thing.

It is not difficult to train oneself in all the intricacies of moral theology. It is intensely difficult, and it demands great patience and wide experience, to be able to understand and to estimate justly the wide variations of human behavior.

In no other way do individuals differ so widely as in the relative strength or weakness of what we call "the will"—the conative reactions of the personality. To the Behaviorist there is no such thing as the will; there are only varying conditionings that are the result of conditioned reflexes, or mental habits. But there persists in the least disciplined individual a sense of something "right" that he might have "done" which he contrasts with the something "wrong" that he wishes he somehow had not done. Human minds seem incurably dualistic. If there be, then, such a thing as right and wrong—no matter how greatly the emphasis on what is right and what is wrong may vary—then it is certainly a fact that the human will is more definitely conditioned towards what is wrong than towards what is right. The good that I would, I do not; the doing of it demands an effort, the overcoming of difficulties, the retraining of a habit. The evil that I would not, that I do; because somehow the doing of it is easier. But, each personality has varying streaks and strains of conative strength and weakness. These *loci minoris resistentiae* of each human will are of infinite variety. Perhaps it would be more accurate to cease talking altogether about the will, and to give up trying to split into air-tight compartments the various ways in which an integrated human personality reacts to its environment. But we might still say that no matter how completely integrated a personality may seem, it has its "spots of least resistance" and pathological streaks that tend to break up the integration, to weaken the purpose, to cloud the judgment and paralyze the will.

In dealing with personalities and their reactions, we should learn to consider and to weigh each case according to its *data, acta, facta,* and *agenda.*

I suggest this very imperfect scheme for examining your cases and for keeping records of them:

A. What are the *data* of your patient, your penitent, the individual or your social group, your parishioner? These "given facts" belong under these two heads.

   1. Heredity. The family history. Racial strains in grandparents, parents. Mental cases. Mental types of father and mother, brothers, sisters. Epilepsy, tuberculosis, cancer. Get the physical and the mental good points, as well as the bad ones.

   2. Environment. Earliest recollections. Relationships to parents, to brothers and sisters. Sources of physical or mental stress or strain in childhood (falls, shocks, frights). Adolescence; sex difficulties. Autoerotism. First sex experiences. Sleep-walking, dreams, bed-wetting. School life and its reactions. Manhood or girlhood. Experiences with opposite sex. Business. University. Careers. Marriage. Marital relations to husband or wife. Children. Success or failure. Disappointments; sudden losses. Religious development. (Get a general outline of the life.)

B. The *acta.* Things that have been *done,* which made the personality what it now is. Or this might include the *passa;* not the things done, but the things experienced or suffered. Here you must block out an outline of what the person has "done" with the heredity and the environment that have been given to him. In other words, the *acta* are the reactions of the personality to its environment and its heredity. Under this head numerous individual matters may be listed. Such as:

   1. Actual illnesses. Mental "breakdowns."

   2. Faulty or wrong habits of thought. Phobias. Inhibitions. Obsessions. Habits of anxiety, etc.

   3. Physical habits that become characteristics. Sex habits, Habits of posture, of business activity, of dealing with others. Marital habits.

   4. Religious life. Baptism, confirmation, etc.

5. Achievements. Handicaps overcome. At home, school, college, business.

6. Failures. Sense of Inferiority.

These two heads should give us a general outline of a case. We must try to set down these facts as objectively, as briefly as possible. Then, if the patient or penitent has come to you in connection with some definite sin. or difficulty, you must consider:

C. The *facta* or the objective result of a certain type of more or less conditioned behavior. In other words, the *deed done*. Or as the Roman theologians say, the *what: quod*. There is an old Latin tag of a verse that contains all the possible circumstances of an action. In English it runs: "Who, what, where, when, by what means, why and how?"[13]

These are useful subheads. But in each *factum*, we are chiefly interested as a rule in:

a. *quod;* the action itself.

b. *quis;* who, the actor himself or herself.

c. *quomodo;* in what way, *i. e.,* whether the action was purely voluntary, partially inhibited, absolutely irresponsible.

d. *quare;* why? The motive for the action.

Finally under:

D. *Agenda.* What is to be done? What advice you will give? How do you intend to deal with your patient's difficulties, weaknesses, sins? Shall you send him to a physician, a psychiatrist, or try to manage the case yourself?

I suggest this outline knowing quite well that it is very imperfect. But every student of behavior, every pastor and social worker, can fill it out according to his own needs as he learns to deal more and more efficiently with the complicated results of human life, thought and emotion.

But no case histories, no methods of technique, none of the routine methods of analyzing or classifying difficult personalities, will take the place of the general motive that must lie behind all

[13]Cf. Slater, *Moral Theology,* Vol. 1, p. 25.

our work as physicians of souls. Our newspapers of late have given great prominence to a certain Mr. Gaw of Chicago. I do not know exactly what his municipal office is; nor how successful his efforts may prove in making people happy in Chicago, even though they are there for only a few days' visit. I do know that his *motive* is a sound one; an unusual one. In a recent interview he said: "When I first came to Chicago I did not have a dime. But I worked my way up. I was successful. And I did it all by liking people. I always liked them. Always wanted to talk to them and make them like me. I guess you might call that my religion—*just liking people.*"

Just liking people! Such a habit of mind may not seem to constitute in itself a satisfactory religion; but it might well form a satisfactory addition to the religion of every clergyman and social worker.

Chapter II

MENTAL ILLNESS

EXPLANATION OF TECHNICAL TERMS. THE PSYCHOSES: MANIC-
DEPRESSIVE CONDITIONS AND SCHIZOPHRENIA. CLINICAL MATERIAL

No one can play contract bridge or any other kind of bridge
until he knows the names and values of fifty-two playing
cards. And likewise no one can understand the conversation
of two physicians until he has been through a medical school
himself, or has at least close at hand a medical dictionary.
Lawyers have their own vocabulary; so do brokers; even
golfers.

But medicine is especially prone to speak in a "language
not understanded of the common people." It must be remembered, however, that up to eighty years ago Latin was the
language of medicine, and that Harvey's celebrated treatise on
the circulation of the blood,[1] even the works of such men as
Marx,[2] in the nineteenth century, were all written in Latin.
Moreover, almost all our anatomical and pathological terms
are taken directly from the Greek. Hence, the young medical
student who knows no Greek has difficulties. He has to
learn by heart long muscle-names like sterno-cleido-mastoid,
when the name itself would tell him exactly where and what
the muscle is, if he could read Homer. And yet, often enough
it is "those common people" who object to our speaking in a
not understandable tongue, that are frequently to blame for
the strange-sounding terms of our medical camouflage. If the

[1]*Exercitatio anatomica de motu cordis et sanguinis in animalibus,* Frank-
fort, 1628.

[2]Carl Friederich Heinrich Marx, professor at Goettingen. Most famous con-
tribution to medical history is *Origines Contagiæ,* Karlsruhe, 1827. See *Die
Medicinischen Classiker Deutschlands,* von Heinrich Rohlfs (Stuttgart, 1875),
Vol. I, pp. 323–479.

rich Mrs. Bevins consults you, and if after hearing the history of her lassitude, her fatiguability, her insomnia and constant irritation, you tell her that she is suffering from a general weakness and exhaustion of the nervous system, she will not be impressed and perhaps she will not want to pay your bill. But she will pay it gladly if you tell her the same thing in Greek, if you say, "Dear lady, you are suffering from a mild case of typical "neurasthenia." Neurasthenia is a term compounded of two Greek words that mean a "weakness of the nerves." But, of course, it does sound better than ordinary English.

In psychiatry also, just as in other domains of medicine, one often needs a pronouncing dictionary; for this game is more complicated than others; worse than chess. You must learn to recognize the different pieces, to know a knight from a castle, a psychosis from a neurosis, before you can really play it intelligently. I must burden you therefore with a few definitions.

1. Psychosis: You are already familiar with that termination "osis." Roughly, it means a sick or pathological condition. Acidosis, that familiar dyspeptic acquaintance of the hurried, anxious American, means a condition of sickness or of ill-health that is caused by too much acid in the digestive tract. With the first part of "psychosis" you should be familiar also. The Greek word "psyche"—which recalls the famous story of Cupid and Psyche by Apuleius—has come to mean "mind," as distinct from "body." A *psychiatrist*—compound of "psyche" and the Greek word for physician—is a mind-doctor, while *psychiatry* is the knowledge or the practice of mind-doctoring. So *psychosis* is used in a restricted sense for illness of the mind, some definite type of mental disease. For just as there are many "oses" of the body, so there are many types of "psychoses," or illnesses of the mind, each of which has well-marked symptoms of its own and which is treated as a sort of disease entity, exactly like tuberculosis, pneumonia, typhoid

fever, in the physical sphere. To say that a patient is "psychotic" means that he is manifesting symptoms of one of the many psychoses. He is not merely mentally maladjusted, tormented by phobias or obsessions; he is mentally ill. And this illness is primarily an *illness of the mind*.

2. Neurosis: People are very prone to blame on their "nerves" mental conditions that they do not understand. When an ordinary patient tells you that he is "nervous," usually his real difficulty lies in his mental machinery, only he is terrified of that word "mental." He imagines that every mental case must be "crazy" or "insane." There is a Greek word "neuron"; it means either a nerve or a sinew (tendon). If you have ever looked into a deep wound in an arm or a leg, you will have seen there string-like formations or tubes, some of them empty, others that look more solid. The solid, firm-looking strings are nerves or tendons; the flabby, empty-looking tubes are blood vessels. Now, the Greek physician could not, at first, distinguish between a tendon and a nerve. He called them both "neura." But in modern anatomy we call the blood vessels arteries, or veins, leaving the word "neuron" for the nerves alone. Therefore, neurosis is a sick condition of the nerves; not "nervousness," by which most people mean jumpiness, bad temper, tremors of hands or legs, or a state of perpetual annoyance by noises or children or husbands. A neurosis is a sickness of the nerve itself. If you feel intense pain every time you move your leg, and if the pain runs down the back of the limb, from hip to heel, then your long sciatic nerve is probably sick, inflamed or irritated. There is nothing "mental" about this. You do not need the advice of a mind doctor, a psychiatrist; you need a nerve doctor, a neurologist.

3. Psycho-neurosis: A neurosis is a physical condition, the result of pathological processes in a definite part of your body called a nerve. Psychosis is a mental condition, the result of some pathological process in your personality—in your "self"; a process that generally cannot be detected by microscopes or

dissected with knives. Between neurosis and psychosis lie states of illness, of discomfort, of maladjustment which are neither purely mental nor purely physical, yet contain elements of both. In these conditions the mental difficulty produces a visible objective result upon the nerves; or else, the other way round, the neurological condition produces some mental habit, some impairment of mental function.

I have already given you an example of a neurosis—a sciatica. Let us suppose that the pathological condition in the sciatic nerve gets well; there is no longer "anything the matter" with that particular nerve. Nevertheless, you insist that you feel pain from the sciatic nerve, and you do not believe the neurologist who tells you that the nerve condition is healed, that you *can* walk if you want to. You do want to walk, yet you can't; or you *think* you can't, which is even worse. Nerves are something like telegraph wires; at one end is the operator sending a telegram. While the nerve-wire is diseased this operator sends pain messages to the brain; but after awhile the nerve heals, the pain operator is gone. Nevertheless, the nerve-wire has developed a sort of habit-consciousness of its own; it goes on sending telegrams, even though there is no operator at the other end; it keeps speeding pain messages to the brain, although the objective cause of those messages has disappeared. Or, one might put it in another way and say that, during the painful months of your sciatica your brain has become sensitized to the reception of pain messages from a certain part of your body. After awhile the sciatica is cured; but your brain-receiving station keeps on feeling the pain messages just as before. And you will lie in bed, month after month, insisting that you cannot walk, that you are suffering from acute sciatica and that your doctor does not understand your case. In all this, you can seasily see the mental and the nervous, or the objective element. Such conditions we call *psychoneuroses*. But, finally, let us suppose that you have never had any sciatica, but that you are suddenly convinced that your leg has been cut off, or has been turned into a glass leg, so that you cannot possibly walk. This is psychotic, a state that is purely mental; this is not a psychoneurosis, not a neurosis either, but a psychosis.

This last statement leads us to a necessary distinction between two symptoms of mental illness, delusions and hallucinations. As I write, a pencil is lying on my desk. If I insist that there is a snake on my desk, then I am merely misinterpreting an object that really exists. Even if there is no snake on my desk, there is a pencil lying there. Such reactions are called delusions. It is a different reaction, however, if I look at my empty desk, on which there is nothing at all, and then insist that I see a snake. Here I have no objective basis of reality. I see something where nothing is visible. Reactions of this type are called hallucinations.

Now, let us close for the present our medical dictionary. We know now at least some of the cards with which this game of psychiatry is played.

It would be impossible in the scope of this book to give you any satisfactory description of all types of mental illness, and to outline all the mental conditions that are called psychoses. You can find such complete discussions in text books on psychiatry.[3] All that I can do is to pick out those psychoses that are the most common; the types of mental illness with which parish priests or social workers will most frequently be concerned. If I can show you general pictures of these common types and suggest methods of dealing with them, I shall be giving you about as much psychiatry as the average pastor or social worker ought to know in order to be a satisfactory physician of souls. But I wish to present the psychoses that I shall try to describe not merely from the standpoint of frequency of occurrence, but also from that of a general classification. The outstanding authorities in the field of psychiatry give varying

[3]E.g. *The Human Mind*, by K. A. Menninger or *Outlines of Psychiatry*, by W. A. White. For further data concerning these two books see Descriptive List of Books, section II, B. and Bibliography.

classifications of the psychoses. But, in general, we may say that we can divide psychoses into different classes according to their outcome, their seriousness, their source, their therapy. Let me set this down in a simple systematic manner.

We may classify psychoses:

A. According to their results into:

1. Benign psychoses; mental illnesses that always get well, and that leave the mind of the patient absolutely unimpaired.
2. Ominous psychoses, mental illnesses that involve a serious disintegration of the personality, and that, at the present state of our knowledge, are seldom, if ever, curable.

Or we may divide them into

B. Psychoses that affect primarily

1. The emotions, the affective life.
2. The intelligence.
3. The judgment.
   An unsatisfactory classification, as it is impossible to separate emotions from intelligence, etc.

or:

C. According to the source of the pathological mental process, into

1. Exogenic; mental illnesses that are the result of some poison, or infection taken into the body from outside. And
2. Endogenic; psychoses that, as far as we can see, are not dependent on external agents but arise from conditions within the personality itself.

Section 1, the exogenic, may be again divided into:

a. Non-toxic psychoses; in which the external cause is not a definite poisonous substance. And *b.* Toxic psychoses, the objective cause of which is some external poisonous agent.

These rough divisions will help you in understanding just why I propose to discuss with you certain types of mental illness.

I wish to present to you, *first,* a psychosis that is benign (*A.* 1) and affects primarily the emotions (*B.* 1) and that is apparently endogenic (*C.* 2). It is commonly called the manic-depressive psychosis.

Secondly, a psychosis that is ominous (*A.* 2), that affects intelligence and judgment (*B.* 2, 3) and that is endogenic (*C.* 2). It used to be called dementia praecox. We now call it, more accurately, schizophrenia.

Thirdly, a psychosis that is ominous (*A.* 2), exogenic and toxic (*C.* 1, *b*). It is called paresis.

Fourthly, a psychosis that is often apparently benign, yet quite as often dangerous and ominous. (*A.* 1, 2) Non-toxic and endogenic. It is called paranoia (*C.* 1, *a;* 2).

Then, psychoses that arise from toxic conditions (*C.* 1, *b*) that vary in their benignity and ominousness. Some are endogenic, such as epilepsy (*C.* 2), others exogenic, such as alcoholism (*C.* 1, *b*).

In this way, I shall hope to give you examples from nearly every class. I shall omit the more unusual mental conditions that you will probably never meet with, but which you may, if you wish, read up in the great text books on the subject.

Before beginning a description of manic-depressive conditions, forgive me if I turn aside a moment, in order to preach a little sermon that I have preached to countless audiences and that I have even printed in a book.[4] It is a homily on our general attitude to mental illness.

There are still plenty of people in this country of ours who regard mental illness as something disgraceful, as God's pun-

[4]*Foursquare* (Macmillan, 1930), pp. 35–37.

ishment on the third and fourth generations of some secret offender. This is natural enough. Up to the days of Pinel (1745–1826) and Esquirol (1772–1840) in France, and of William Tuke (1732–1822) in England, the men who at the beginning of the nineteenth century were most responsible for a change in the inhumane treatment of mental patients, mental illness was still believed to be the direct result of "sin." If the sin was not manifest in the patient, then it had been latent in his forebears; or else, the patient was "possessed of the devil." I have no desire to suggest the impossibility of what theologians call demoniacal possession. I have seen too many mental cases that at least suggest the unseen presence of some inimical foreign personality hiding beneath the tormented personality of the patient himself. Nevertheless, "possessions" in mental cases are the exception, not the rule. But even in our present age of enlightenment, the first automatic reaction to mental disease of many modern men and women is a reaction of horror. If such illness touches their own family, there develops at once a conspiracy of silence, a determination to cover it up, to pretend that it is not there. Why? Because people still think of mental disease in terms of sin; and if the mental patient be boy or girl, then since the sin can scarcely be theirs, it must be the sin of father or mother, or grandparents, or perhaps of more remote ancestors. And modern parents, no matter how hard they may be on the "sins" of their own children, are very anxious about any possible past sins of their own and strive to deny their existence by denying also the existence of the mental case in their families that seems to point the finger of discovery at themselves and to cry out "Thou art the man." No one would quarrel very bitterly with these people if their methods of reacting to their own past sins did not cause them to commit a much greater offense in concealing a case of mental illness until it is too late to give treatment and permanent help.

Still greater is the fear of many people who notice mental symptoms, not in others, but in themselves. The "fear of going

insane!" What agonies of mind it has caused! How much unnecessary tragedy and distress! As long as a person "fears he is
losing his mind," just so long may he be sure that he has a fast
hold on the tail of it. For the victim of real ominous mental
illness has no such fear. He knows that *he* is sane; infinitely
saner than the mad people who inhabit his world and who
shut him up in a hospital and tell him that he is *not* Napoleon
Bonaparte or John the Baptist. Why will people not accept
mental illness as quietly and as simply as they accept illness of
the body? Few patients who have a severe attack of influenza
feel sure that they are going to die; but a man whose mind is
temporarily blocked, so that he can't make ordinary use of it, is
always perfectly sure that he is "going insane."

Pastors and social workers who come so much closer to
their people, than even the most prominent psychiatrist comes
to his patients, can do endless good, and can help not only
mental patients but even the poor psychiatrists themselves, by
teaching their people the right attitude toward mental illness
and mental difficulties. We must get rid of the old idea of
mental illness and the hereditary horror that has for so many
centuries enveloped it. Sensible men and women still speak
with bated breath of "mental hospitals"; their very names—
"The Phipps," "Bellevue," "Bloomingdale"—have acquired
under- and overtones of horror. As for the fortunate person
who happens to have been a patient in one of them, why,
people still shrug their shoulders when he passes, or grin
and put their index-fingers to their foreheads in a significant
manner. To have had a "mental breakdown," to have been in
a mental hospital, an "insane asylum"—God save the mark!—
is a black stain on a man or a woman's social or economic
record. Even in our universities the form of application for
admission to some advanced type of academic training frequently contains the question, "Have you ever had a mental
illness?" And some unfortunate young man or woman who
may have had a mild depression or elation and have entirely

recovered, has to decide whether it would be better to develop a temporary amnesia for that experience, or else tell the truth and quite possibly be rejected as a candidate for admission.

But my sermons on this particular text have been so numerous and so much alike, that I shall take for granted that you have already heard or read one of them, and will have profited thereby. I can therefore go on to the description of a psychosis which is so common, and at the same time so tormenting to the patient, that it will surely, at some time or another, come within the sphere of your work as pastors or social workers. It is a kind of mental upset that might happen to any one, possibly to myself; and therefore I have done my best to arrange for my treatment while my mind is still unclouded by depression and my judgment still unimpaired by excitement. For I have drawn up a paper, properly witnessed, in which I set down the mental hospital to which I am to be taken, the psychiatrist who is to take charge of my case, these same instructions to be relentlessly carried out, no matter how forcibly I may, in my disturbed state of mind, rebel against all the provisions that I, myself, have made. If I knew that my gall-bladder was functioning inadequately, that I was possibly forming inside of me certain gall stones which might at some future time make an operation necessary, no one would think it peculiar if, before the acute condition developed, I should set down the name of the surgeon to whose skilful fingers I preferred to entrust my internal anatomy, and the hospital in which I wished the operation to be performed. But if I attempt to guard against the possibility of foreign bodies, like gall stones, not in my gall-bladder but in my integrated personality, in my mind, then every one feels all the more assured of his belief that all psychiatrists are more or less crazy themselves.

We call this type of mental-upset a manic-depressive psychosis. In my own student days it was often called "Circuläres Irresein" or circular insanity, because it seemed to go in a circle, from a depression to a normal level, from normal level to

excitement, and so on. But the new name is much more satisfactory, for it gives in one name the two phases of the attack.
Now, one patient may develop only a depressive phase. Another only the excited period. Still another may go from a depression into an an excitement. Let me illustrate with a dia-
gram familiar to every psychiatrist.[5]

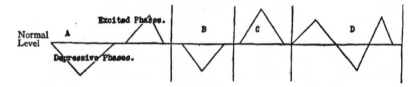

The straight line represents the normal level of our emotional life. Below this line are the depressive conditions; above
it the excited ones. Just as we say: "He is *up* in the air" (excited); or *down* in the dumps" (depressed). Depression, excitement and normal level may alternate in many combinations. The four commonest types are noted on the figure *A, B,
C* and *D.*

A begins with a depressive phase, comes up to the level of
normal reaction, and then goes up into an excitement. It
might, of course, begin with an excitement, go from that to
normal, and then into depression. *B* is the type in which there
is no elated phase, only a depression. *C* has no depressive
phases, merely an elation. While *D* is what used to be called
circular insanity, as it goes from excitement to depression, or
vice versa, without any intermission of normal reaction. There
are also mixed states, a kind of maniacal stupor, or what is
much more common, an agitated depression.

You all understand the word "manic." But you must get
away from your common ideas of "mania" as used in antiquated expressions like kleptomania, pyromania, etc. By
"manic" we mean simply "excitement" or "elation."

[5]See White, *Outlines,* pp. 143–144.

We are dealing, therefore, with a psychosis that is, first of all, benign, apparently endogenic and non-toxic, and which affects primarily the emotional, not the intellectual life. That means,

a. that you may tell your depressed or excited patients that they *will surely recover.*

b. that, when they do recover, their minds will be absolutely unimpaired.

c. That every moment they live they are nearer the end of their suffering. The end of the tormenting depression is sure to come. If they will only stay alive, they can't help getting well eventually.

One thing you *cannot* tell them. How long the attack will last. It may last months, even years. But somewhere in the future there is a definite end of it.

In dealing with manic-depressive patients, you will notice at once that it is their emotional life which is most affected. For instance, you can tell a depressed patient that he will surely recover, that a true depression which does not lift is not known to science, that you yourself have had thousands of similar patients, and that all of them eventually recovered completely. For a few moments the patient can work over this knowledge with his intelligence, and can reason out the encouraging fact that you, with all your experience, must know what you are talking about. For these few moments he has a little glimmer of hope. But soon comes a rush of emotion; he is overwhelmed by his general sense of depression. And he states the matter clearly when he says to you: "You tell me that I am going to get well. I believe you. I can reason out an acceptance of your statements. But I *feel* that you are all wrong. I *feel* that I shall never get well. I *feel* that my case is an exception to the rule; that you do not understand it. I *feel* that I am eternally lost; that for me there is no hope anywhere."

So with the elated patients. You may make them see, from the standpoint of objective reasoning, that they have no right to charter an airplane to fly from New York to Washington, when they really have scarcely enough money to pay their railroad fare between the same two points. But they charter the airplane just the same, because they *feel* that it will be all right somehow; they *feel* that they must hurry as fast as possible from one place to another. And the only way to stop them is to put them somewhere where they simply cannot spend on airplanes money that they do not possess.

There is no use in trying to reason with an elated patient. Occasionally, with depressed patients, you can appeal to the intelligence and give them a few moments of hope before the emotional cloud of depression descends upon their minds again. As a general rule you may take it for granted that depressed and excited patients need hospital care. Many are the tragedies that might have been prevented by recognizing in time these depressive or elated mental conditions. And yet it is often difficult to differentiate between a patient who is developing a psychotic elation and a woman who is temperamentally emotional, excited, or what she calls "nervous"; between a man who is mentally blocked, depressed, suicidal, mentally sick, and one who is by temperament over-anxious, introspective, and who enjoys looking always on the dark side of life.

The reason for this difficulty is evident enough. There is nothing "abnormal" in being elated occasionally, in feeling so "bucked up" that you do rather foolish, thoughtless things. There is nothing pathological in feeling depressed occasionally; in realizing, when you wake up at four in the morning, that you are, in many respects, a failure, a poor business man, an unsatisfactory husband, and a poor sort of father. Therefore, it is not always simple to discover just when the depression or the elation reaches a point when it is becoming a psychosis, a real sickness of the mind that cries out for the protection and the treatment that only a mental hospital can afford.

But, after all, the pastor and the social worker are not going to practice psychiatry. All they need is to be able to say, in such and such a case, that this or that individual is showing marked symptoms of some emotional mental upset and needs medical care. Let me, therefore, try to give you a few simple rules by which you can usually pick out the cases that need the psychiatrist or the hospital.

Let us begin with a case of elation or excitement. You hear, first of all, that a woman in your parish seems to be in a constant state of feverish activity. When you see her, you notice that she talks and talks incessantly, and that her stream of thought is liable to turn abruptly from one subject to another. A single word from you will divert it altogether. She may be talking about the rummage sale of a Woman's Auxiliary, but if you merely mention that it is raining, she will switch off into a discussion of the climate of Palm Beach as compared with that of Los Angeles or the Riviera. She will also tell you that she does not sleep much and that she does not need sleep. Her mind is going so fast that she cannot stop it long enough to get much rest in bed. All day long, she is dashing from one thing to another, and the most apparently insignificant things often become to her matters of intense importance. *She has lost her sense of relative values.* It becomes as important to interview the ash-man as to give a dinner to twelve people. She may be able to hold down this mental activity while she is talking with you, and therefore you must not depend too much on a single interview. Moreover, you must get from others confirmation of her statements. If you inquire of her friends, you will probably discover that she is buying a lot of clothes, that she has suddenly determined to throw out all her old bedroom furniture and get new furniture that she does not need. You may hear that she has decided, although she has no dramatic ability whatever, to go on the stage. Especially you will notice that *everything seems easy to her*. Her ideas of a dramatic career, for instance; she does not see or appreciate any of the difficulties involved. She sees herself already on the stage playing a prominent part, and with her name in letters a foot high over the door of some important theatre. Meanwhile, her mind is continually on the go. You wonder that she shows no signs of fatigue. This absence of fatigue is always a suspicious sign. Such a mind is like a stationary engine that has lost its governor and is whirling and whirling around, not working, but simply going and going.

In this condition, you will notice at once three outstanding characteristics. First, your patient's *judgment* is impaired: her sense of relative values is upset. She sees no reason why she, a woman of middle age without any experience, should not become at once a great emotional actress, or a power in big business; if she needs one new frock, she does not understand why she should not buy a dozen; if she wants to come up to town for a few days, she cannot see why she should not take an entire suite of rooms at the most expensive hotel, although her husband may be a bank clerk on a very limited salary. Secondly, she is filled with what we call a sense of *euphoria;* a sense of well-being; of happiness, of intense emotional satisfaction. Everything is for the best in the very best of worlds. She is "Pippa" raised to the thousandth power. Not only is God in His heaven and the world quite right, but she herself is even happier than the Almighty and will show Him a thing or two in the general management of the universe. Thirdly, and perhaps most important, is her lack of *insight*. For instance, she is "going on the stage"; you cannot make her see that she has neither talents nor opportunities. She orders a new motorcar; you cannot make her see that her old car is only a year old and that she has not enough money to pay for a Lincoln or a Pierce Arrow. If she were not psychotic, mentally ill, you would be able to make her understand the insuperable difficulties of a dramatic career; you could make her acknowledge that she could not afford a new car.

Therefore, as soon as you have established these three points, lack of insight, euphoria, and an impaired judgment, together with the constant unbroken stream of mental and physical activity, you will do the woman and her family an inestimable service if you will go to her husband and tell him that his wife is not making a fool of herself and trying to ruin him financially because she is "a devil" or in love with some other man, but that she is mentally ill, and for the moment quite irresponsible. And the only way to keep her from making a fool of herself and ruining him is to put her, with her own consent or without it, in some "neutral atmosphere," in some mental hospital, where she will be protected against herself, until she recovers and can return to her family as well and as mentally sound as she ever was.

In depressive cases the diagnosis is often much easier. You find the same impaired judgment, the same lack of insight; but in place of the euphoria, the sense of well-being, you have before you a picture of mental agony and torment that beggars the most appalling descriptions of Dante's lowest level in Inferno. And, in the depths of a real depression, the patient is absolutely helpless; he can do nothing to help himself—nothing.

Therefore, be on your guard against cheap and easy advice. Don't tell a depressed patient to "pull himself together" and to "snap out of it." He *cannot* snap out of it, any more than he could snap out of a pneumonia or an attack of influenza. If you make him *try* to snap out, you only force him to expend a tremendous amount of mental energy in an attempt to do something that is beyond his power to achieve; for the man's mental processes are *blocked*. Keep your eye out for this symptom of blocking; it will help you to recognize a true depressive psychosis.

Let us look briefly at a typical case. One of your male parishioners has had to give up his work at his office. You call on him. You notice, first of all, that it is hard for him to talk. His usual easy stream of conversation has become a tiny trickling brook. He says little more than "yes" or "no," and even that seems to cost him an effort. But, as he loosens up a little, you learn that he had to give up work because he "could not concentrate." If he were reading a law-case, he would read and reread the same sentence four or five times before he could grasp its meaning. If he were adding up a column of figures, he, who could once add such a column correctly at a glance, now has had to go over it time and time again. It seems to him as if mental activity of any kind were blocked. He could force himself to do a little work; but that little was done at the expense of intense mental fatigue. And then, worse than the inability to concentrate has been the inability to decide, even the simplest things, especially the writing of letters. He has important letters to write; but he puts off writing them day after day; he can't decide to start writing; he can't decide what to say when he does start. And when he is walking down to the office in the morning, he may stand for five minutes at the corner of two streets, unable to decide whether he will turn down State Street or keep straight on down the Avenue.

Of course, he knows what is happening to him—this he admits only after he has come to trust you. He is "losing his mind," and he knows too just why he is losing it. For example, when he was a boy he acquired certain sexual habits. They stopped when he was married. But now he knows—he *knows* that they "ruined" him, that he is now a "hopeless case," that he is headed straight for the "insane asylum." And who—who will take care of his wife and children? Then the disgrace. People will all guess just why he has "gone insane." Would it not be better to end the whole thing now? Every time he passes over the high bridge or crosses the railway track on his way to the office, he thinks how much easier for every one it would be if he—if he——.

You cannot fail to recognize a mental picture such as this. And you can do much to help. You may not only help to save a valuable life, you can also give some comfort to a tormented soul. You will find in such a depressed man the same lack of insight that we saw in our elated patient. You cannot reason him out of his ideas of utter failure, of hopeless loss, of sin against the Holy Ghost. You cannot appeal to him from his past religious experience. He has lost all faith; he is an outcast from God. And, of course, his *judgment* is impaired; he cannot see things as they are. Suicide is no longer a crime, or a sin; but merely the "only way out." But the "blocking" of the mental processes is usually the outstanding symptom. If the mental machinery of the excited patient is like a racing engine in a motionless car, then the machinery of the depressed patient is like a motor-car that has all the brakes set and is still trying to make its engine lift it up a steep hill. I suppose that a motor-car, with all brakes set, could possibly move a little; but it would move at the expense of so much friction that the engine would be strained, if not broken. And when this same "blocking" becomes such a mental torment that ideas of self-destruction begin to intrude themselves into consciousness, then it is high time for you, as the pastor, to interfere; for a depressed patient with suicidal ideas belongs in a mental hospital.

Together with this blocking, you will usually come across persistent tormenting *ideas of guilt*. These are often of the most peculiar types; but you cannot reason them out of your patient's mind. He has a "feeling" that at some time in his life he has done something wrong, for which there is no forgiveness. At some time he missed the "right road" and now he can never, never regain it. He looks back over his past life and selects some happening, some incident, some habit, which he makes the operating cause of his present condition.

Let me recapitulate these depressive symptoms. The blocking, the inability to concentrate or to decide; the overpowering sense of guilt or of loss; the impaired judgment; the lack of insight; the artificial selection of some past happening in the patient's life as the cause of his depression; the powerlessness of the patient to help himself, except in one way—suicide.

Even if the patient does not produce definitely any ideas of self-destruction, you had better not be too sure that such ideas are not lurking in the back of his mind. Do not wait for this last symptom before you insist that the patient needs psychiatric treatment, although, in manic-depressive cases, the mental hospital does not, in any great degree, shorten the length of the attack. Many psychiatrists believe, and I among them, that a manic-depressive attack will run its course, and that nothing we can do will shorten its duration. The patient will get well anyway, *if* he lives. *But* excited patients belong in hospitals because society must be protected against them, while depressed patients belong in the same place, because they must be protected against themselves. Moreover, the carefully regulated life in a hospital makes it easier for the patient to bear his particular burden. This is especially true of the depressed patient whose power of decision is blocked. Let him be placed in a neutral environment where everything is decided for him, where his blocked mind may lie fallow until it begins to work again. In a mental hospital such a patient has all the alleviations of the new systems of occupational therapy, that have already accomplished so much.[6]

So, get your elated and especially your depressed patient into a mental hospital. But, before the depressed patient goes, you can help him in several ways. Tell him, first of all, that he is *not* losing his mind; that he could not "go crazy" if he wanted to; that he is suffering from a temporary mental upset, which in the mental sphere is about as serious as an attack of influenza in the domain of physical illnesses. Impress on him the fact that he is *sure* to get well in time; that his mind, when the depression lifts, will be as unimpaired as it was when the illness began, and that he will look back on his present sufferings as an awakened man looks back on some horrible dream. Beg him, above all, not to give up the routine practices of his

[6]W. R. Dunton, M.D., "Occupational Therapy," *Proceedings of the Congress on Medical Education*, Feb. 16–18, 1931. Am. Med. Ass., Chicago.

religious life. Even though he has lost his faith, even though he feels himself an outcast from God, even though his private devotions seem empty routine and his church attendance a farce, even though he cannot *"believe,"* beg him to keep on "doing." At his Confirmation he promised to "believe and to do" what his sponsors once promised for him. If the "believing" part of the contract has become impossible, let him cling all the more tenaciously to the other half. If his mind is so blocked that he cannot say his prayers, let him at least get down on his knees and let God the Holy Spirit say his prayers for him. Above all else, persuade him to keep on going to church, to make his communions, and, if it is his custom, to make his confessions also; to hear mass as often as he can; to make a few minutes' visit each day to some quiet church where the Blessed Sacrament is reserved, or, if this be impossible, at least to enter some church where he can sit or kneel for a few minutes, and let his blocked tormented soul rest in the presence of God. He cannot, he knows, help himself. But God will help him, if he will give God a chance to do so.

Moreover, while he is a patient in a mental hospital, go to see him. He may not be able to say to you a single word; he may feel that he does not want to see you at all. Do not stay too long; but put before him your assurance of his ultimate recovery. Say a prayer with him, not necessarily on your knees, and make him, at least, say "Amen." You will probably go away feeling that you have done him no good at all. But later on, when he has recovered, you may find that your brief visits have given him a few moments of relief in the midst of his mental suffering. The physicians in the hospital are often chary of clerical visitors; but they will judge your visit by its results. If you can leave the patient a little less tense and apprehensive, a little less agitated, they will be only too glad to have you visit him again.[7]

[7]K. M. Bowman and A. F. Raymond, "A Statistical Study of Delusions in the Manic Depressive Psychoses," pp. 111–123; also L. E. Hinsie and S. E.

The most important period in a manic-depressive attack is the period of convalescence, at which time you can be of great help. Your elated or depressed patient is coming gradually back to a normal mental level, beginning to feel "himself" again. A very great deal depends on whether or no the convalescent patient can acquire what we call "insight." It is very important that he should be able to talk over the details of his past illness, to accept it, as one accepts some operation or physical illness from which one has recovered. Most people are only too glad to bore you with all the details of their appendix operation; they are much less willing to tell you about their manic-depressive psychosis and their experiences in a mental hospital. If however they try to forget it, try to pretend that it never took place and push it far into the background of their lives; if in a word they refuse to accept it as part and parcel of their past lives, and so never acquire "insight," then they will be seriously hampered in dealing with a similar condition if it should recur. For that is the important element in manic-depressive attacks; they do tend to recur. And you, as a pastor, must learn how to teach a patient to accept the possibility of a recurrence without becoming terrified or discouraged. You must say something like this:

"You are better, my friend; the elation is subsiding, the depression is lifting. You are yourself again and can look life in the face once more. I am glad to see that you are able also to talk about your depression or as much of it as you remember clearly. Now, the physicians here have already told you that such mental upsets as this may recur. They told you this, not because they are hard and unsympathetic, but because they want to help you in the future. They want to show you how to deal with these same mental conditions if they should ever begin to develop again. Let me, as your pastor, urge you to accept the possibility of a recurrence without any undue anxiety, Suppose, instead of a mental difficulty, you had some chronic

Katz, "Treatment of Manic Depressive Psychosis, A survey of the Literature," pp. 131–185. *American Journal of Psychiatry*, Vol. XI, No. 1.

physical ailment, hay-fever, for instance. Past attacks of hay-fever would have taught you just how to deal with its early symptoms; you would avoid certain places at certain times of the year; or, if your nose began to run and your eyes to weep, you would seek immediately a change of air, and get into an environment that would be free of the unseen sources of infection that bring on your hay-fever. You must treat your attacks of depression in the same way. You have just gone through one attack, so let us hope that it has taught you something. You know now the general symptoms, the premonitory signs. Very well, don't be afraid of them. If, at some future time, you should find that you are having difficulty in concentrating, that your mind is getting blocked, that you are having trouble in deciding things, you should know then what to do. You must stop trying to concentrate, you must drop your work as soon as possible and get yourself into some simple neutral environment—in the country or on a farm—where you can reduce your daily life to the lowest common denominator of physical and mental activity. You may then keep these same symptoms from developing. In other words, if you can get a clear insight into your past attack, if you can accept without fear the possibility of a recurrence, because now at last you know what these attacks are and what mental symptoms precede them, then you will have learned how to deal with your own particular handicap so that you can control it, instead of it controlling you. Every man and woman has some handicap, some spot of lesser resistance, either mental or physical. One man may have an old tuberculous process that has become stationary, which he can easily take care of if he accepts it and regulates his life in a certain way; another has recurrent attacks of sinus trouble. You have had one excited or depressive attack; you *may* have, at least, the beginnings of another. On the other hand, if you readjust your life, or reform some of your mental habits, you may be able to make this past attack the last you will ever have."

These "imaginary conversations" which I am suggesting are the best means I can think of for getting into your own minds the way in which you should react to various types of patients. They should prove somewhat more useful then the mere stating of an imaginary case, with symptoms, therapy and prognosis.

I have merely touched upon the surface reactions of manic-depressive patients. Other types that I have not yet described are the mixed states, in which excitement and depression are mingled. The commonest type is an "agitated depression." It has all the usual symptoms of mental blocking; but also a state of excitement, not the euphoria of the elated cases, but an excitement of intense fear—fear of impending death; of social disgrace; of financial ruin. All these fears express themselves in a constant tormenting state of mental and physical tension. Such patients sometimes produce peculiar "somatic delusions"; ideas that they have no stomachs, that all their intestines have been taken out, their brains removed. Such delusions suggest a much more ominous mental state than a clean-cut elation or depression. I cannot describe such cases in detail, as I am not attempting to write a text-book on psychiatry. I am merely trying to describe to you those less complicated types of mental illness which are the most frequent, and with which you will surely, at one time or another, be brought into contact.

I am intentionally omitting a detailed discussion of two important matters: the whole question of heredity, and the question of causation.

As for heredity, it is true that the family history of manic-depressive cases often shows a depressed or an elated ancestor or two.[8] But we must leave this whole question to the authorities of the experimental laboratories and research stations. I

---

[8]"Heredity in Nervous and Mental Disease," Vol. III of *Reports of the Association for Research in Nervous and Mental Disease*. Also M. Bleuler, M.D., "A Contribution to the Problem of Heredity Among Schizophrenics," *Journal of Nervous and Mental Disease*, Vol. 74, No. 4, October, 1931.

must however warn you against one danger in this direction. I have frequently come across domestic tragedies that arose entirely from a false concept of heredity in mental conditions. I have known a young woman, deeply in love with an estimable young man, who refused to marry and to have children because her father or her great-grandmother had "died in an insane asylum." I have known men who deliberately cut themselves off from the happiness of having a home of their own, because one of their parents was either an epileptic, an alcoholic, or a paretic, or even because such a parent had committed suicide during an acute depression. The heredity of mental illness should never be made into a bug-bear of this type. There is no more danger that the child of a schizophrenic mother may itself become a dementia præcox case, than the child of a perfectly normal mother. You must look to it that such a false idea of heredity in mental matters shall not poison or ruin the lives of modern men and women.

Then there is the vexed question of causation—the answer to the question, "Why and how do people become mentally ill?" It would lead me too far afield to consider the various theories. I prefer to hide myself and my readers also behind a general admission of ignorance. When two apparently healthy men are both exposed to the same source of pneumonia infection, we do not know exactly why one develops pneumonia and dies, while the other develops nothing at all. Nor do we know, when two people are exposed to the same sources of mental stress, shock or strain, why one reacts by developing an acute depression, while the other passes through the difficult situation entirely unscathed and untroubled. There are few psychoses of which we can say that the exciting cause is absolutely known. Some eminent authorities have insisted that many psychoses, especially those of the manic-depressive type, are the direct result of some chronic inflammatory process, or of persistent intestinal stasis. Cure the infection, these men say; take out all the infected teeth, the infected tonsils; cure the constipation, if necessary remove surgically the entire lower bowel as far as the sigmoid flexure, and you will get surprising results. In one famous mental hospital in which these ideas were put into surgical practice, surprising results were apparently achieved. Of course, in depressive conditions, the whole organism is blocked. There is not only a stasis of the mind, but the whole personality is costive. In the depressed patient everything slows up. Therefore, the chronic constipation may possibly be a secondary result, and not the sole cause of the depressive psychosis itself. But I am not an eminent authority on such matters. I am not competent to interfere in the strife of the mental giants of my profession. So, if you persist in asking me what is the *cause* of this or that mental illness, I shall persist in answering that, so far as I myself am concerned, I really do not know. There are many men who know much more than I do. So please ask them.

After all, the illness of a personality is not so easy to trace under the microscope or on the autopsy table as an illness of that same personality's liver or lungs. Our pathological technique has not developed far enough to make it possible for me to answer such a question as was once propounded to me by a man on a coroner's jury, who had been present while I was making an autopsy on a man who had suffered from delusions of persecution, who had tried to kill his imaginary persecutors, and who had luckily jumped off a bridge and drowned in his attempts to escape them. I had removed the man's brain and was sectioning it, when this juror leaned over my shoulder and pointing to the surface of the brain asked, "Doctor, will you kindly show me those delusions of persecution." I pointed to a part of the brain cortex, and in my turn, I asked, "What do you see there?" "Nothing," said my friend, the juror, "nothing except something that looks like swiss cheese." "Well," said I, "that's all I can see myself. And it looks like swiss cheese to me too." That juror did not think highly of my professional ability. My readers may have the same opinion when I skim over so lightly this whole question of "causation." However, I cannot show you now the delusions of persecution on the cortex of the human brain. Some day perhaps, but not yet.

If you should visit any state hospital for mental cases and ask the psychiatrist in chief what type of mental disease was represented by the majority of his hundreds of patients, the chronic cases that will never get well, he would answer you with one long Greek word—schizophrenia. In the old textbooks you will find this psychosis called by two Latin names, dementia præcox. We used to call it that, because physicians had noticed that it manifested itself very frequently in young people. It was, so they thought, a "dementia," a loss of "mens" or mind that occurred "precociously," that is, at an early age when one would not expect to find an objective deterioration of the mental machinery. There was, so the earlier writers said, "a dementia of old age, a senile dementia" that must be a natural result of the wearing out of the body. But this other "dementia" was not senile, but "præcox." Then the Germans, who are great sticklers for accuracy in medical terminology, and who would much rather take their medical expressions from Greek than from Latin, made up a new name for this mental illness and called it "hebephrenia." This was Greek right enough; but it did not make sense. Phrên, in Greek, is another word for mind. But Hêbes means youth or adolescence. So hebephrenia must signify a condition of the youthful mind, not necessarily a pathological condition at all. In the strict sense, every young person is "hebephrenic." But not every one is necessarily a case of dementia præcox; or is necessarily "schizophrenic." That long word "schizophrenic" is not only Greek, it makes sense also. And as there are fashions in psychiatry as well as in gowns, as no well-dressed woman to-day would be comfortable in the very short skirts of five years ago, so a psychiatrist, unless he is "way back with the mental buggies," never uses the expression "dementia præcox." He speaks of schizophrenia. For there is a Greek verb "schizo," which means "to split"; and a schizophrenia is a condition of the mind in which the integration or unity of the personality has begun to split up into separate subsidiary entities, that start their thinking and acting on their own accord, until the personality disintegrates so completely that all sense of normal personality is lost.

Let me at least try to explain this "splitting off" in the words of every-day life. You are on your way to your office or to the university. Last night you had been reading a Life of Napoleon Bonaparte, and when you went to bed you had just finished the description of the Battle of Waterloo. This morning, as you walk along, you turn over in your mind the story of the battle. "If I had been Napoleon," you think to yourself, "I could have won that battle. I should have done thus and so, and not all the unexpected Blüchers in the world would have upset my plans." But although in your thought you temporarily identify yourself with the Emperor of the French, you keep this identification within the unity of your personality. You are still you. You have no difficulty in disentangling yourself from Napoleon when you are through thinking about him and have to get off the trolley-car or park your own automobile. But suppose that same compact sense of unity has begun to loosen a little; suppose that the function of your mind, by which you temporarily identify yourself with Napoleon, gets "split off" from the rest of your personality and begins to function all by itself. You can no longer call it back into yourself and distinguish yourself from the Emperor, and very soon you begin to realize that you *are* Napoleon Bonaparte. There is no necessity of parking your car. Have you not marshals and generals at your command? Are not policemen less important than they? So stop your car in the middle of the street and tell that fat "cop" on the corner to park it. If he looks at you questioningly, why explain things to him courteously. Tell him who you are—the Emperor Napoleon. Of course, if he is insolent, if he refuses to obey orders, then you get angry, quite naturally. You happen to have left your official sword behind; you cannot run the miscreant through the body as Napoleon would doubtless have done. But there is a heavy spanner handy in your car. Hit the "cop" over the head with that. You do hit him. And then you cannot understand why every one should make such a fuss about a little thing like that. You try to explain. You do your best to make people realize who you are. But they will not listen.

One of the most pathetic schizophrenic patients I have known believed, nay, he *knew* that he was Jesus Christ come into the world a second time in order to make men happy, to make them love one another. He knew the great secret. If people would only listen to him he could tell them how to put an end to all the pain, all the injustice on earth. No one would listen, except an occasional doctor or a dull orderly, neither of whom understood what it meant to be the Savior of the World and to be prevented from saving it.

Another example. Again imagine yourself on your way to your morning's work. You have a hard day before you. You will need all your ability, all your mental and physical strength in order to get through it successfully. But as a matter of fact you are feeling very seedy indeed. Your head aches. Your hand isn't as steady as it ought to be. And it is all the fault of that "party" last night. Whatever possessed you, knowing that you had a hard day ahead of you, whatever tempted you to go out with that gay crowd, to eat an expensive dinner that you couldn't afford, to drink too many cocktails, to go from the theatre to that night-club, and to get home at three o'clock without a cent left in your pocket? What a double-barrelled idiot you are, lazy, good for nothing, weak willed, yielding to the slightest temptation, spending money you haven't got, and doing a lot of other things—things that you remember only hazily and the mere thought of which makes you "hot under the collar." You're a failure. You're no good.

"Oh, longing no research can satiate,
Or seek to reveal what is hid.
For alas it were vain to expatiate
On deeds more depraved than I did."[9]

Yet, all the while you are calling yourself names, kicking yourself, swearing at yourself, you are carrying on this light interchange of graceful compliment within the unity of your personality. You are blaming *yourself*. And you can very easily disentangle yourself of the previous night from yourself of this morning, you can stop at a drug-store and get a bromo-seltzer, and by the time you arrive at your office or the university, you are interested in the day's work and are telling your-self that you probably do not look half as wall-eyed and washed-out as Johnny Jones who was one of your partners in crime last night.

But, suppose that the unity of your mental reactions has begun to loosen; suppose the part of your mind that is calling you bad names and telling you painful home-truths gets "split off" and starts functioning by itself. You are no longer able to say, "This is I, talking to myself, or calling myself names." You begin to say, "This is some one else outside me, some one who is talking to me, calling me names, insulting me. I hear some one, some one not myself, telling me that I drink too many cocktails, that I am a wash-out, a failure. What business is it of his what I am?" And so you are constantly in a listening attitude. You begin to hear voices from outside yourself; you tell other people about it; and they make fun of you. You think they must hear the voices because you hear them so clearly. If they insist that they hear nothing, then they are deceiving you. They must believe the insulting things that the voices are saying. They must be your enemies. Perhaps it is from them that the voices come. But you hear the insulting

9"Brandy and Soda," After Swinburne by Hugh Howard. In *The Humbler Poets*, edited by Slason Thompson (Chicago: McClurg, 1888), pp. 447–8.

voices when nobody is about. That however is easy to explain. These enemies of yours that send the voices are sending them over some unseen radio. Wireless telegraphy, of course. The messages come straight out of the air. After awhile, you begin to reason it all out. It is the Catholics who are "after you." Or the Masons. It may be the man next door. You are surrounded by enemies on every side. And nobody will believe you; nobody will help you. Finally, while you are riding on a trolley-car, you realize abruptly that it is the motor-man who controls with his hand the electric current and who is directing toward you the insulting, intolerable stream of wireless telegraphy. You can't stand it any longer. Shoot him, then, if you have a gun. If not, go up to him. Tell him to stop the talking. And if he refuses, pick him up and throw him out of the car, and turn off the current yourself.

This may give you some slight conception of the torments that beset the schizophrenic patient when his personality first begins to disintegrate. He is conscious that something strange is going on in his mind—his "thoughts are leaking out." And he soon comes to externalize his mental difficulties; to connect them with some material agency.

Schizophrenia is an endogenic psychosis; it acts markedly in the sphere of the intelligence, and it is ominous. As a general rule schizophrenic patients never return to a normal mental life. There are a few cases that are able sometimes to adapt themselves to a simple type of existence; but such mental healings always heal with a "permanent mental defect." At the very best, something of the integrated personality has been irretrievably lost.

Your schizophrenic patient, just like the manic-depressive, will lack insight; you will not be able to reason him out of his hallucinations. You will notice too that his mental symptoms are not delusional but hallucinatory; no sounds are audible, yet he hears voices. Moreover, the disintegration of his personality is frequently accompanied by a complete dulling of the emotions. The sudden death of his father brings no tears to his eyes; take him to the most thrilling motion-pictures, and he remains as emotionally stolid as if he were looking at a blank wall; he loses all affection for those he once loved. In this way he is the direct antithesis to the manic-depressive, who is all emotion. Finally, such a schizophrenic patient will talk and act in a way that can only be expressed by the French word *bizarre*. He shows peculiar tricks of speech; he attitudinizes, holding his hands or his feet in certain peculiar and noticeable positions. These attitudes and positions all have a mental significance to him, some strange, quite impossible connotation; for example, he maintains a definite pose of his arms in order to minimize the effect of the electric currents that are being passed into his body from a distance by his unseen enemies.

Moreover, at the beginning of the psychosis, the patient may develop unsocial habits. He will remain for long hours in his room, doing nothing; he will refuse to get up in the mornings; or will walk the streets alone all night; at table he is moodily silent; he is often boorish and rude. Sometimes he will tell you that he has discovered he is not his father's son; that he is an illegitimate child, with some important mysterious ancestry. With his disintegrating personality he is no longer able to adjust himself to the ordinary ways of home or school or business life. He feels that "something is going wrong inside his mind," and the split-off elements of his thinking force him to locate the trouble, not in himself, but outside himself.

I do not think that you will have any great difficulty in recognizing a schizophrenic case. Of course, you may sometimes suspect that a very introverted, shy and peculiar young man is developing this type of psychosis, and you may wrong him grievously. But if you keep him under observation and find that his peculiarities do not tend to turn into hallucinations, in other words if there is no "development," no progressive disintegration, then you can be fairly sure that your patient is not psychotic, not mentally sick. He may be what we call a "psychopathic personality," with all sorts of phobias and inhibitions, but with insight and some self-control. He is not developing a definite mental disease.

If you are in doubt about the matter, it is better to be on the safe side of the fence. Persuade your patient to see a psychiatrist, on some pretext or other; this experience, if he is not mentally ill, will surely do him no harm. If he is really schizophrenic, you will prevent him from doing harm to others.

The really pathetic cases in a mental hospital are these schizophrenic patients who show little or no gradual mental deterioration and whose personalities are still sufficiently integrated to be able to adjust themselves to routine hospital life, but who could not possibly meet the complex demands of an extramural existence. The ultimate results of schizophrenia, the complete dementia, the absolute mental blankness, the tiny spark of mental life that still flickers in a sound body—all these lie outside the scope of this book. You may see and study them, if you care to do so, in any large mental hospital.

Here we are interested only in giving such knowledge as will enable you to recognize an incipient schizophrenia, so that you may take the necessary steps to protect the patient as well as the community. Many a murder might have been prevented, if some parish priest, minister or social worker had been able to understand what was going on in the mind of one of his parishioners, or cases.

If any of you have an opportunity of acting as chaplain to a mental hospital or of holding occasional services in such institutions, you will have a chance to study those numerous cases of hopeless schizophrenia which have become merely a matter of custodianship. The over-worked physicians of such a hospital have little or no time to waste on these incurable, disintegrating cases. But no one has ever yet shown just what might be done to help these helpless people—not by sermons, not by an occasional reading of Morning Prayer, but by the use of Catholic sacraments. Many of these partially clouded minds are capable, I am sure, of making good communions, good confessions, of saying simple prayers and of coming close to God. For they have come very, very far away from man and from the world of logical thought in which man lives. Religion, not Protestant expositions and long extempore prayers, but Catholic faith and practice, has never really been tried out as therapeutic agents in connection with mental cases. Today physicians are no longer as antagonistic as once they were to the intrusion of "the parson" among their psychotic patients. They have no patience, and I sympathize with them, no patience at all with a type of religious service that merely stimulates the emotions of emotionally unstable people and "upsets the whole ward for a week." But the peaceful, quieting atmosphere of an early mass, not mumbled, but said plainly in an even well-modulated voice, could do the most excited patient no harm, even if the mass itself were viewed by the hospital authorities merely as a somewhat theatrical Eleusinian mystery: while not even the greatest psychiatrist can tell what help these starved, dislocated, twisted minds might find in coming, for those few moments, into the immediate presence of Him, who once cast out devils and who is still, although many physicians may doubt it, the Great Physician of human souls.

As to the etiology of schizophrenia, I can tell you nothing definite. There are theories enough. I will mention two; one a theory of purely mental causation, the other a theory of a more tangible, more apparently objective cause. Some authorities believe that the schizophrenic is inherently incapable of meeting life as it really is. In his recoil from actuality, he creates an imaginary world of his own, which finally cuts him off completely from all adjustment to reality. He hates his home; therefore he begins to imagine that he is not his father's son, but the adopted illegitimate child of some millionaire. Gradually he finds himself actually at war with the life of the world; and this conflict flares up in some sudden outbreak of violence or peculiarity. He may withdraw himself from reality so far that he refuses to think at all; refuses to eat, to move, and lapses into a so-called catatonic state of complete inactivity.[10] The other theory thinks it has found a possible explanation of schizophrenia in an inadequate and improperly adjusted functioning of those mysterious entities, the ductless glands.

A very great deal of our unconscious life, our automatic physical functioning and development, is guided by the hormones, or the chemical products of these same glands; thyroid, adrenals, pituitary, interstitial cells of the testicles and so on. Most glands, as you know, have ducts or outlets, like round rubber tubes at the end of a bag. Your mumps gland, for instance, the parotis, on either side of your face, is a gland with a duct. It produces saliva, and it sends this product through its duct into your mouth. But ductless glands are set directly in the blood-stream. They have no single outlet. And they control a very great part of our daily lives by the manner in which their products act on what is called the autonomous or vegetative nervous system. These are the nerves that you yourself cannot control by any impulse from your brain. By means of your "volitional nerves," you can make your legs run, instead of walk; but you cannot make your heart go faster by sending it an order from your brain. Its action is controlled by a different type of nerves. And it is this type that is set in motion or inhibited by the products of the ductless glands. I cannot go into the complex subject here.[11] But some modern investigators have thought that the exciting cause of schizophrenia may lie in the imperfect correlation of these ductless glands and of their various products. Another very interesting line of investi-

[10]For a study of the mental elements in the causation of psychoses, see *Psychopathology*, by E. J. Kempf, M.D. "The autonomic-affective cravings do not reason. Like other physical forces, they cease to strive just in proportion as they are neutralized. Therefore, when the perfect reality cannot be obtained, a substitute is adopted or accepted, as an image, delusion, hallucination, fetich, ritual or symbol." *Ibid.*, pp. 38–39.

[11]*American Journal of Psychiatry*, Vol. I (1921–1922), old series Vol. 78, pp. 589–607. John Rathbone Oliver, "Emotional States and Illegal Acts in Connection with Schizophrenia."

gation along the lines of endocrinology, that is the science of the ductless glands,[12] has divided human beings into two principal physical and mental types. One type, called the pyknic type, develops manic-depressive psychosis, if it has any mental illness at all. The other type, the asthenic, becomes schizophrenic. But I have said enough, I hope, to make it comparatively easy for you to recognize manic-depressive conditions and schizophrenic symptoms whenever you come across them in your work. These two psychoses are the most frequent. You will surely, at some time or another, have to deal with them. But how successfully you deal with them will depend on your ability to absorb such information as I have been able to give you into your own experience, to make it part of your own personal technique in dealing with mental difficulties. I can give you the tools. But you yourself must learn how to use them. With the very same box of tools, one man may create a masterpiece while another only succeeds in cutting his own fingers.

CLINICAL MATERIAL

A. Manic-depressive Cases:
(1) Mild Elation.

James Doe, a young man of average mental ability, is a freshman. His father is a country lawyer, stolid, unimaginative. The mother is emotional, over-anxious; she has always surrounded her only son with an atmosphere of fear, fear of getting his feet wet, fear of getting drowned if he goes swimming with other boys. Her two daughters are several years older than their only brother, who has always been "the baby" of the family. As a child he was afraid of the dark and of thunderstorms, but concealed these fears from every one except his mother. There is a history of occasional somnambulism, night terrors and bed-wetting up to the age of eleven. First school contacts were difficult. James did not make friends easily. But he had no serious illnesses; he was phys-

[12]Ernst Kretschmer, *Koerperbau und Charakter*. Eng. ed., *Physique and Character*.

ically strong, although very imaginative and self-conscious. During his early years at a public school, he was teased because he "would not fight." One day, at the age of thirteen, being teased into a sudden fury, he flew at his tormentor and nearly annihilated him. This sudden realization of his own physical strength seemed to change the boy's character. He became truculent, often provoking a fight, rather a bully of smaller boys, rude at home, swearing, refusing to go to church. He was evidently over-compensating for a sense of inferiority. By inflicting pain on others, by being rude at home, he kept proving to himself that he was "not afraid" of any one. Beneath this external adjustment he was still introspective, still fearful and shy. In his home town, at high school, he was not very popular. Younger boys were afraid of him. He was always flattering and toadying the bigger ones, especially those more powerful than himself. At home he became more and more rebellious, rude to his mother and his sisters, but avoiding his father and still afraid of him. During adolescence he developed autoerotic habits. He had intense fears of their results, but could not control them, and was too afraid of his father to ask his advice. In order to prove to older high-school boys that he was a "rounder," he went once to a house of prostitution, but became so terrified by the intimate advances of the woman whom he had chosen that he was impotent. She laughed at him. And he believed that his autoerotic habits had "ruined his manhood."

When he came to the university, he knew no one. But by chance he met another freshman who was living in one of the large dormitories, whose roommate had fallen ill, and who asked James to share his double room. This young man had many friends. James soon found himself caught up in the midst of all kinds of gaiety—girls, theatres, parties, synthetic gin. He was pledged to a good fraternity. He was, for the first time in his life, gloriously happy. But he was doing no work in his classes. He was in debt. He was taking little exercise and smoking too many cigarettes. Abruptly he realized that examinations were only two weeks off. His roommate, who had been living the same type of life, cut down his own smoking, gave up parties, kept away from the fraternity house, and got out his neglected text-books. He worked twelve hours a day and more. James did the same thing. The examinations came on. James did fairly well on his first examination. But during the next few days he found that, when he went to bed, he could not sleep. His mind kept on going and going. Other men in the dormitory complained that James kept them from studying. He was always dropping in, and continually talking. His roommate shut himself up in his bedroom so that James would not disturb him. But he heard James talking to himself in the study. James was not doing any work for the second examination. It was all easy enough. He knew it all anyway. On the morning of the examination, when the examination itself was half over, James suddenly burst out laughing, took up his examination book, and walked laughing out of the room. In a few moments, he came dashing back again, went to the proctor in charge and handed in his book. The proctor refused to accept it. James had carried the book out of the room with him. That was absolutely forbidden. James could not understand this. He talked in a loud, high-pitched voice. The examination was too easy. He had answered all the questions. Anyhow, there was his book. If the proctor didn't want to accept it, that made no difference. James didn't think much of the college anyway. He was going to take up aviation. Admiral Byrd had promised to take him on his next trip to the South Pole. Finally, James had to be escorted from the room by two of his class-mates. He was not unpleasant or quarrelsome. On the contrary, everything was all right. The proctor discovered that James' examination book was filled with unconnected sentences that made no sense. Before looking at the book, he had thought that James was intoxicated. Now he hurried over to the dormitory. But he was too late. James, who had been locked in his room by his impatient class-mates, had climbed out of a very high window, slipped down the branches of a tree to the ground, and was, at the moment, walking about the campus, clothed in last summer's straw hat and nothing else.

This period of elation lasted for about two months. It was followed by a very short phase of mild depression, after which James recovered completely. After three months in the mental hospital, and a summer on a farm, he returned to the university and settled down, and while in his sophomore year made up the lost work of his freshman semesters. He has been perfectly well ever since. At the mental hospital, one of the residents, who took an interest in James, taught him how to recognize symptoms of elation and how to deal with them if they should ever appear again. James graduated last year with honors. Fortunately, he is going into business. If he had wanted to become a lawyer or a physician and had applied for admission to some distinguished medical or law school, he would probably have been rejected because he had once had "a mental illness." For James would not have lied about it. He is rather proud of having been once "a mental case." That attack brought him a lot of precious information about himself that he guards as one of his most valuable assets.

(2) Depression.

Louisa Small is an unmarried woman of forty. She holds an important position as one of the chief department-heads in a great department store. She has great executive ability and also a vivid imagination. She knows, years ahead, just what women will be wanting to buy at a certain definite period. She is the third of a large family of ten, and has been always the "family buffer," the arranger of all domestic difficulties, the recipient of all secret troubles. Her father, a professor in a small New England college, was also a Presbyterian minister, rigid in matters of morals, setting a very high standard but living up to it himself; an almost violent prohibitionist, because his father, who had suffered from recurrent "melancholia," had been an alcoholic. Louisa's mother, a very repressed, drab little woman, had been exhausted by child-bearing, and had died after the birth of her tenth child. The two eldest children had died in babyhood. Louisa had become the head of the family when she was just entering adolescence. In childhood, she showed no psycho-neurotic traits, no phobias or faulty mental habits. She was always efficient, always obsessed by a sense of duty; a student of medium ability, for her household duties came first. Her father was the centre of her little world. She ran his house, brought up his seven other living children. She might have married several times; but she felt that her father could "not spare her." When she was thirty-two, her father married again. Her brother and sisters had emancipated themselves from the home atmosphere. The new stepmother was kind enough, but "there could not be two mistresses in one house." So Louisa had torn herself free from the habits of many years. She had found work easily enough. And now after eight years of it, she held an important position. Her salary was more than adequate; she had a charming apartment; every year she went the rounds of the great designers of women's dress in London, Paris, Vienna. She had friends of a kind. She entertained a little. She read a little. And she rode horseback occasionally. But of late, she noticed that small things had begun to annoy her. Her immediate chief, a man, the more or less autocratic head of her department, got on her nerves. Whenever he walked through her department, she became uncomfortable; if he criticised anything she got panicky, said or did the wrong thing, was clumsy, dropped something, made some idiotic mistake. She began to avoid him as much as possible. As a result he became very friendly with her chief assistant, an attractive younger woman, who was, as the patient knew, ambitious, very critical, and determined to make her way in the big shop. Gradually it became harder and harder for the patient to get through her day's work. She often had to make very important decisions that would involve the expenditure of a great deal of money. In the past, she had made these decisions quickly, confidently, successfully. Now she was not sure of herself any longer. She kept putting off these same decisions. And when she did finally make them, she would feel sure that she had decided wrongly and would try to alter them. One such alteration involved the department in difficulties and loaded it down with a type of frock that did not sell. Her chief had not said much, but she knew he had said a great deal to her critical subordinate. Finally, she decided that she was "getting stale." It was time for her annual trip to Europe; she was glad to go. But no sooner was she on the ship, than she made up her mind that her going had been a mistake. Her chief had seemed altogether too anxious to get her away. He was probably planning all sorts of things behind her back. While she was gone, her assistant, who was taking her place in the shop, would doubtless be making herself indispensable. Louisa spent only a few days in London, unable to decide on any orders. Then, the night she got to Paris, she had an acute attack of indigestion. She thought that her heart was going to stop beating, that she was going to die. She must get home—home. And at once. Without cabling her employers, she caught the next boat to New York. While at sea, she was standing one night alone in a dark corner of the deck, looking down at the rushing water below. A sudden surge of emotion, just like the water around the ship, seemed to surround her. She was a failure. She would without doubt lose her position, for she had spent the shop's money on an expensive voyage, and had accomplished none of the commissions with which she had been charged. No one would miss her. Her family did not need her. There was no single person in the world who really loved her. Moreover, there was something seriously wrong with her heart. She had no more courage; she couldn't face life any longer. How much easier it would be to—. And then, by chance, one of the ship's officers, who chanced to have been watching her, joined her, and in an attempt to cheer her up, sent for a steward and persuaded her to drink a hot toddy. She had scarcely ever tasted alcohol before. A glass of light wine, or a few swallows of beer was the most she had ever taken. But the whiskey seemed to clear her head; to lift, for a moment, her sense of failure, her depression. After that, she kept a bottle of whiskey in her cabin. And she had drunk more than one bottle by the time she landed. When she got to her apartment, she went to bed with another acute digestive attack. The physician whom she called in was a very general practitioner. Naturally, all that he saw was a middle-aged woman who had been using too much alcohol. He took away her alcohol, gave her a little bromide that only made her feel more mentally depressed, and left her alone in her apartment, for she had returned so unexpectedly that she couldn't get in touch immediately with her maid. Meanwhile, the shop had heard nothing from her since her last letter from London. She was all alone; she could not eat, she could not sleep, she could not concentrate her mind on two lines of print. The bromide soon ceased to affect her; she went out and bought veronal, a very great deal of veronal. It so happened that her maid, who chanced to be passing through the city, decided to visit the apartment to see that everything was in order. She found her mistress in a stupor, that the maid thought was death, or at least the approach of it. And as she was a religiously minded woman, she sent for her priest, after she had summoned a physician.

Here is the case. Suppose you were the pastor who was called to this woman. Suppose, that after she had recovered from her veronal poisoning, under the physician's care, you had a chance to talk with her. How would you deal with her? How would you get at the real mental elements—the causative factors—that seem so covered up and distorted by the surface symptoms of veronal poisoning and alcoholism? The possibilities of your service to this woman would be tremendous. If you saw only a thoughtless, self-indulgent, selfish woman, who had allowed herself to "drink because she got discouraged"; if you rebuked her for "sins" and told her "to pull herself together and to keep away from the whiskey bottle," you might find her name a few days later among the names of those who have "found the wrong way out." On the other hand, if you could recognize the beginnings of a typical depressive psychosis, if you could put her in the care of a psychiatrist or in some mental hospital, you would surely have saved a soul alive. If you could do more than this—if you could keep in touch with her during the depressed period, walk by her side while she went down into her mental hell and then help her during her period of readjustment, you would prove yourself indeed a physician of souls. Finally, when she had completely recovered and had secured the same or even a better business position, if you could make her see the danger of a self-centred life that has no emotional outlet, if you could persuade her to adopt one of her dead brother's many children and to find something or some one on whom to expend the dammed-up powers of her love—if, above all, you could teach her to love God and to walk in His ways and by His side—then you would have proved yourself something even better than a good physician of souls—you would have proven yourself a faithful able priest of Jesus Christ.

B. Schizophrenia.

Abraham Cohn is an able young Jew about twenty-five years of age. His father was an orthodox Jew, a tailor in a small way, a good man, but not particularly successful. The mother is a different type; ambitious, scheming, clever in the management of money, and determined that her children shall "make good." She laughs at her husband's out-worn orthodox ideals. To get on in this world you must do as the "Goim" do. You must go them one better. With one exception, none of her children have fulfilled her hopes. Two daughters have married poor men; one a push-cart peddlar, the other a clerk in a pawnshop. Two of her three sons are no better off; they hurried through the eighth grade of school so that they could get jobs. And what jobs! One has a small news-paper route, a scolding wife and three children. The other is a waiter in a Kosher restaurant. But the third son, Abraham—he is different. Even as a little boy he was always fond of his books; he would much rather read his geography than play on the street with the other boys. He was seldom ill, like the others. He did not even look much like his brothers. His mother secretly rejoiced in this because, if Abraham had not a Jewish name, he might be easily mistaken for a gentile boy. He was never noisy, never rude. And if the other children bothered him, he would go to his bed-room and read a book. At school he always stood at the head of his class. And by the time he had reached the eighth grade, his teacher had told him that he ought to go to high school. Of course the other sons objected. Why shouldn't Abe go to work and earn something? They weren't going to feed an extra mouth while he was "getting an education." Nevertheless, in their hearts they were proud of him. So Abe went to high school. In his free time he sold papers and did odd jobs. He could be an efficient money-getter when he knew that the money he earned would help him through school. He graduated. And then—no, he would not go to work—he, Abraham Cohn, the son of Elias Cohn the tailor, he was going to be a lawyer, and have an office of his own, and go into the court-house and be able to talk straight out to the judges themselves. Three hard grinding years as an undergraduate at the local university. Up at day-break to take out his papers; working in lecture room and library all day; dashing home to help deliver the suits that his father pressed and cleaned, and then sitting over his books until long after midnight. He had one intimate friend, Jonas Friedman, a young Jew of his own age, who had similar ambitions. Both men came from the same type of environment; both were "working their way" through college. But Jonas was self-sufficient, satisfied with life, jolly and friendly with every one; while Abe, so Jonas thought, kept too much to himself, worried lest people should not want him around because he was a Jew, and frequently complained that he was not "getting a square deal." Jonas was rather proud of his ancestry. If people did not "want him around," well, he could go somewhere else where people did want him. And if any one did not "give him a square deal," he would find out the reason why and get himself a square deal somehow. Abe was by far the more brilliant student. He was do-ing especially well in his economics and history courses. But Jonas was more popular. He got odd jobs around the grandstands of the athletic field; came to know the managers of some of the teams. Abe looked down on all "thick-headed athletes." He had other ways of earning money; doing occasional tutoring, helping, for a price, panicky freshmen who had done no work during the term and who had to pass certain insignificant examinations. When Abe took his B.A., Mrs. Cohn almost fainted with pride. She and Jonas' mother sat side by side in the back room of the academic theatre. Jonas had found them better seats, further towards the front, but they would not sit there; such prominence would have embarrassed them. Nevertheless both mothers seemed to be reach-ing the goals of their ambitions. There remained only the last lap in the race. The law school for Abe; the medical school for Jonas. Jonas had by far the more difficult task. His work at the medical school would not leave much time for money-making. And he needed all his mental energies for the medical work, if he did not want to be dropped at the end of the first semester. But, through one of his athletic friends whose father was in a bank, Jonas was able to borrow a certain amount of money, taking out an insur-ance policy on his own life as a security for the repayment of his debt. Abe could have done the same thing, but he dreaded debt; he was afraid of involving himself in difficulties that he might not be able to meet. Besides, the bank might cheat him in some way, perhaps put some clause into the promissory note that would make Abe have to pay twice as much as he had borrowed. And the mere idea of a life insurance policy made him panicky. He was not going to die. It was bad luck to think about dying. Besides, he was suspicious of these insurance salesmen; they tried to put something over on you, to make you pay more than you could afford. Yet Abe, in his way, was lucky also. Abrams, Sonneborn and Abrams, the most important Jewish legal firm in their city, would give him a place as clerk or errand boy in their office. Mr. Sonneborn, who maintained his orthodoxy in the face of his partners' liberalism, had often seen Abe's father at the synagogue. And for years Mr. Cohn had pressed Mr. Sonneborn's trousers. This office position would not pay very much; but it would give Abe a great opportunity of "learning law by experience"; the theory he was to get at the law school. This particular school was not what is now called a "full-time institution," but it was a very good law school nevertheless. The lectures did not begin until four o'clock in the afternoon, so that a young man who had to have a paying job could work on this job until four o'clock, on five days of each week, and could then dash down to the school, where he would listen to difficult lectures from four until eight or nine, and then drag himself home to sit up until midnight with his law books and his lecture notes. There are thousands of eminent lawyers who have passed unscathed through three years of such mental effort as this. Therefore, it can be done. Although one often wonders why more young law-students in similar schools do not develop some type of mental up-set or exhaustion. Abe went through two years of this with flying colors. During the summers he worked hard in the law office; and his two weeks' holiday was spent at home with his books. Then in October of his third year something went wrong. Abe came home one day at two o'clock, when he should still have been at the office. He explained to his mother that he and the chief clerk, Mr. Isaacs, had had a misunderstanding. Mr. Isaacs had been trying "to put something over on him." When Abe had brought him a certain set of documents, Mr. Isaacs had looked at Abe in a very peculiar manner. His look intimated that he believed that Abe had altered the date of a certain paper. And Abe was not going to stand that. Next morning Abe would not get up. His mother thought he was ill. But he insisted that he was not going to the office that day. In a panic his mother took her courage in both hands, and going to the law office, managed to intercept Mr. Isaacs as he went out for luncheon. He reassured her that he had said nothing to Abe.

Everything had been quite all right. If Abe wasn't feeling well, let him stay home for a few days. There wasn't much important work just now. Then he laughed; "I guess, Mrs. Cohen," he said, "your son must have got himself a girl. He sits looking out of the window sometimes, just doing nothing, and sort of mumbling to himself. I think her name must be 'Merriman.' Same name as the Governor of the State. Your boy must be getting into high society." Mrs. Cohn went home utterly puzzled. Abe was still in bed, staring at the ceiling. "Mother," he said, "I wish you'd speak to the people next door. I keep hearing their voices through the wall. Tell them to turn off that radio." Mrs. Cohn was too anxious to realize that, at this time of the day, the neighbors were all out at work. So she told Abe what Mr. Isaacs had said, that if he were sick he could stay at home. But he'd better go to his law-school lectures. Then, in simple curiosity, she asked about "the girl." Abe shook his head. He had no time for girls. But "Merriman"? That name? To her surprise, Abe flushed to the roots of his hair. And she persisted with her questions until she got an answer that terrified and wounded her. "I've always been sort of different from the rest of the family, haven't I, mother?" Abe asks. "Well, for some time I've been thinking that I can't be your son—I mean that there must be some sort of mystery about my birth. You've always concealed it from me. But whenever I write down the name "Merriman" it looks so familiar. You know, the Governor had a son who was sort of wild in his youth. So I might perhaps be—" Poor Mrs. Cohn breaks into sobs. Her own son; the fruit of her own body. Wouldn't she know her own child? Doesn't he love her any more? And strangely enough it seems as if Abe does not love her very much. He makes no attempt to comfort her; he pushes her caresses aside. Her grief does not touch him in the least. At four, he goes to the law-school. During the first lecture, the man who sits next to him notices that he is not taking any notes, but writing one name over and over again. When the lecture is over, a small group of men is gathered in the hall. Abe Cohn walks past them. Abruptly, he turns, comes back and puts his hand on one man's shoulder. He is shaking with suppressed rage. "You stop calling me that," he says. "Oh, I heard you. But I won't stand it." There is a moment's pause of astonishment.

"There you go again," Abe shouted. "I told you to stop. I don't care whether I am a Jew. You haven't any right to say—." He stops, seems to be listening and then, clenching his first, suddenly strikes one of the men in the face. There is a row. At first, every one imagines that Abe is drunk. He has gone off muttering to himself. But the man, who had been struck, has heard more clearly than others, some of Abe's excited statements, and as soon as his lectures are over, he takes the trouble to find out Abe Cohn's home address. On his way he meets Jonas Friedman, a man whom he had known at the university, and who is now in his third year at the medical school. He tells Jonas about Abe. And Jonas, having already had two semesters of psychiatry, gets a chilly sensation of fright down his spine. He and the law student find Abe at home sitting in his bedroom, with his ear close to the wall. In his hand he is holding a revolver that he has just borrowed, on some pretext, from his brother the clerk in the pawn shop, who had, among his unredeemed pledges, all sorts of "guns." Abe is not particularly surprised to see Jonas or his friend from the law-school. "I'm just waiting," he says quietly, "until the people in there begin talking to me through the wall again—calling me names—calling me—calling me— I won't have them call me *that*. If they do it again I'm going in next door to stop it—listen!" He holds up his hand. Then, leaping to his feet, he seizes the revolver and starts from the room. It takes the combined strength of the two men to prevent his going next door and "stopping the voices." The next morning he has quieted down. But Jonas persuades Abe to accompany him to the medical school so that he can show him the work he is doing this semester. He leads Abe into the mental clinic and turns him over to one of the assistant psychiatrists.

If you were that psychiatrist, how would you go about an examination of this case? How would you approach Abraham Cohn? You only know that of late he has done and said some peculiar things, that he attacked a fellow-student without any apparent reason and that after borrowing a revolver he made threats against some neighbors whom he does not like. That is about all the information that you can get from the law-student who has accompanied Abe, while Jonas has gone off to his work in the surgical dispensary. On the basis of this information, how would you get at Abe's fundamental difficulties? How would you deal with his statements about being called names, not getting a fair deal, and being annoyed to a pitch of frenzy by some kind of a peculiar radio in the house next door to his? What help could you give him? not only now, but later on, if he is sent to a mental hospital? Or, if you yourself were a rabbi, or a member of Abe's own race, how could you offer him the help that religion is supposed to be able to give? If Abe were a Christian, and you his pastor, what would you say—and do?

Chapter III

MENTAL ILLNESS
(continued)

PARANOIA, EPILEPSY, PARESIS. CLINICAL MATERIAL

WE have now discussed two types of mental illness, two psychoses, which are the most common types and with which you, as pastors and social workers, will almost inevitably be brought into contact. Before I pass on to conditions that are definitely exogenic and toxic, I must describe briefly a mental state that is usually called "paranoid." The Greek word "nous" is another word for mind. And the preposition "para" means "along side of" or "besides." As Doctor William White says, "The term paranoia was used by the ancient Greeks to designate a kind of thinking that was 'beside itself.'"[1] Just as we speak of "a mind distraught" or distracted. Once it meant "mental disease," or "insanity" in general. Nowadays, we mean by paranoia a mental illness, that is endogenic, that does not apparently affect the intelligence except at one single point and that may or may not unfit the patient for the activities of ordinary life.[2] The outstanding elements in it as they would strike the casual observer are these. First, the apparent mental soundness of the patient. You may talk for a long time with such a patient and never realize that he or she is not mentally normal. But, if you touch on *one* certain subject, you will bring from the patient a whole mass of pathological mental material. Yet this same mass is always mentally co-ordinated, and this is the second noticeable symptom; for, if you once

---

[1] *Outlines of Psychiatry*, pp. 113 ff.

[2] See the full discussion of paranoia in White, *loc. cit.*, and in Menninger, *Human Mind*, pp. 83, 87, 239–241 and p. 94.

grant the patient's premises as true, then the rest of his statements are logical deductions from those premises.

In almost every court-house in the country, the judges, lawyers and attendants there are familiar with at least one paranoid individual. He is usually an anxious-faced man with
shabby clothes, whose pockets are stuffed with worn, tattered
papers, and who carries a little brief-case bursting with soiled
documents. Or, a determined precise little woman, who can
produce from an ancient reticule or from the secret intricacies
of her clothing, the same kind of legal-looking papers. Day in
and day out, they appear in the corridors of the court-house;
they will interview judges, they buttonhole hurrying lawyers,
they will even pour out their woes to bailiffs, or to any by-
stander who seems to know something about "the injustices of
the law." They are all interested in "some important case"—a
damage suit that was settled years ago; a once disputed title
to a piece of land or a house, that was proven unsound just after
the Civil War. They all have a legal grievance; they have all
been "cheated of their just rights." Their lawyers have deceived them; the judges who heard the case have been corrupted. They suspect every one who ever had any connection
with the case, or who has ever tried to tell them that they have
no case at all. Their statements are logical enough. Once grant
their major premise, for example that the United Railways
does owe them compensation for an injury, that a certain piece
of property does legally belong to them, and you must admit
that their complaints about injustice and prejudice are justified.
Talk with them on any subject except law or the administra-
tion of justice, and you will find them sane enough. But mention a certain judge's name, speak of some lawsuit of your
own, and you will release at once a whole torrent of complaint,
of abuse; a story of persistent injustice, mingled with warped
ideas of persecution, that you know are the delusions of a sick
mind. Usually, this type of legal paranoid is permitted to har-
ass unhappy judges and to take up the time of the district at-

torney, and they are put off from day to day with vague promises because every one in the court-house knows and is sorry for them. They are usually harmless.

Sometimes, however, they are far from harmless. President Garfield was assassinated by a paranoid individual. Guiteau was declared sane and was hanged. But to-day no one doubts that he was a mental case. He believed that he had rendered great service to the Republican party, that he had as just a claim upon the newly elected president as that prominent gentleman whom the President had just named his Secretary of State. Guiteau did not claim any such high office as that. But, considering his services, it was only fair, only just that he should be given one of the less important diplomatic or even consular posts—minister to one of the smaller South American republics, for instance. Naturally, the President and his advisors had never heard of Guiteau. His letters, his applications, if he did make them, were put into the waste-basket. Meanwhile, Guiteau waited from day to day for his "promised appointment." I daresay that during the weeks before the assassination, he talked with many people, and these people may very well have sympathized with him; for, granting his major premise, namely that he had given distinguished service to the Republican party, his complaints about the ingratitude of politicians would have to be granted also. Such ideas of persecution are of course based on delusions. But while that same delusion is hidden from you, you would feel inclined to sympathize with Guiteau and his likes.

Of course, the paranoid has no insight in the particular field of his delusional system. In other matters, he has insight enough. You will surely be brought into contact with paranoid cases of this kind, and you ought not to have much trouble in recognizing the type. Many sane people, however, act in a paranoid manner when they allow one grievance, one social slight to develop in their minds until it becomes a kind of obsession.

"Mrs. Pennyfeather deliberately ignored me on the street a month ago," says Mrs. Jinglepencil. "I could not imagine what I had done to offend her. Then, I remembered that her husband and mine work in the same office. In the last promotions, my husband was advanced; hers was not. She evidently suspects that I exerted some influence on Mr. Indigo, who is the head of the office. Of course, he is a good friend of mine; but not so good a friend as all that. I shall warn my husband against the Pennyfeathers."

This is paranoid thinking. As a matter of fact, Mrs. Pennyfeather did not ignore Mrs. Jinglepencil on the street. She simply did not see her. Mrs. Jinglepencil's system rests on a delusion. Grant her major premise of Mrs. Pennyfeather's rude action, and the rest of her ideas might logically explain it. Mrs. Jinglepencil's paranoid thinking is not perhaps immediately dangerous. She does not shoot any one as Guiteau did. But she may well sow seeds of distrust between two friendly clerks in an office, and create an atmosphere of jealousy that may not kill anybody, but that may make some one often wish he were dead.

A great deal of gossip that goes by the name of "harmless" or "good natured" is paranoid. The premises are frequently delusional, while the system erected on that delusion will sound logical enough. That is what makes "paranoid thinking" so dangerous.

Here is another example. The rector, in getting off a trolley-car one night, slipped and twisted his ankle. As he limped up the street to the rectory door, his ankle gave way; he fell, picked himself up, and staggered up his front steps. Miss Paranoid, across the street, knows that the rector has been out to dinner, she has seen him stumble and fall. He has—just whisper it—been drinking. On this delusional foundation, a whole superimposed system grows. Given the fact of his drinking, it is logical enough to demand "some changes" in the parish; to believe that the empty bottles in the rectory ash-can are whiskey bottles, and that the man who comes to see the rector on Saturday nights is his bootlegger. The unfortunate rector who, while nursing his swollen ankle, is supposed to be "recovering from a debauch," is surprised when one of his vestrymen, his best friend, takes him aside and in a whisper suggests that "he should go easier on the booze." The men or women who have paranoid tendencies seldom "think straight," for they see and hear the things that they *want* to hear or see. If Miss Paranoid had not disliked the rector and been interested in the senior curate, as that rector's possible successor, she would never have seen what she thought she saw.

In dealing, however, with real cases of paranoia, it is often hard to tell when such a patient ceases to be "a harmless nut." Usually, if you find that the persecutory delusions of such a patient are associated with a large group of people, for example, the Masons, the Roman Catholics or the Jews, you need not feel bound to hurry him or her off to a mental hospital. On the other hand, if the delusions seem to be concentrating themselves on a small group, or on a single individual, then it is time to take some steps to let that same group or that individual know what is going on.

I suppose that every pastor has had, at some time or other, the following experience. During some service, for example during the high mass on Sundays, or while he is preaching, he suddenly hears a loud, inarticulate shout or snort from one of the pews or seats. Then comes the sound of a fall; of heels or hands hammering against wood. There is a moment's confusion. Several men gather around the pew, and the priest sees that they have picked up some one and are carrying him or her into the vestry or out into the front porch of the church. After the service is over, while the priest is standing at the front door speaking to his parishioners, he asks what the trouble was. He may get several answers. It was, some one says,

(1) A young man who had an epileptic seizure. Or,
(2) A young girl who fainted. Or,

(3) An old man who had "a stroke." Or,

(4) A middle-aged man or woman who "got feeling funny and fell over."

If, before that sound of the fall at the back of your church, you heard the kind of shout or snort that I mentioned above, you can be fairly sure that the answer you will get from your parishioners at the front door will be No. 1. But, before I go on to speak of epilepsy let me interpolate here—where it does not belong—a very brief discussion of the other three answers.

If some one has "fainted" (No. 2), then even the youngest Boy Scout of the parish troop will know that he must loosen the clothing about the woman's neck and chest, and not *lift* up her head, but let her lie flat. If the disturbance during the service comes under No. 3, then the quicker your Boy Scout can call an ambulance and get the unconscious man to the hospital, the better. His face will be congested; his breathing stertorous. Keep *his* head up. If his lips are blue, then it may be a heart attack. To the hospital with him as fast as you can. But, if your case comes under No. 4, if it be the result of what we call a "psychogenic" seizure, that is a state of clouded consciousness induced by some mental cause, such as fright, anxiety, or the like, then, after you have assured yourself that your patient is neither in a faint, an epileptic attack, nor the victim of a cerebral hemorrhage, go away and leave her alone, or with one person to watch her. Do not stand around her in a curiously interested group. Don't give her a "gallery." She will recover all the more quickly if she finds that she is not holding the centre of the stage. About all these matters, I shall have something more to say in another chapter.

But epilepsy:[3] pastors and social workers will surely have to

[3]For the most modern treatment of epilepsy see "Epilepsy and the Convulsive State," being Vol. VII of the *Proceedings of the Association for Research in Nervous and Mental Disease*. See especially sec. I, "Historical Survey and General Considerations of the Convulsive State," chap. 1, Presidential address by Dr. Walter Timme, pp. 1–5; and "A Note on the History of the Convulsive State prior to Boerhaave," by Dr. E. C. Streeter, pp. 5–30.

deal with it. The question of etiology or causation is a very complex one. I refer you to the classic text-books.[4] It is usually classed among those psychoses that are associated with organic diseases of the brain or the central nervous system. The expressions of this organic condition are so varied that White[5] prefers to speak of "the epilepsies." The Greek word "epilepsis" means seizing hold of, or as we say, a "seizure." The Greeks[6] called it the "sacred disease," distinguishing it from all other diseases, because they attributed the convulsions of epilepsy to the invasion of the human personality by some divine agency. And even to-day, any sort of a "convulsion" is, to the layman, an appalling picture of human suffering that terrifies him and makes him feel helpless.

When you are called on the street to help some convulsed person, or are suddenly faced by a convulsion of one of your people, you must not think that every convulsion is a symptom of epilepsy. Convulsions, as symptoms, appear in the toxic conditions of alcoholism, of kidney disease, in those psychogenic states that we call functional psychoneuroses, and in organic diseases of the brain, such as brain tumor, and in a type of psychosis that we shall discuss very shortly, "paresis." But as a general rule, the type of convulsions that you will meet with most frequently are the convulsions of idiopathic epilepsy. By "idiopathic" we mean a convulsion that is not a symptom of some other disease (allopathic), but of the organic brain condition that we call "the epilepsies."

In dealing with epileptic individuals, you may not often have a chance to see them during an acute convulsion. You will usually see them and talk with them during what we call the "interparoxismal" period, the times in between convulsions. And roughly, you may judge of the seriousness of an

---

[4] See White, op. cit., pp. 287–294.   [5] Op. cit., p. 287.
[6] See the book on the "Sacred Disease" in the Hippocratean Corpus. [Oeuvres completes d'Hippocrate, par Emil Littré. 10 Vols. (Paris, 1849), Vol. 6, pp. 352–397, or Hippocrates by W. H. S. Jones in 3 Vols., Loeb Classical Series. See Vol. 2, pp. 127–184.]

epileptic case by the frequency of these same convulsions. A case in which major convulsions appear every week and then, in spite of treatment, persist in their weekly occurrence or increase to a convulsion every other day—such a case will soon demand hospitalization. Fortunately there are many, although not nearly enough, excellent epileptic hospitals or colonies to which you can send your patient. After he or she gets there, a definite mental deterioration may begin to appear and may develop until the patient is quite incapable of caring for himself at all. But with such extreme chronic, almost hopeless cases, you will, as a usual thing, have little to do. The people that you are interested in, the people to whom you may be of inestimable help, are those men and women who have occasional epileptic seizures, but who are still able to live outside of a mental hospital.

First of all, you must be able to distinguish two types of epileptic seizures: what is commonly called "the grand mal" (taken from the French, for a change, instead of from the Greek, and meaning "the big sickness") and the less marked convulsive state, called "petit mal" (the little sickness).

A grand mal attack has certain definite symptoms. Often, but not always, it is preceded by what is called the "aura." The patient feels the attack coming on, as if some cold wind were blowing on his face. And he often, not always, reacts to this "aura" by that strange half-strangled shout, that once heard can seldom go again unrecognized. After that, there begins a contraction, a twisting of the muscles of the limbs, especially of the arms, of the neck also. The patient foams at the mouth, his teeth grind together and he often bites his tongue or the inside of his cheek, so that blood is mingled with the foam on his lips. Sometimes there is an involuntary passage of urine, even of feces. If you are doubtful about the symptoms of an attack, look at your patient's tongue and the inside of his cheeks. If you find there scars of bites, you may be fairly sure that he has had grand mal attacks. Gradually, the twisted tormented muscles relax, the teeth cease to grind, the face looks less distorted; then the body relaxes, and the patient sinks into a deep sleep. He may sleep for several hours. Usually, when he wakes, he remembers nothing about the attack itself, except the warning "aura." Often these grand mal attacks come at night. If no one is living with the patient, or if no one hears him, he may have such an attack every night, come out of it, fall into deep sleep, and then wake up with a feeling of general lassitude perhaps, but with no memory of what has happened to him.

Differing greatly from these grand mal seizures are the petit mal attacks, which often take the place of the major seizures. Hence, they are sometimes called "vicarious cloudings of consciousness." In them, the patient does not fall; there are no muscular contractions, no foaming at the mouth, no tongue biting. But for a few minutes the patient loses immediate contact with the world of reality; for those few minutes "he is not there." He comes to himself abruptly, winks his eyes, shakes himself, and *is* himself once more. Unless you are a very keen observer, you may not notice the attacks' at all. But for the patient himself, they are a source of great torment. He never knows whether such a petit mal will or will not develop into a major seizure and fell him unconscious to the ground.

Such cloudings of consciousness may last longer than one imagines. Moreover, during the hours immediately preceding a grand mal attack, the patient may be tremendously, dangerously excited. "In this state, the patient is a veritable wild man. Fortunately his efforts are diffuse and not coherently directed."[7] Still, this "furor epilepticus" is not frequent. The vicarious cloudings of consciousness are of greater behavioristic importance. During them, epileptics often do very peculiar things; they simulate robberies, attempt murders, even rapes.[8] In a sense an epileptic individual has much less power than a non-epileptic to resist mental strain and stress. It is unfair, I

[7] White, *op. cit.*, p. 288.
[8] See the casuistical and case material at end of this chapter.

think, to say, as some authorities do, that an epileptic is never entirely responsible. Of course, no one of us, even the most highly specialized university professor, is always absolutely responsible, in the sense that he always knows exactly what he is doing and why he is doing it. In this sense, but in this sense only, one may say the same thing of the epileptic. The treatment of epileptic cases you must leave where it belongs, in the physician's hands. The new preparation, luminal, has proved infinitely more helpful in preventing major attacks than the old huge doses of bromides. But, although you cannot *treat* your epileptic patient, you can do a great deal to prepare him for treatment. In fact, you can do something that the physician often cannot do. You can show the patient how to be an epileptic and yet to keep on being himself—his best, most useful self. For as I have already said, convulsions, seen or experienced, terrify people's minds. Nothing frightens the grown man and woman so much as the realization that, at any time during the day, when they are on the street, at the theatre, in church, they may suddenly "get that awful feeling"—may lose consciousness, and only wake after hours to find themselves in utterly strange surroundings, with no memory of what has happened, no knowledge of where they are or of how they got there.

You will have such cases to deal with, I can assure you. Some good-looking young man may find his way to your study or your church or your confessional, so frightened that he can scarcely speak, and only able to give you a hint here and there of the source of his terror. You must be able to recognize the situation. He may tell you that he is doing well at his work—he will always begin with that—that he has lived a "pretty decent life"—that he is interested in a girl. When he was a baby, he had an occasional "convulsion," so his mother told him. But she is dead now. He doesn't know how bad the convulsions were. During his school years, he had one or two "funny attacks," mostly at night. In the morning his tongue would be sore, and he would find—that he had wet the bed. But he thought nothing of these things, until two months ago. Then one day, while he was at the office, he began to "feel queer." He came to himself in his boss's room, lying on a couch, so sleepy that, after being sent home in a cab, he slept for six hours. Next day, at the office, no one mentioned the matter. He thought he had "just fainted." But two days ago he had another "funny attack." And his boss asked him to see a doctor. The doctor, after hearing a description of his "fainting attacks," said one word, "epilepsy." The young man knew what that meant; he had a first cousin, a girl, who was now a hopeless epileptic case. His life then, so he thinks, at least so far as usefulness or happiness is concerned, is at an end. At the best, he will soon be a useless burden to his family. If it were not for the disgrace and the publicity, he would get a revolver to-night and——.

That is the situation. Fortunate indeed is the young man who, finding himself in such a tragic crisis, seeks help from some well-trained pastor. For the pastor can turn that life from despair toward hope, toward more than a mere glimmer of hope—much more indeed than that. Therefore, face the issue squarely with such patients. Say to them, "Yes, you may have discovered that there is a handicap in your life of which you formerly knew nothing. But to know and to prepare is far better than to go on blindly to some future development that may prove truly tragic. No human being is without some handicap. But there is no handicap in the world that cannot somehow be turned into an achievement, if you will only accept the handicap, and not be afraid of it or pretend that it does not exist. First of all, let us get another medical opinion from some psychiatrist or neurologist. If your attacks are really epileptic, well, there have been many epileptic individuals who have done great work in the world. Your attacks have not been very frequent. Moreover, medical science can do a great deal to control them, to reduce their frequency.

We will see what can be done along those lines. But even suppose that, for the rest of your life, you *are* going to be subject to an occasional seizure; in other words, to a temporary loss of consciousness that may last a few moments, or cut a few hours from your conscious life. *Are you going to let those few occasional hours of unconsciousness ruin all the conscious hours of your existence?* Think of the people who have some much greater handicap that is with them, not for an occasional hour, but most of the time. They don't give up and shoot themselves. But above all, don't be afraid of your attacks. Do what you can to provide against the likelihood of their occurring on the street or in some place where you cannot easily lie down at once. If you were working in a factory, at some machine, I should advise you to change your type of occupation. But as a clerk, or a business man you are reasonably safe. And do not feel that you can never marry. Let us see, first of all, what the specialist says. If the attacks can be reduced in frequency, then, if you are interested in some young woman who seems interested in you, do not be afraid to tell her about them. If she really cares for you, she will not be greatly disturbed. Should you two marry, then it might be a good idea to leave the hurrying life of a city, with all its elements of emotional stress, and find yourselves a place in the country, where you could work in the open air and not be constantly hurrying to catch trains or to keep appointments. But put out of your mind forever that thought of the revolver. *There is no exit that way.* Finally, if your religion has ever meant anything to you, it should come to mean all the more, now that you need a strength beyond your own in order to adjust yourself to this new burden, in order to make out of this unexpected handicap a real spiritual achievement."

If you are able to speak in this way to the cases with which you come in contact, you will not only have given back hope to a hopeless man; you will have made a devoted and grateful friend, who will stand by you to the very last ditch, because you stood bravely, manfully, by him in the hour of his greatest need. The next type of mental illness we must consider is in many ways the most tragic, the most irreparable of all psychoses. We call it *páresis,* with the accent on the first syllable. Until a few years ago, physicians had a careless, unscholarly way of pronuncing medical terms derived from the Greek. They said, for example, "enéma," with the accent on the second "e," instead of on the first "e." So they said "parésis," accenting the second syllable. All this was very bad and sad, and a little mad. Now we are better scholars, and if we are really up to date, we say "páresis" with the accent on the "a." Sometimes, you know, one jests about a painful matter; one laughs a little, so that one may not cry. For what we know about "páresis" is sad, and painful and tragic enough.

As I have already said, we do not know very much about the objective cause, the etiological factors of many psychoses. But when we come to deal with paresis, we know the remote cause. This remote cause is always a syphilic infection.[9] Various theories have been brought forward in order to explain why only a very small percentage of people who have acquired syphilis later develop paresis. These theories do not concern us here. We must merely remember four facts: first, that all cases of paresis have, at some period in their lives, been exposed to syphilic infection; secondly, that only a small number of those who have had syphilis develop paresis; thirdly, that the paresis develops from ten to twenty years after the primary infection; and lastly, that it attacks the male more frequently than the female, there being about one female paretic patient to every three males. These are the basic facts.

We are only interested in these matters in so far as they may come within the range of a pastor's or a social worker's activities. But we must not forget the dictum of a distinguished

[9]See White, *op. cit.,* p. 163. "The opinion that syphilis is a necessary precondition to the development of paresis has been held for a considerable time and is at present a settled issue."

physician, who once said: "If a physician encounters in a patient symptoms or conditions that he cannot assign to any definite disease entity and that therefore puzzle him, he will not go far wrong if he takes it for granted that these conditions and symptoms are the results of syphilis." In discussing paresis, I cannot avoid speaking of syphilis; and I cannot hope to give you much help in dealing with certain types of people unless I speak very briefly about this particular disease, and also about another condition. often classed with it as "venereal"—gonorrhea.

We inherit, not only the sins, but also the fears of our forefathers. There is no disease in the whole medical calendar of human woe that is so closely connected in the human mind with horror and dread as this disease, that derives its harmless-looking designation from the imaginary name of an imaginary Greek shepherd in a Latin poem of the sixteenth century. The great physician, Fracastorius,[10] of Verona, who was one of the first to forecast the modern germ theory of disease, was especially interested in a type of infection, apparently new, that was ravaging all Europe. Each nation tried to palm this new evil off upon its neighbors. The Italians called it "The French disease"; French and Germans spoke of it as "The Italian plague." But it had no definite name. Men spoke of it as a "lues," a plague. Its effects on the human body were appalling; medicine was utterly unable at first to cope with it. Strangely enough, one of the best descriptions of it is to be found, not in a medical book, but in Erasmus's preface to his little treatise, *de Lingua,* on "The Tongue" and its peculiar sins.[11] Erasmus also calls it "lues." Fracastorius

---

[10]*Hieronymi Fracastorii de contagione et contagiosis morbis et eorum curatione,* Libri III. Translation and notes by Wilmer Cave Wright, Ph.D. (New York: Putnam, 1930.) See pp. xxv–xxxi.

[11]*Des. Erasmi Roterdami lingua sive de linguae usus et abusu* (Lugduni Batavorum, 1624). *Epistola dedicatoria,* pp. 7, 8. First published in 1525. See "Medicine from the Standpoint of History," by John Rathbone Oliver. *International Clinics* (Phila.: Lippincott, 1928), Vol. I, Series 38, pp. 244–245.

doubtless called it by the same general name; he had no intention of inventing a new name, and yet that is exactly what
he did. For in order to spread a knowledge of the dangers of
this new "Morbus Gallicus" and of the best remedies against
it, he wrote a little Latin poem, the form of which is copied
from the *Eclogues* or the *Georgics* of Virgil. Surely there must
be many men and women who remember how they stumbled
through the translation of Virgil's *Eclogues* in order to be
able to pass their college entrance examinations. They may
not remember very much about these same poems; but one
thing they probably have not forgotten, namely, that these
same poems are set in the form of rustic dialogues and that
most of the speakers are shepherds, goatherds or farmers. So
Fracastorius wrote an eclogue, and in it two shepherds are
described as discussing the new disease and its possible cures.
One of these shepherds is called Syphilus. The exact derivation
of the name is doubtful. Perhaps it comes from two Greek
words, "sus" and "philos," and means a man who likes pigs;
not a bad name for a swineherd. However that may be, this
name of the disputing swineherd, Syphilus, came in process
of time to denote the disease itself.

But modern physicians have been anxious to get away, as
far as possible, from the inheritance of fear and horror that
even to this day clings to the name of Fracastorius' swineherd. So among physicians you will not hear the word "syphilis" very often. We have nowadays another name for it, a less
terrorized word; the same word as a matter of fact that the
great Erasmus used. We speak of "lues venerea," or simply
"lues." Of "a luetic" instead of a syphilitic patient, and so on.
It is a sound idea to turn men's minds away from hereditary
horrors that have grouped themselves around the name of a
swineherd in an old Latin eclogue. I mention all this for a
very definite reason, and in the hope of giving you the means
of helping frightened people.

I feel sure that almost every pastor or social worker of some years' experience has had to deal with the "mental horror" of lues. I shall not use the word syphilis any longer. Some one of your young men will surely come to you in a state of acute terror. He will be even more terrified than the epileptic patient that I have already described. Or the matter may be mentioned in the confessional. At any rate you will hear the same tale of agonized remorse. Your infected penitent may have been living a promiscuous sex life for years; on the other hand, he may have experienced only one act of intercourse. If he has been fortunate, he has at once noticed what is called the "primary lesion," the small, round sore with its hard crater-like edges, and he has gone to a physician at once. If he has been less lucky, he has either paid no attention to the sore, or has been afraid of what the doctor might tell him, and so has waited until what are called "secondary symptoms" develop—rash, sore throat, and many other typical reactions; until he is forced to go to some one—perhaps to you. If he has seen a physician, he knows what is the matter with him. If he has put off consulting one until the secondary symptoms have appeared, he suspects. In either case, he is in intense agony of spirit. All the horror of this special disease that has accumulated through centuries, until its very name is tabooed and only mentioned in whispers, has come upon him. I have known more than one suicide under similar circumstances.

I beg you, therefore, not to let any back-wash of these old horrors touch your mind; not to show by look or act that you shrink from the man who comes to you in such agony of remorse, in such fear for the future. Ten to one, this disease is to him a sealed book of a far worse Inferno than Dante's.

You have here a great opportunity. But, in whatever you have to say, do not confuse material issues with spiritual ones. Do not confound sin against the seventh commandment with a venereal disease. Don't tell the young man that he is "being punished for his sin." Perhaps he is. But this knowledge will not help him much now. Keep the two issues apart. Reassure him first of all about his physical condition. As a matter of fact, he is more afraid of the physical disease than of losing his immortal soul. Keep away from the word "syphilis." Tell him that we speak of it now as "lues." That will help a little. Tell him that nowadays lues can be as easily and as completely cured as tuberculosis; that the cure may take months, perhaps a year; but that this will not mean entering a hospital, unless the disease has developed into the secondary stage. Tell him *not to be afraid* of it. He can be so completely cured, that in two years' time he can marry and beget sound children. When you have reassured him about the physical results of his actions, then you can begin to talk about his sin—his lack of self-control, his self-indulgence. If you reverse the process, and begin to preach to him about sin while he is still in agony of mind, you will only increase his agony, but will not greatly help him. He doesn't want to be told that he has been a sinner and is suffering the due reward for his deeds; he wants to learn from you that, although he has done wrong, there is a way back to health and to forgiveness.

Reassure him first as to the physical results of his excesses, and then make him see how these same excesses and this lack of self-control have involved him in all sorts of physical difficulties, from which he can only escape by the aid of medical science; and have tainted his mind, his memories, his thoughts, just as it has infected and upset the processes of his body. Make him see "sin" as a "lues" of the soul. He'll understand that. He has, before his own eyes, a good example of what a "lues" can do to a human body.

When we speak roughly of "venereal diseases," we mean the two common afflictions of lues and gonorrhea. But, while lues and its symptoms are associated with horror and disgust —over-emphasized, so gonorrhea is under-emphasized and too often accepted by young people as a merely "temporary inconvenience." The average young man and woman of to-day thinks nothing of having had a gonorrheal infection or two.

But just because this infection is considered of such secondary importance, it is often followed by very serious results. Chronic gonorrheas unnoticed, uncared for, often cause all sorts of tragic complications. The gynecologist, for example, could tell you many stories of married women infected by their husbands, women who did not know what was the matter with them until some serious ovarian trouble drove them to the specialist. It happens sometimes that when a woman is pregnant, her husband seeks a temporary sexual partner, and from that same partner he brings back a gonorrhea, and after his baby has been born and he and his wife come together again, he all unconsciously infects her. The inflammatory process creeps up into her tubes, these become swollen, chronically inflamed, so that no ovum can pass through them into the uterus. So the woman becomes sterile. People wonder why, after having one child, she has never had another. I do not mean that there is a suspicion of gonorrhea in every "one-child family," but gynecologists will tell you that such a suspicion is often warranted.

After this necessary diversion into matters connected with venereal disease, matters which are certain to be brought before you as pastors or social workers, I must beg you *not* to ask me one question, that is probably on your lips or in your mind. What *is* lues? Where did it come from? I can answer the first question by telling you that the cause of lues is a micro-organism, called the spirochæta pallida, discovered by Schaudinn[12] in 1905, and found by Nagouchi, the famous Japanese scientist, in the spinal cord and the brain of paretic patients. But where it came from? If I could answer that question in a satisfactory way, I should be great indeed among medical historians. Some schools of historians believe that lues was first brought into Europe by the sailors of Columbus, who acquired it in some part of the newly discovered conti-

[12]Fritz Schaudinn (1871–1906). See F. H. Garrison's *History of Medicine,* 4th ed. (Phila.: Saunders, 1929), p. 708.

nent through intercourse with natives whose bodies had acquired a certain amount of immunity to the invading ravages of the first infections. Another school believes that lues can be traced to antiquity, long before Columbus. I do not know which school is right. You can easily read up the subject for yourself.[13]

In connection with lues, you have probably all heard of what is called a "Wassermann" test or reaction. This is a laboratory process to which human blood is subjected, and the outcome of which shows whether the patient, from whom the blood has been taken, has had a luetic infection or not. A similar test is made with the spinal fluid, easily drawn through a hollow needle from the canal in the patient's spine, the canal that contains the same fluid as that in which the brain is suspended like a round sponge swimming in a large, deep round cup. I have said that in psychiatry we were *sure* of not many things. But here is one thing of which we can be sure. If the spinal fluid of a patient, who has begun to show peculiar mental symptoms, is sent to a good laboratory, and the report comes back that this same fluid shows "a positive Wassermann" and what is known as a "paretic gold curve," then you may be *sure* that your patient has paresis. Not more than ten years ago, such a diagnosis was indeed a death warrant. Paretic patients did not live more than a year or two after the disease had begun to show itself. But you are not interested in the "end symptoms." When the final stage is reached, there is almost nothing that you can do, for the mental deterioration may become so profound that the patient "ceases to live a mental life and leads only a vegetative existence."[14] Your interest must be concentrated on the beginnings of this psychosis, so that you may be able to recognize it and secure a definite diagnosis before the patient harms others or harms himself.

[13]See an excellent concise statement of the question in Garrison, *op. cit.*, pp. 189–91, especially the fine print on p. 190.
[14]White, *op. cit.*, p. 179.

The early manifestations of paresis are so manifold that it often goes unrecognized. And yet there is scarcely any other psychosis in which the early diagnosis may prevent more unhappiness and make impossible many tragic happenings. The best description of these symptoms that I know is to be found in Doctor White's *Outlines of Psychiatry*.[15]

"Manifesting itself in its incipiency by symptoms of defectice intelligence, lack of judgment, memory defects and moral obtuseness, we frequently see the most pitiable of pictures—a previously respected citizen, father of a family, occupying an enviable position, yet becoming at the height of his career an ardent worshipper at the shrines of Venus and Bacchus. Friends and relatives see nothing in these manifestations but the outcropping of original sin and are distracted by their inability to stay the career of drunkenness and vice upon which their erstwhile respected relative has entered. How many heartaches, how many pangs of anguish, how many blushes of shame could be spared the wife and children of such a man, if the family physician did but recognize in these occurrences the symptoms of the onset of a mental disease and advise them what course to pursue.

"Here we have a disease afflicting one when at the very zenith of his physical and mental powers, insidious in its onset, yet capable of so changing the character in a few weeks that the votary of every form of vice sinks to the depths of drunkenness and debauchery, and may even stain his hands in blood. But this is not the worst. It often happens that such a man as I have pictured is the guardian of the family exchequer. When this is the case, it almost invariably happens that he wastes considerable amounts of money in his debaucheries, becomes involved in ill-advised speculations—and finally when he has succeeded in hopelessly entangling his business affairs and plunging himself into debt, is committed to an

[15]See pp. 163–190, passim. (Used by permission of the author and the Nervous and Mental Disease Publishing Co.)

institution, the disease having at last been recognized, and his family only then comes to the realization that they are penniless. *The pity of it all is that it might have been prevented."*

The first mental symptoms of paresis, then, are those of a gradual change of character, and of progressively failing mental and physical powers. The patient cannot keep at his usual work; his memory is not good, he forgets important engagements. When he begins to drink too much, to go to houses of prostitution, he does not do these things in decent secrecy, but often openly, without shame, in direct contradiction to all his previous habits. His judgment, especially in business matters, is impaired. Moreover, he grows careless about his personal appearance; he wears dirty linen, forgets his collar, leaves his trousers open.

Into this general picture there come some physical symptoms. The loss of co-ordination, the unsteady gait, used to be summed up in a special entity that was once called locomotor ataxia. It is merely a part of the paretic process. A paretic patient cannot shut his eyes, put his feet close together, stretch out his hands horizontally, and still stand up straight without swaying or falling over. So there are a few simple tests that you may make without trespassing on the domain of medicine and risking arrest for attempting to practice medicine without a license.

Try first the test that I have already mentioned. Make the patient put his feet close together, pointing outwards; have him stretch out his arms horizontally at the level of his shoulders, and then tell him to shut his eyes. If he loses his equilibrium, you have one positive paretic symptom. Then test his memory; ask him what he had for breakfast, or to give a brief account of his doings of yesterday. You may find a very hazy uncertain reaction. Next, ask your patient to pronounce some difficult words, "Third Riding Artillery Brigade," or best of all, "Methodist Episcopal." If he slurs his syllables, runs them together, you have another symptom. Finally, take him to the window, cover one eye with your hand, and then remove the hand suddenly. Watch the pupil of the eye. If it contracts freely when the hand is removed and the light strikes it, then your test for paresis has been negative. But if the pupil remains "stiff," if it does not contract to the stimulus of light, then you have elicited an important reaction; for "stiff pupils" are always suggestive of cerebro-spinal lues of some type. If then you have a parishioner who shows these physical symptoms, and if in addition you have noticed signs of some mental deterioration, a change in character, a lack of judgment, carelessness about his personal appearance, then you must persuade him to see a doctor "just to run over his general health." Among the tests that the doctor makes, be sure that he has laboratory tests made both of blood and of spinal fluid. If the report on the spinal fluid comes back negative, then you may be sure that somehow you have made a mistake—and you may thank God for having made it. But it is better to make it a dozen times, than to miss the chance of recognizing a paresis in its incipient stages.

Sometimes your attention may be first called to a case of this kind by what is commonly called a "paretic seizure." Such seizures usually occur at the beginning of the second state of paresis, or at the end of the prodromal or incipient stage. These attacks, Doctor White says,[16] "may vary in severity from light syncopal (fainting) attacks with pallor and temporary prostration to severe apoplectiform or epileptiform crises." Seizures of this nature, if described to you by one of your parishioners, should stimulate at least your curiosity. Do not make light of them; but do not frighten your patient. Find out what you can about his present behavior; make one or more of the simple tests I have mentioned, and get into touch with his family physician. The family physician may think that you are a meddler and an alarmist; but in the end he will be grateful to you, if you give him an opportunity

16 Op. cit., p. 171.

to recognize an arterio-sclerosis of the brain, an epilepsy or a case of paresis. For it is quite possible that he may have been unable to make a correct diagnosis himself, simply because he is not in possession of the facts that you, the patient's pastor, happen to know.

Paresis, then, is an ominous psychosis; exogenic, since its primary cause is the spirochæta pallida, which for some unknown reason attacks the central nervous system and lies hidden there for years, until the final outbreak comes; and up to fifteen years ago it was one of the hopeless problems of psychiatry. Of late a little hope has begun to dawn, and the manner of its dawning forms one of the many romances of medical history, which is, if people only realized it, as closely packed with exciting adventures as the latest detective novel. The story goes that, some years ago, in a Viennese mental hospital, there was a severe outbreak of influenza. In one ward there were many paretic patients—sent there to deteriorate and to die—paretics in all stages of that hopeless disease. Many of them had bad bouts of "flu," and it was noticed that those patients who had the severest attacks and the highest temperatures showed a peculiar remission of their paretic symptoms. Their gait was less ataxic, less unco-ordinated; their minds seemed to clear a little; the process of mental deterioration seemed to have been slightly arrested. Vienna has always been a centre of great medical discoveries. From Semmelweiss to Freud, that city has written its name large on the canvas of medical history; so these strange happenings in a paretic ward did not pass unnoticed. I will not bore you with a description of all the research, all the laboratory tests, that made the discovery possible. But it *was* discovered that an elevation of the body temperature was able somehow to inhibit, to hold up the development of those poisons which the spirochætes were producing in the central nervous systems of paretic patients. Therefore we have found a way, or just the beginning of a way, to treat paretic patients, by giving them another disease.

It sounds incongruous. The last time that I was in Vienna, I watched the procedure. The paretic patient is injected with a large dose of malaria germs of a certain type. The patient is then allowed to have at least ten acute attacks of chills and fever. After the tenth attack, he is dosed with quinine, which is, as you know, a specific remedy for malaria, and the malaria is cured. Such a bout of chills and fever has had remarkable results in arresting the paretic process. Of course, in advanced cases, it can accomplish little. But I was told of paretics in the second stage of the disease—a hopeless disease until then—who showed so much mental improvement that they were able to go back to the ordinary duties of life. Just how long such an improvement will last, I do not know. Perhaps it is only a temporary remission. But at any rate, the principle that has been discovered gives us some hope of being able, in the future, to remove paresis from that class of psychoses that is marked with the black cross of hopelessness and of death.

CLINICAL MATERIAL

A. Paranoia.

Paranoid individuals are not difficult to recognize. I will set down two paranoid cases, from my own experience, without any general history because I was never able to examine these patients in detail.

(1) An old lady, in a mental hospital, seemed perfectly normal so long as you did not mention the subject of "tea." She was of English parentage, I believe. Five o'clock in the afternoon was a bad time to visit her. If you did come at that time, her mind seemed obsessed by the idea of tea. She would stand with her left hand crooked on her hip, to represent the handle of a teapot. The right hand she would stretch out, bent, like a teapot spout. Then she would bend sideways from her hips, as if she were pouring out tea through her bent right arm. She insisted on such occasions that she *was* a teapot. At any other time of the day she would be quite normal, unless you mentioned tea, then she would assume her characteristic attitude and say, "Let me give you a cup of tea."

One day I found her in the surgical ward, badly burned. On the previous day, just before five o'clock, she had stolen, unseen, into the hospital kitchen and had seated herself on the stove, which fortunately was not very hot. She explained her action by saying that she was expecting company and had "to warm up the tea." If you admitted her major premise, namely, that she *was* a teapot, then her actions were logical enough.

(2) Several years ago, I was sitting in my private office, after having dismissed my last patient. Some one knocked. A young man came in, feeling his way, and leaning on a stick. Over his eyes was a green shade, pulled down so far that it hid his eyes. I thought, at first, that he was a blind beggar, but he did not ask for money. Then I thought that he was looking for one of my colleagues, an ophthalmologist, who had an office next to mine. But when I suggested this, he shook his head. I was puzzled. He began to talk, in a quiet educated voice, about the difficulty of finding work. All sorts of people wander into my office, anyway, so I supposed that he was "looking for a job," and had heard that I was a soft-hearted individual whom he could "touch" for a dollar or two. I asked him to sit down; he refused, but stood beside my desk. Finally, during an embarrassing pause in our talk, and while I was reaching for my purse, I asked, "How can you get the kind of a job you are looking for if you are blind?" "Oh," he said simply, "I'm not blind." "Then why do you pretend that you are, why wear that eye-shade? You have no business to counterfeit blindness and rouse people's sympathy on false pretenses." He dropped his right hand into his coat-pocket. I did not pay much attention at the time. "But I don't pretend to be blind," he said, "only I have to wear this shade." I thought that he was suffering from some sort of psychogenic blindness—some habit of mind—and I became interested. "Let me look at your eyes," I said; "anyhow, let me take that shade off." Still keeping his right hand in his pocket, he held me off with his left. "I shouldn't touch that eye-shade if I were you," he said in a matter-of-fact voice. "I've heard that you're a decent sort. I don't wish you any harm." I admit that I was very stupid, but then I was very tired after a long, hard day's work. I supposed that he might have some disease of the eye which he thought infectious, and which he did not wish

me to touch lest I should possibly infect myself. "Oh, I'm not afraid," I said, and stretched out my hand to lift his green shade. As I did so, I happened to glance down at my visitor's right hand, and saw that it was tightly clasped around something in his coat-pocket. In my police court experience I had seen that gesture before. I drew back my own hand. "That's better," my visitor said; "it wouldn't have been safe for you to lift that shade. You see," he went on casually, "I have funny kind of eyes. The thing people call the Evil Eye is nothing to mine. If I look at any one straight, that person dies." I began to feel distinctly uncomfortable. My waiting-room was empty. I had no means of calling my secretary, even if he had been in the next room. But I was curious. This man and I had been talking together for half an hour. I had noticed nothing mentally abnormal, until I spoke of "eyes." "That's why I have to wear this shade," my young friend went on, "if I don't want to kill people. But if I do look at them, if they look straight into my eyes, they die." Then, a little less certainly, he added, "They have to die, you know." I suppose that I was tempting fate, but I felt impelled to ask one more question. "But," I said, "suppose you looked at them, and then they didn't die." "I said they'd have to die, didn't I?" he answered. "That's why I carry a loaded automatic." I do not remember very clearly how I got that man out of my office. I do know that I was very careful not to touch his eye-shade, and was in agony of mind lest somehow it should drop off. I remember that I was lucky enough to meet the policeman on our beat, who is an old friend of mine. Pointing out to him the man with the eye-shade I suggested that he take him to the police-station on some pretext or other, but without removing his eye-shade until he had removed the automatic—it was really there—from the man's coat-pocket.

Perhaps, had I been able to follow up this case, I might have had to classify it as a schizophrenia with paranoid trends. But as I saw it, during those exciting minutes, I thought of it as a paranoia. Except for the one fundamental delusion, everything was so logical, even the eye-shade, and especially the loaded revolver.

B. Epilepsy.

In the last chapter I have already sufficiently described the symptoms of grand mal epileptic attacks. The cases suffering from petit mal, with vicarious cloudings of consciousness that take the place of a grand mal seizure, are more likely to be brought to your notice.

(1) Not long ago I found in the daily press the following case: It was reported that a Protestant minister, while alone in his little church, had been attacked by masked men. These men had not stolen anything; there was nothing to steal. But they had hung the minister from an electric-light fixture, and had left him there to die. Fortunately, they had hung him directly over the Communion Table; he could just reach the surface of it with his toes. Also, the rope, with which he had been hung, had stretched a little. He had managed to free himself; and half strangled, his clothing in disorder, he had rushed out of his church, in great excitement, to the police station. For two days, the little town was in a state of intense excitement. The masked robbers were looked for in vain, they had disappeared without leaving a single clue. Naturally, the young minister was the centre of interest. On the next Sunday his church was crowded. Unfortunately, one of the local police was a trained policeman of the modern type. He did a little detective work on his own; examined the ropes with which the minister had been hung, looked for the footprints of the two assailants, and soon convinced himself that there had been no masked assailants at all. When he brought his evidence to the young minister's attention, the young man broke down, and admitted that he had strung himself up on the chandelier, and had set the entire stage with his own hands. But he could give no valid reason for his actions. Probably, he was hooted out of town, and was unable to continue his ministry. People doubtless thought that he had tried to "play a practical joke," or to "get some advertising without having to pay for it." That young minister may have been a mild epileptic, emotionally unstable, and with periodic cloudings of consciousness. If he was, he needed understanding and treatment, not abuse.

(2) The following case came within my own personal knowledge. A young man of average intelligence and education, aged about twenty, was employed as a junior clerk in a small country bank. In a nearby town there had been an attempted hold-up in a similar bank, but the robbers had escaped without getting any

money. One Saturday there had been a lot of extra work, in re-moving some old records and accounts from the bank itself to a small garret or attic just over it. It was a simple job. The cashier and the other clerks left the bank at three, telling the youngest clerk to finish piling up the records in the attic and then to lock up and go home. On Sunday morning, as the policeman was pass-ing the bank, he noticed a light still burning in the attic. He was a careful man, so, on passing the cashier's house, he told him what he had seen. The cashier, suspecting nothing wrong, but unwill-ing that the bank should waste money on needless electric light, went to the bank and up to the attic to turn off the light. A mo-ment later he telephoned for the police. The attic floor was cov-ered with old records thrown about in heaps; the filing cabinets were tipped over, their drawers emptied on the floor. On a beam that ran across the top of the attic, lay the youngest clerk, tied with a rope. He had a vague, confused story to tell about having been struck down from behind while he was carrying the last arm-ful of records to the attic. But he had not seen his assailant. He seemed dazed. He slept soundly almost all that Sunday. The police examination showed that nothing had been stolen, that there were no foot-prints, no traces of any forced entry. But the young clerk persisted in his story. It was discovered that he was an epileptic case. And there was no doubt in the minds of the police that he himself had staged the whole robbery during a period of clouded consciousness. How he ever got up onto the high beam and man-aged to tie himself and remain there for so many hours was hard to understand, unless one remembered the many impossible things that can be done by an epileptic during such clouded mental periods.

One must of course distinguish these and similar cases from cases of feigned robbery or rape in which there is some definite reason for the fictitious statements. A woman who has spent her husband's last week's salary on a new dress, who is afraid to tell him and stages an imaginary robbery, is not epileptic, or suffering from an attack of clouded consciousness. She is rather a quick thinker and often a careful, clever worker. In epileptic cases the fictitious events show no adequate motive and betray a childish-ness, a lack of judgment, that stamps them as the product of a sick personality.

C. Paresis.

(1) Samuel Brown is a man of thirty-five, very happily married and with two healthy children. His wife has had two miscarriages, each in the early period of her pregnancies. Brown has been reasonably successful in business and has an assured future. He has just made the last payment on the purchase of his home. Every one speaks well of him. Although not markedly religious, he goes with his wife to mass every Sunday; he has had all his children baptized; and he is thinking of being confirmed when the bishop makes his next visitation. His family history shows no cases of mental illness, no cases of tuberculosis or cancer. His father died at eighty-five; his mother at eighty-seven. He comes from a long-lived, sound stock. During childhood and adolescence there were no symptoms of poor adjustment, no fears, no sleep walking. He was popular among boys, always able to "keep up with the gang," a good mixer. At high school he played on the football eleven. He is a sound, fine looking, pleasant fellow, not very brilliant perhaps, but steady and sure. At the office he has just been promoted to a position of trust and responsibility. One of his boyhood friends will tell you that Sam never "sowed any wild oats." From eighteen to twenty-six, that is from his graduation from high school until his marriage, he lived for the most part with his parents, except for one single year, when he was twenty-four. During that year his father had died, his mother had gone to stay with an unmarried sister, and Sam had to "board out" in a house with a group of other "unattached" young men. Sam's friend will tell you that this group was rather "a fast lot," and that for a few months he felt a little worried about Sam. But just then Sam met the girl whom he afterwards married, and cut loose from his "gay friends." One morning, while you are in your study, Mrs. Brown, Sam's wife, comes to you on some parochial business. Incidentally, she tells you that her husband has had a "queer kind of attack." He had taken her out to a dance in the parish house. The room had been very hot. He had danced a lot; he had been having a good time, for everybody likes Sam. Suddenly, he dropped his partner in the middle of the floor, turned ghastly pale, fell and began to twitch all over. "When we got him on his feet," Mr. Brown says, "he was dizzy and got sort of hysterical, laughing and behaving like

a naughty little boy. Of course every one thought he was drunk; but he hadn't touched a thing. He doesn't drink, Father; you know that. With the confirmation classes coming on, which he wants to join, I wouldn't wish you to think he's been doing anything wrong. I've got him in bed at home to-day. He's pretty weak on his legs yet. When he tries to get out of bed, he staggers. He won't take his sickness seriously, he just giggles. He won't see any doctor, and I dare say he's right."

There is your opportunity as a pastor. No matter how overwhelmed you may be with parish work; make time in which to go and see Sam Brown at once. If you can persuade him to let you test the reaction of his pupils, if he will try to say "Methodist Episcopal," you can satisfy your mind as to two important symptoms at least. You will probably find him quiet enough, like his usual self, so far as you can see. Do not frighten him. But, inasmuch as he is thinking of being confirmed, tell him about the necessary preparation for receiving that sacrament. If your people make general confessions before being confirmed, explain to him how he is to prepare for it. If they do not, then at least you have a right as his pastor to go over with him the sins and mistakes of his past life. And you may find that during those fatal six months that he spent in the boarding house, in touch with that "gay crowd," he went to one or two "gay parties" that ended up in a place that was strange to him and that he does not remember very well because he had had too much to drink. After he met Mattie, his wife, he never wanted to see a place like that again; he wanted to forget he had ever been there. Now, you have a chance to tell him something of the dangers of going to such places. He may shake his head. "Oh no, I was lucky. I was lucky. Nothing happened to me. I did, several days after one of those parties, notice a little sore, round, with hard edges. But I didn't think anything of it. I asked one of my friends; he said if I didn't have a burning pain when I urinated, I was all right. So the sore healed up. I've never even thought of it since. It can't have meant anything, can it?" But such a thing as a neglected luetic sore may mean so much. It may mean a man's life, and almost the life of his family. Let us suppose that you persuade Sam Brown to see a physician; that a spinal fluid test is made and the result is positive. He is, more or less, a doomed man. At the worst, he may be dead in a few years, and those years will be spent in a mental hospital. He may not suffer much actual physical pain. For, in many cases of paresis, a sense of euphoria, or well-being, persists until the last. At best the process may be slightly retarded. But he will never be a well man again; never able to hold his business position, to support his family, to see his children grow up around him. You, as his pastor, cannot prevent these things. However, you can still do something for your patient. The physician, to whom you send him and who makes the final diagnosis, will probably not want to tell your parishioner the truth. If, in his case, mental deterioration has already begun, perhaps the truth will not help him much. But if he is able to appreciate the situation, it seems to me that he has a right to know what is the matter with him. But I should not tell him until he is safely in some mental hospital and protected against the temptation of utter dispair. The wife, surely, ought to know the truth. If she has really loved her husband, it will do her no harm, for one of the chief causes of her husband's condition was ignorance. Modern young men of to-day may be better instructed in all these matters. I hope that they are. Yet, cases like Sam Brown's do happen still. As for Sam Brown himself, if he can prepare himself to meet the truth like a Christian and a man, he may be able to use the days of unclouded consciousness that are left him to set himself right with God, to do what he can to prepare himself for leaving this world, or for facing a long period of mental and physical deterioration.[17] A man faced with paresis needs all the strength and help that Catholic faith and practice can give him. Why keep him from these same sources of comfort by pretending that there is nothing seriously wrong with him? But the wife will need you even more than her husband needs you. Her whole future happiness may depend on the way in which she adjusts herself to her husband's illness. At first, she may be bitter and blame him for everything; or, like Job, will want to curse God and die; for the whole thing seems so unjust, so unnecessary, so devilishly cruel. But if you, as her pastor, know how to stand by her during her first week of de-

[17]This whole question about "telling the patient the truth" will be discussed in Chapter IV.

spair, you may indeed save a soul alive out of Hell. Many people still do not believe that the wages of sin is death.

(2) I might mention here the famous story of a distinguished English physician. Sir Arthur Conan Doyle, I think, used the material in one of his medical tales. This physician, who in his youth had lived a rather promiscuous sexual life and had never married, was lecturing to his medical students one morning on paresis, or as it was then called, locomotor ataxia. He described what is called the Sign of Romberg, the symptom of being unable to stand straight with outstretched arms and eyes closed. One student did not understand. The lecturer, in order to make his description clearer, put himself in the required position, with arms outstretched, feet close together. Then he closed his eyes—and fell sideways. He went out from the lecture room a doomed man.

CHAPTER IV

MENTAL MALADJUSTMENTS

TELLING THE PATIENT THE TRUTH. ALCOHOLISM. MEDICINE AND
DRUG HABITS. MENTAL DEFICIENCY. CLINICAL MATERIAL

BEFORE I proceed to a description of what are commonly
called "toxic mental states," such as alcoholism, let me here
touch upon a matter that in a sense lies outside the domain
of mental disease, but that involves a question which is frequently discussed between physician and pastor: the question
as to whether or not the patient shall be told "the truth." Let
us take a common example. One of your parishioners has suffered for some years from "chronic indigestion," and finally
he or she goes to some good diagnostician. An exploratory
operation is necessary, apparently a minor one; and you are at
the hospital when the operation is performed. The surgeon is a
friend of yours. A few hours after the operation, you waylay
him in a corridor of the hospital, and ask him about his
patient. He tells you that the operation has disclosed an inoperable carcinoma of the intestines; he could do nothing
except sew up the wound again. The patient has about six
months to live. You know that in a few hours you must go in to
visit that patient who will be anxious to hear something about
his or her operation. What are you going to say?

Some physicians, I am afraid, do not think it wise to tell
such patients the truth. It is far better, they think, not to
"upset the patient," not to make him or her terrified, unhappy;
that it is much better to "jolly them along," to keep them as
contented as possible. And yet this attitude of mind seems to
me illogical. Even if one has no belief in any life after death,
death is still an important biological change. A man with any

power of logical thought would surely like to know if that change were imminent. He has things to set in order before he goes, even if he supposes that he is going nowhere at all. To the Christian man or woman, death is something to be prepared for. We pray to be delivered from sudden and unprepared death, and a few months is a short time in which to make that preparation. It is silly to say that a good Christian is always prepared to die; few of us are as good Christians as all that. Moreover, I have seen too many cases in which the hopelessly ill patient does more than suspect his or her real condition. And yet the doctors and the nurses are always trying to keep such patients "cheered up," while all the time the patient suffers more from the sense of uncertainty than he could suffer from knowing the truth that even he suspects. My own mother, one of the bravest women I ever knew, used to say: "I ask only one thing. Don't *spare* me. Tell me the truth. I can face it if I know it. But I can't face being 'spared.'" The few remaining months of life that such dying patients have may be of inestimable value to them, if only they know what they are facing. To deceive them with false hopes is to rob them of the greatest opportunity of their lives.

In this connection I cannot help remembering, with thankfulness to God, the name of one physician, who, at the very height of his usefulness, was found to have an inoperable carcinoma. He insisted on knowing the truth. During the last months of his life, so far as was possible, he went about his ordinary duties, but in the spirit of one who was trying to do his work well up to the very end. And those who were privileged to be with him during those last months and weeks learned lessons far more valuable and impressive than could be taught by ten thousand sermons preached by as many bishops.

Of course, in deciding such a matter as this, you must try to work sympathetically with the physician in charge of the case; but if it comes to a definite divergence of opinion, I believe that you will seldom go far wrong if you insist on telling the patient the truth. A great deal will depend on the way in which that truth is told. But if you yourself are living in close contact with the unseen world, with the things that are eternal, you will be able to make out of the truth that you tell, not a sentence of death, but a sentence of life everlasting.

Under the head of Toxic Psychoses, we class those mental disturbances which are caused by the introduction into the body of a poison, some toxic substance. Most of these substances are exogenous; that is, they are introduced from without. There are of course endogenous toxins,[1] which are produced by the body itself, and are usually called autotoxins. But auto-intoxications fall usually in the domain of medical practice. They do not directly interest the parish priest, except in so far as they produce mental conditions of anxiety or fear in persons who seek the priest's help. The most important exogenous toxic conditions or psychoses are those connected with alcoholism. Less important to the priest are those associated with the use of narcotic drugs.

There is no chapter in practical psychiatry that is more complex, more puzzling than the chapter of alcoholism. I need not waste time on a description of the condition called "delirium tremens" except to point out that during the delirium the hallucinations are always visual and take on the form of animals. Moreover, there is a horror associated with these hallucinations in the patient's mind that can never be forgotten by any one who has sat by the bedside of a delirious alcoholic patient. The pastor is more deeply interested in the mental and physical habit of alcoholic indulgence.

Here is a man who, with your help, has just pulled himself out of the gutter. When he came to you he was just recovering from an alcoholic indulgence of two weeks. He was dirty and neglected; had pawned almost all his clothes; spent all his money; lost his position; and had been separated from his wife.

[1] See White, *op. cit.*, p. 262.

Alcohol, then, had cost him a great deal. It had cost him his home, his good name, his physical health, his power of clear thought, his own self-respect. That is a great deal for a man to pay for anything. Now he "wants to stop" paying. But he has no money; no job; nothing but a confused mind and a tremulous body, tortured by the lack of the poison that has been the cause of all his troubles. He is moving in a vicious circle. In order to be able to live and think, he needs the alcohol that is gradually making it impossible for him to think and to live at all. With your help, he pulls himself out of the gutter; his body begins to get rid of the poison; he can eat and sleep once more; he is properly clothed; and you find him work. He becomes reconciled to his wife; he has a home of his own again. You think your job is done; that your patient is cured. But after some six months the wife tells you that her husband is becoming restless, depressed. She knows the symptoms and she does what she can. Perhaps you find time to see your patient occasionally; but, in the moments of his greatest temptation, he cannot get hold of you. Finally, one evening when he is with friends who are having "a few drinks," or during some hour of intense depression and nervous tension, he takes "one drink" too. He is the type of alcoholic to whom "one drink" is poison; to whom "one drink" means a thousand or more. You hear that he has not turned up at work, and has disappeared from his home. A year later you may pick him out of the gutter again.

The remarkable element in such cases lies in the power of the temptation, the overwhelming strength of the motive. Such a man, when he is tempted to take the "one drink," knows perfectly well just what alcohol has cost him in mental and physical suffering, in disgrace and in degradation. Yet, the urge is so strong that, in spite of such knowledge, he chooses to endanger all that he has achieved at an infinite cost to himself and others, chooses to throw it all away and to start again on his Way of Sorrows. Of course, one can hardly say that he "chooses" with the freedom that a non-alcoholic possesses when he decides to stay sober rather than to get drunk. What I want to impress upon you is the strange, overwhelming power of attraction that "makes" the man choose the alcohol and all the suffering and disgrace that its use involves, rather than a glass of ginger ale, and with it, home and position and economic security, not to speak of happiness and mental peace. I do not believe that we, as yet, understand the mental mechanism of chronic alcoholism. We deal with alcoholics in a sort of hit and miss way that makes our efforts at treatment so often unsuccessful. Some physicians and pastors seem to have had greater success with their alcoholic cases than I have had with mine.[2]

Of course, it is not difficult to theorize. One knows that an alcoholic does not drink because he deliberately *wants* to break his wife's heart, because he deliberately desires to ruin himself, to debase his body and confuse his mind. He does not do all these things because he is a devil incarnate and rejoices in making others unhappy, although it sometimes seems as if the Devil had more to do with alcoholic cases than we realize. No, the reason why a man must have alcohol no matter at what cost to himself and to others, is that alcohol gives him something that he needs, something that he cannot find in anything else. If you can discover what this mysterious thing is and give it to him or to her in some non-alcoholic way, then you will have cut away the roots of the overpowering need.

Sometimes it is easy to discover what it is that a man finds in alcohol. A great many alcoholics go through life on the entirely false assumption that "every man has a right to be happy," and by "happiness" they mean a general sense of well-being and of satisfaction with things as they are. When they do not find what they call happiness in their daily lives —when a wife is cross, or children ill, or a "boss" unjust— in other words, whenever such men discover that the world

[2]See E. Worcester and S. McComb, *Body, Mind and Spirit*, pp. 225–238.

is not going the way they want it to go, then they assimilate
a certain amount of alcohol and behold, the world is all set
right again. Or, if the world still seems a little awry, then
they themselves have acquired a new attitude toward it which
enables them to look down upon it and to despise it from their
own alcoholic heights. There are more men than you think
who are able to go through the drudgery of a week's work
only because they are upheld by the reasonable hope of being
able to get more or less drunk on Saturday night.

Other men have a more logical reason for their alcoholism.
The man who suffers from recurrent waves of depression, who
feels that his mind is "slowing up" and who has to force himself through each day's work, gets from alcohol a temporary
relief. It enables him for a time to speed up his blocked mind,
to get through his day's work. Others who are obsessed by
some persistent mental habit of anxiety, who are inhibited by
some chronic fear, find in alcohol a temporary release. But still
more numerous are those men who suffer all their lives long
from a sense of physical or mental inferiority.[3] They are intensely shy, afraid of other people, obsessed by the idea that
they can never compete successfully with other men. This
mental habit hinders them in their work. If they are salesmen, they have to force themselves every time they visit a possible client or buyer. To them, alcohol is a godsend—for a
while. Two or three "drinks" raise their sense of individuality,
give them self-confidence, make them feel that "they are as
good as any one else and probably a damn sight better."

Once you have discovered what a man "gets" out of his
drinking, your problem appears solved. All you have to do, in
the case of the man with a sense of inferiority, is to give him
a sense of his individual worth in some non-alcoholic way. In
the case of the fearful, over-anxious man, take away his fears
and he will not need alcohol. If some one suffers from periods
of depression, show him how to deal with the depression with-

[3]This subject of the inferiority sense will be discussed fully in Chapter VII.

out alcoholic assistance. It sounds so easy, but in reality it is tremendously hard.

If a man is merely an occasional alcoholic, and if the habit or the obsession has not been deeply rooted, you may be able to help him in some such way. But with the periodic alcoholic who disappears for weeks or months, or the chronic case who is always more or less under the influence of alcohol, you must do a lot of surface reconstruction work before you can get at the fundamental sources of weakness. Alcoholism is like all habits: to overcome it, you must create another habit. The alcoholic must have a chance to say "no" so often that he no longer even thinks of saying "yes"—until it has become *easier* to say "no" than to say "yes"; until the results of saying "yes" seem so unpleasant that the saying "no" is a protection against things that he does not want to have happen. To achieve this takes time.

The only really satisfactory results that I have obtained have come through placing the alcoholic in an environment where it was almost physically impossible to get alcohol, or where it was to be obtained only at the cost of such trouble and danger that the danger and the trouble were not worth while. The old idea of sending an alcoholic on a trip around The Horn in a sailing vessel, on which the only alcohol available was locked in the captain's cabin, was not such a bad one. Nowadays it is possible to get a man work in certain parts of the United States that are so thoroughly "dry," that it would require unusual determination and involve a great deal of trouble in order to get some very inferior type of liquor. In such an atmosphere the forming of a new habit is made comparatively easy. But it is useless to send a man into such surroundings until he has been under medical supervision and treatment, until his body has been cleared of the alcoholic poison and he no longer can be considered a sick man, whose sickness can be at once temporarily eased by a little of the stuff that has poisoned him.

Let me warn you, however, against attempting the sudden absolute withdrawal of alcohol from a sick alcoholic patient. Such a thing is highly dangerous. If you have an alcoholic patient who breaks a leg, and if his wife says to you, "Now that I have him helpless at home I can take away the whiskey" —do not let her desire to keep her husband sober send him into an attack of delirium tremens and make him suddenly walk out of the window in an acute alcoholic confusion. Let him have a reasonable amount. Reduce it slowly, if you wish, but unless the doctor who is visiting him approves, do not try to pin a white ribbon on the broken leg. It may lead to a broken neck.

I fear that I am unable to give you any very great help in dealing with alcoholic cases, except to beg you never to lose patience with them. Sometimes a man has to go down into the gutter six times before he learns to want to stay out of it. For, after you have done everything you can for the alcoholic, after you have made his body sound, and have helped him to begin the creation of a new set of mental habits, there is still one important element you have not touched at all, that is, the man's will. He must *want* to keep away from alcohol; not merely when he is so poisoned with it that he never wants to smell it again, but later on when he feels well, when he is bored by the routine of daily life, or depressed, or when he is faced by some difficult, trying situation. For, like everything else, the will has habits of its own. If you cannot teach your will to function almost automatically in a certain direction, you will never be quite safe from the danger of its slumping in the opposite one.

I do not wish to go into detailed discussion of the influence of religion on alcoholic cases. The struggle with alcoholism as it comes before the priest in the confessional, the pastor in conference with his parishioner, or the social worker in an interview, is made up of the same mental stuff as the struggle with habits of dishonesty or of sexual indulgence. No priest with any experience will attempt to deny the value and the help of the sacraments in such cases as these. The alcoholic who has made a fresh start, but who is suddenly overtaken by a period of intense temptation, can find a new source of strength and of resistance in his communions and his confessions. He has an infinitely greater chance of success in his struggle than the man who, without faith and without supernatural help, is fighting it out alone. When the unbelieving alcoholic falls, he tends to fall far, and dispair is always close to him. For the Catholic-minded man who, after a fall, makes his way directly to the Sacrament of Penance and then to his Communion, the fall is never so great, the recovery is easier, and there is no place for hopelessness, for discouragement or despair. Even in churches where there is no confessional, the pastor should make himself easy of access to his alcoholic cases. Often, a man who has seemed half drunk has been sent away from a rectory or a church, when he had come to seek human contact with his priest or his pastor in order that he might not get drunk entirely. If you cannot keep in personal touch with such cases, encourage them to write to you; and be sure to answer their letters promptly. Persuade them to send you a few lines, when everything is going well, but especially when they are depressed, tempted or already falling away from their purposes of amendment. It is a hard struggle—and you know nothing of its bitterness. Believe me when I tell you how bitter, bitter hard it is. Be patient, not sentimentally soft, but understanding and just; understanding, because when a man falls you must remember the fifty times that he has successfully resisted. And just; because when he does fall, the force of the old temptation has been so great that even you yourself —had your feet been set in such slippery places—might not always have been able to stand upright.

I am carefully avoiding any mention of prohibition.[4] But in

---

[4]My personal reactions to prohibition have been set down in my book, *Foursquare*, pp. 109–118.

your dealings with the alcoholics of our present day, there are one or two matters that you should keep in mind. I shall not take it upon myself to criticize the forces that have produced the present situation; but the fact remains that we, as a nation, are to-day consuming a great deal of immatured or artificial spirits. In pre-war days the physician or the pastor knew fairly well what his alcoholic cases were consuming, and what the results of certain kinds of beers, wines and spirits usually were. Nowadays, we are frequently puzzled by new post-alcoholic conditions.

There is no doubt in my mind that the average type of alcoholic case that one sees to-day in the cells of a jail is much more toxic than the cases of twenty years ago. Moreover, the mental results are more marked. I have seen a man who had been arrested for being drunk and disorderly—not so very drunk at that—and given ten days in jail, develop not a delirium tremens—he had not been drinking hard enough for that—but an acute hallucinosis of fear and persecution. He knew that he was to be murdered; he attacked every one that came near him; he would not eat because the food was poisoned. Before we came to recognize these cases as post-alcoholic, some of them were committed to mental hospitals as cases of schizophrenia; and after a few days, when the poisonous alcohol was out of their bodies, they suddenly recovered completely, to every one's astonishment. Recovered, except for one thing. They could not remember how they got drunk or how they got into jail.

What we call "amnesia," or loss of memory, used to happen occasionally in the old days in connection with alcoholism. An undergraduate who drank too much champagne would not remember how he got to bed that same night. But "amnesia" has become very much more frequent in these days of unmatured spirits. After three or even two "small drinks" I have known men and women to lose all memory of the events of the following hours. A dangerous thing indeed.[5] I feel

[5]See cases at end of this chapter.

sure that alcoholic cases to-day are going to be more difficult to deal with than were similar cases before the War. Nowadays, alcoholism, and not chronic or extreme alcoholism either, is associated as never before with mental disturbance, and especially with amnesias or losses of memory.

The whole question of "drug addiction" I can pass over with a very few words.[6] I do not look upon it as a source of such serious complications as the use of our modern unmatured, synthetic spirits. And I do not believe that the average pastor or social worker will ever see enough drug cases to make it worthwhile for me to discuss the subject in detail here. Roughly, there are two types of what we call "users" of narcotic drugs, of cocaine or of the products or derivations of opium. First, those who use these drugs in order to attain a certain state of mental happiness or relaxation or stimulation; and secondly, those who have acquired, in some way or other, the habit of taking every day a certain amount of these same preparations. The first class, in order to attain its end, has to increase the dose; and that is dangerous. Such people may become so filled with morphine that they are in a continuous state of drowsiness or sleep; or so stimulated with cocaine that they are excited, overactive, uncontrolled. The second class scarcely ever increases the daily dose. They get no stimulation, no pleasant sensations out of it; but they have acquired the habit, and in order to be able to live, to work, to eat and sleep they need a certain number of grains of a white powder. Usually they are quiet, respectable, hard-working men and women, who live more or less in constant fear—fear of discovery, and fear of not being able to get their daily supply. Although they would gladly get rid of their habit, yet they know that in order to get rid of it they will have to go to a hospital or undergo treatment for many months. This would mean the loss of their position, this would make other people point them out as "dope fiends" and would, at the same time,

[6] See *Foursquare*, pp. 118–127.

entail a period of intense physical and mental torment for themselves. So as long as they can get their "supplies," they go on their quiet way, bothering no one and doing no harm. Yet they are breaking the Federal Narcotic Law every time they buy a few grains of cocaine or of morphine from a "drug peddler." No one looks down on the rich man when he orders a case of champagne from his bootlegger—whose activities are as illegal as those of the drug peddler; but if the unfortunate drug user is caught with morphine or cocaine in his possession and cannot show a physician's prescription for it, he is in for all sorts of trouble.

If you are ever brought into contact with a drug case, let me give you one piece of good advice; at least, I have always found it good. In your city or near it there are Federal Narcotic officers. Many of the chiefs of divisions are medical men whom you will, I am sure, find very understanding and anxious to help. If you come across a narcotic case, who is suffering agony of body and mind because, for some reason or other, he has run out of "supplies," take him at once to Narcotic headquarters; or, if that is impossible, take him to a physician registered under the Federal Narcotic Act, who can prescribe for your patient enough of his drug to keep him out of agony until you can get into touch with the Federal officers. If your patient has been buying his supplies from "peddlers" and you give him money to go on buying, you are assisting him in breaking the law; and you will not do him much real good. If he is really a worthwhile case, or if the physician to whom you take him feels that he is suffering from some illness that would make it dangerous to deprive him of his usual dose, then you will find the Narcotic agents more than anxious to co-operate with you and to help your patient. If they decide that he really needs what he has been accustomed to take, they will refer him to some physician whom they trust, and then your patient can secure what he needs without breaking the law. If, on the other hand, your patient really wants to

get rid of his addiction the Narcotic Service will advise you
where to send him.

The whole question of drug addiction in this country has,
I believe, been greatly exaggerated. If you are anxious to get
at the real facts, ask your nearest Narcotic agent to send you
some of the reports of his department. But be on your guard
against any printed circular that comes to you by post asking
you to enlist in a great anti-drug crusade, membership in this
same crusade being only open to distinguished men like yourself on payment of the small registration fee of five dollars.
Should you send in your five dollars, it will probably go into
the pockets of some crook who is using the mails to defraud
and whose only crusade is one against your pocketbook for
his own benefit. The Narcotic agents have investigated many
such crusades; ask them about any circular you may receive
before you deprive yourself of five dollars.

Thanks to our Federal Law, it is now almost impossible for
ordinary people to get hold of narcotic drugs. The old days,
when a woman who took cocaine could get all she wanted at
the nearest chemist's shop, are long since past. At present a woman of the upper classes who uses morphine, and who naturally
does not know what drug peddlers are or where they hang
out, can get her supply from only one source, a physician.
Forunately there are few physicians, if any, who would keep
on prescribing morphine or cocaine unless the case demanded
it. I mean that the old type of self-indulgent woman who was
a morphine or cocaine user because she could get it so easily
has, I believe, ceased to exist. But there are people who use
other kinds of procurable drugs. Occasionally you may come
across some one who has a veronal habit; some woman, who
goes on using larger and larger doses, in order "to quiet her
nerves" and who is found some morning in a deep coma from
which she is aroused only with great difficulty.

In all such cases there is not only a physical habit of body,
there is also a peculiar habit of mind. I have known many men

and some women who have gone through all the torments involved in a withdrawal of their habitual drug, and have been without it for months, yet who suddenly drop back into using the drug again. They will tell you that, although they have been "off the drug" for months and feel no physical discomfort, they are nevertheless constantly tormented by a sense of "something lacking." The hypodermic use of morphine, for instance, is rather a complex process. The sterilizing of the needle, the dissolving of the drug, the injection itself; these manual acts may have been performed many times a day for months or years. A sort of mental habit has been formed. Even when the drug itself has been eliminated from the patient's system, there remains that half-conscious urge to take up again those familiar actions that have attained an almost obsessive power over the mind.

Watch a child standing before that mysterious medicine closet in which her mother carefully locks away those strange liquids and powders, which the child sees only on some interesting occasion, the illness of some member of the family; an occasion that has been stamped on the child's memory on account of the unusual happenings that accompany it. So the medicine closet becomes to the imaginative child a fascinating Blue Beard's chamber. Such a child, if left alone, may find the key to this source of mysteries; or the mother may forget to fasten the lock. And the child , with trembling little hands and in an ecstacy of dangerous exploration, takes down one bottle after another, or examines the boxes of colored powders. From a mere handling, it is no far cry to a tasting of this or that liquid; not enough to hurt the child perhaps, but enough to form in its mind an association between "medicines" and a blissful sensation of achievement and power. For she holds in her hands those magical things that "stop stomach aches" or "keep people from coughing." On such a basis there may arise, in one case, an interest in chemical substances that may make of the child a distinguished chemist or biologist, a lover of laboratories, of strange smells, of Bunsen burners and retorts. In another case, on the basis of the same association, there may develop a dangerous fascination for drugs, for testing their power, for "seeing what they do to you." When this second child grows up and is, in later life, confronted with periods of anxiety or of great disappointment and loss, the old memories of the medicine closet and of its powerful contents lead easily to an effort to escape from the unpleasant realities of the present by the use of some "sedative" or even of some narcotic. This may sound fanciful; but if you have ever been called upon to give help to some man or woman who has this urge to escape reality by way of the medicine closet, and who has a perfect obsession to take medicines, drugs, sedatives, anything that is to be found in a drug store or in the drug room of a dispensary, you will realize that I am not painting an unreal picture of acute human distress.

The habit of taking, not narcotics, but "medicine" is a hard habit to eradicate. Thousands of people who believe themselves to suffer from costiveness, set the clock of their daily happiness by the regular action of their lower bowel. If that bowel does not empty itself at a certain time each day, that day is ruined. The man or the woman has a headache; and inasmuch as such unhappiness and such headaches are to be avoided, there grows up the habit of depending either on irrigations or on so-called purgatives. I remember the case of a man who developed an acute emotional panic while in a nursing home because his habitual laxative was taken from him. He had told the nurse on entering that he had given up all his "medicines." But into the pocket of a pair of pajamas he had carefully sewn a phial of his usual purgative. When this was discovered, and the nurse, in very natural annoyance, threw the "medicine" out of the window, the patient became unmanageable. He said, and he believed, that "without his daily laxative" he would die. He would have a "stoppage of the bowels" and expire in agony. And that patient was not an introspective, imaginative woman, but a hard-headed man of business.

There are no real "drug fiends" in the accepted sense of those words. But there are plenty of "medicine devils" who are quite willing to go into the first drug-store to ask for "something for nervousness," and to take blindly what is given them. If a reputable physician gives them a prescription, they will ask the drug clerk who makes it up to read them the names of the various chemical products contained in it; but they will devour a box of "headache powders" without a tremor; they will buy and eat "aspirin tablets" by the bottle. The modern indiscriminate use of aspirin, which is a specific and a godsend in certain types of rheumatism, is, I believe, decidedly dangerous. Fortunately, most people do not know how to take a dose of salicylic acid in the proper manner; they usually swallow down the white, button-shaped tabloid; and I am glad that they do. But they would be better off if they left aspirin to the rheumatic people who really need it.

Self-discipline has gone out of fashion. It does not occur to any one to bear a headache patiently, to bear it for the sake of being able to control themselves, if they happen to be pagans; or to offer up the pain and the discomfort to Our Lord, if they happen to be Christians. No. If they have a headache, they must at once "take something to stop it." Pain as a means of discipline—even discomfort—has no place in modern life. No one rebels against the infliction of unnecessary pain more than I do; but it is a poor kind of mental habit always to be running to the medicine closet when you feel uncomfortable or are suffering from the results of your own inordinate appetite for food or drink. There would not be much money made on Bromo-seltzer or Coca-cola, if our age had not lost hold on the old Spartan ideas of pain patiently born, on ideals that we dub "Victorian" and throw into the waste basket of civilization.

Finally, the connection of "drug users" with crime or delinquency has also been greatly over-emphasized. Criminals in preparing for a daring hold-up do not fill themselves with morphine, for opium is a narcotic, a sedative. And the morphine user is a quiet, peaceable soul, unless he has been deprived of his drug. I have known shop-lifters to use cocaine, or more cocaine than usual, when they were making a raid on the crowded counters of some large store. They say that an extra "sniff" or two gives "nerve" to take long chances. But the "extra sniffs" often make raiders take such long chances that they are caught and sent to a place where they can get no "sniffs" at all. Of course, I dare say that many delinquents are habitual users of drugs; but so are many estimable people who are not criminals in any sense. The hold-up man who starts out to "pull off a job" wants his mind as clear as possible. If he is in the habit of using a certain amount of cocaine or of opium every day, he will want just that dosage and no more. He doesn't want to be either over-stimulated or sent off to sleep in the midst of a robbery.

Thus far we have tried to study examples of mental illness, various types of psychoses. I have outlined, very imperfectly, the general symptoms of three common psychotic states; the manic-depressive, the paranoid and the schizophrenic. As an example of exogenic, toxic states, we have studied paresis, and the problems connected with alcoholism and the use of drugs. If you will glance through the tables of contents in Doctor White's or Doctor Menninger's book,[7] you will realize how much material I have been forced to omit. We have said nothing about the pre-senile psychoses and those that depend on the development of an arterio-sclerosis; nothing about the mental conditions that are the result of infection or of exhaustion; very little (except in connection with paresis) about the psychotic states that are associated with organic diseases of the brain or with brain injuries. Again, we have had to pass

[7] White, op. cit. Menninger, The Human Mind.

over the mental disturbances that appear in cases of uremic poisoning and of diabetes, or that are connected with the excessive or the imperfect secretions of the thyroid gland. Conditions of definitely "nervous" origin, using the word nervous in its proper connotation, belong to the neurologist, although many of them may present decidedly mental symptoms. Chorea, or St. Vitus dance, paralysis agitans, multiple sclerosis and other similar disease entities lie somewhat out of the field of our study. Still further away lie other physical diseases, that react on the patient's mental state; heart disease, or even influenza.[8] For information on these conditions, in case you should ever be brought into contact with them, I must refer you to the text-books. Before we pass on to the complex subject of mental maladjustments, those mental conditions that are not psychoses, I must at least touch on the subject of what is commonly and often erroneously called mental deficiency; for this is a matter that will often be brought to your attention.

Idiots and imbeciles, so called, have been known and recognized in every civilization; even the smallest village has always had its "village idiot." But the two words were more or less synonymous until modern psychiatry began to evolve the conception of mental deficiency—not a new disease, not a psychosis, but an hereditary condition, a biological handicap. Every one nowadays knows about "mental tests." At the time of our entrance into the World War, they had become sufficiently accepted to be used in connection with our examinations of the drafted men; yet even then many people made fun of them. The men detailed to give the tests were "the nut doctors" and were considered not on the same level with the doctors who examined eyes and hearts and lungs. And yet it was thanks to those same "nut doctors" that our expeditionary force was the only unit of the allied armies in which there

---

[8]White, op. cit., p. 305. See also Menninger, "Psychoses Associated With Influenza," Archives of Neurology and Psychiatry, 1919, Vol. 2, No. 3, pp. 291–337. Also Journal A. M. A., Vol. 72, p. 670.

were almost no mental deficients—no men whose inability to reason, to judge, to act quickly, might imperil the lives of many thousands of their comrades.

There are, as you know, many types of mental tests.[9] A mental test is, for the psychiatrist, a definite set of tools. It will not perform all kinds of mental operations; nor will it test everything mental. If you go into the office of a general practitioner of medicine, you will see lying around various boxes and bags. One bag is the obstetrical bag, which contains those instruments that are necessary for helping babies into this world. There will be a flat box, which contains the instruments suitable for an abdominal operation. In still another box is an ophthalmoscope and other machinery for eye, nose and ear work. So it goes. When the physician is called out on an obstetrical case, you would not expect him to snatch up his ophthalmoscope and his instruments for the inspection of eye, nose and throat. If he did, he might be able to examine his patient's eyes and nose in a very satisfactory manner, but he would not deliver many babies. So it is with mental tests. They form a certain definite box of tools, and are very useful in their *right* place. The same thing is true of psychoanalysis, which is so popular nowadays; it forms a useful box of tools. But it is not suitable or intended for every mental job the psychiatrist has to do. If this is the only box of instruments that he knows how to use, he will have to limit his practice, or else he will be examining a patient's mental ear and nose while the patient is trying to have a mental baby.[10]

Doctors Binet and Simon were the original framers of the first sets of mental tests and they tried to draw up a group of questions or mental tasks that could be answered by children of a definite age who had ordinary intelligence. Therefore,

[9]My general reaction to them all has been set down in my book, *Foursquare*, p. 29.

[10]"The Present Status of Psychoanalysis as a Psychologic and Therapeutic System," Address by Dr. Franz Alexander, with discussion following, *Archives of Neurology and Psychiatry*, Nov., 1931, Vol. 26, No. 5, pp. 1108-1112.

these mental tests measure, not the emotions, not the judgment, not the experience, but only the intelligence. It is quite wrong to call them *mental* tests. They are *intelligence* tests. And we make a fundamental mistake when we classify a certain child and say, "This child has a *mental* age of eight years," or "This patient has the *mental* level of an eight-year-old child." It is not mental age, or mental level, of which one should speak, but level of intelligence. Since the original Binet-Simon investigations, psychiatrists have attempted to invent tests that will measure, not only the intelligence, but the emotions and the judgment also. Emotion and judgment, however, are not as easy to measure as intelligence; at least not so long as the test is an imaginary one, given in an office, by asking questions; and not in the material or actual life, on the playground, in the home or during a study hour. However, all these statements are beside the mark. All that need interest you is what follows.

There are, roughly speaking, three grades of mental deficiency, or to use a discarded term, feeble-mindedness. The lowest grade is idiocy. An idiot child cannot learn to speak, much less to read; to attend to natural wants; to acquire habits of cleanliness. It is almost an unthinking animal that reacts as animals do to external stimuli, but that is often less teachable than the dullest terrier. There are, of course, grades of idiocy. And there are no absolutely clean-cut divisions between idiocy and the next highest grade of mental deficiency, imbecility. The outstanding element in imbeciles is that they are, partially at least, *teachable*. They cannot learn much; but they can learn something. Doctor White's definition is a good one. "Imbecility is a condition of mental deficiency that can be improved by training but not sufficiently to enable the subject to take and to keep a place in the world."[11] Idiots and imbeciles are not responsible for their actions. It is unnecessary to go into the details of the mental testings by which imbecility

[11]*Op. cit.,* p. 327.

or idiocy is determined according to the I. Q., or intelligence quotient, or of the results obtained by the mental examination. Roughly speaking, again, the idiot's mentality never develops beyond the intelligence of a three-year-old child; the imbecile does not get beyond that of a child of seven years of age. But imbeciles and idiots do not bother psychiatrists or pastors very much. The bothersome, difficult class is made up of those mental deficients whose extreme intellectual development lies between that of a seven and of a twelve-year-old child. This class we call morons. That is, again, a Greek word; it means "fool" or "idiot." In the domain of mental deficiency the terminology is symptomatic of a marked lack of intelligence on our own part. Since "idiot," the lowest grade, is another Greek word meaning "an ordinary, somewhat simple-minded individual"; while for "imbecile" we have to jump over into Latin and then with "moron" jump back into Greek. Etymologically speaking, a moron is a much bigger idiot than an "idiot." But we twist the matter round the wrong way.

However, we hear in these days a lot about morons and moronic behavior. But we must remember that the morons are the hewers of wood and the drawers of water in this world; they are the people who do the simple routine work and who are incapable of anything more complicated. This is especially true of the higher grades; those with an intelligence of a twelve-year-old child. But just because a man or a woman, after being tested, is assigned an intelligence level of, let us say, eleven years, we must not forget that a normal child of eleven is responsible for its actions in a very wide degree and may act with more apparent intelligence than many grown men and women. Moreover, a high-grade moron, with his *intelligence* level of eleven years, has an emotional level of his own actual age, and has had an experience of a similar extent. Never think, then, of a high-grade moron as a man or woman with a *mental* age of eleven. His or her *intelligence* may be eleven years old in ability to reason, but his or her experience is a different thing. In all such cases, you will find that the weak spot of the moron lies in his inability to reason on the basis of his experience. He does not *learn* from experience. Send the normal boy to jail for stealing, and after a while he will realize that boys who steal go to jail and are very uncomfortable there. A moron steals and goes to jail and comes out and steals and goes in again. He cannot reason out the connection between his stealing and his jailing. Moreover, morons are often emotionally unstable. They are up in the clouds or down in the dumps; and most important of all, they are unable to adjust themselves to new situations. There are millions of morons working successfully all over the world at routine jobs; but take any one of them out of his daily routine, face him with some unexpected, some difficult situation, and he will be unable to deal with it—or else he will deal with it in a wholly unexpected manner. Give him a regular job, and he will keep faithfully at it. But let him be thrown out of work—let him have to go round hunting work, and he will not find it. He does not know how.[12]

This is a very imperfect statement of the whole problem which during the past twenty years has been so frequently and so widely discussed, that I may take for granted your knowledge of its practical importance in your work.

CLINICAL MATERIAL

A. Alcoholism. Cases from my own experience.

(1) A lawyer, aged forty-five, perfectly sound in body and mind, accustomed to take a cocktail or a whiskey-and-soda occasionally, but never to excess, is on his way home from his office, where he has been doing some work in the evening. It is about ten o'clock. His partner is with him in the car. As they reach

[12]Any one interested in mental deficiency should get into touch with his local Society for Mental Hygiene, or with the National Committee in New York (450 Seventh Ave.). Many interesting studies have been published in the Committee's periodical, *Mental Hygiene.*

the partner's house where the lawyer intends to drop his friend on his own way home, the partner asks the other man "to come in for a moment and have a drink." The lawyer does not care much for alcohol at night; but he is tired and tense. He goes up to his friend's apartment. He takes about two fingers of whiskey and a little soda. His friend urges him to have another drink. He does not want it. The friend urges, so he takes another small drink—two small drinks of whiskey in about forty-five minutes. He bids his partner good night, goes out to his car and drives home. There is a good deal of ordinary traffic; he has to drive rather slowly. Finally he gets to his home in the suburbs. He has a tricky garage which is not easy to get into without scratching the car. But he manages it well, turns off his ignition, closes and locks the garage door; goes to his own door, opens it with one key on a bunch of twenty. His wife meets him on the stairs. He says to her: "I'm rather tired. Had a hard evening's work. I think I'll go straight to bed." To bed he goes, and sleeps soundly. Next morning, he comes into the breakfast room and looks at his wife in a puzzled, ashamed way. "Maria," he begins slowly, "was I all right last night?" His wife looks up surprised. "Of course," she says; "why do you ask?" "Well," he replies, "I stopped at John's apartment on the way home and had two small drinks of whiskey." His wife begins to laugh. "You showed no signs of it," she says. "You put the car in so quietly, I didn't hear it. And you know how narrow the garage door is! You walked straight up the stairs, spoke to me in the most normal way, and then went quietly to bed. Are you trying to play a joke on me?" Her husband does not answer her smile. "There is no joke about it," he says. "From the time I got into my car at John's front door, *I don't remember a single thing until I woke up in my own bed this morning.*" In other words, he had a complete amnesia for nearly ten hours. While he was driving home through all the traffic, he was like a car travelling along by itself with the chauffeur in a dead faint at the wheel. If such a car is on a straight road, if nothing happens that necessitates the unconscious chauffeur's action, then all goes well. But if another car comes along unexpectedly, if one out of a thousand possible things happens, what then? Our lawyer feels his knees go weak beneath him.

While he was driving home, automatically, through all the traffic last night, suppose something out of the ordinary had happened —suppose the door of the garage had not been open, suppose any slight deviation from the routine conditions—there would have been an accident. People would have noticed the smell of whiskey on his breath. "Drunk and driving carelessly." Many a man's career has been ruined by less than that. And yet he only took "two small drinks" of unmatured stuff that was labelled Scotch Whiskey.

(2) Simon Scales, aged forty, a workman in a big railroad engine-house, was arrested and charged with having entered three houses during the early hours of the morning, between six and seven, and having stolen various articles from various rooms. There could be no question about his guilt. All the stolen articles were found hidden away in an old trunk in his attic. He must have been doing this for some time. Before his arrest it just chanced that a policeman noticed him one morning, a little before seven, coming out of one of the houses. He protested that he had never stolen anything, that he had never entered any one's house without permission. His statements were naturally not believed. Various small thefts had been reported of late in that neighborhood. Simon's wife denied all knowledge of his misdeeds and would not believe him guilty, until in her own garret all the articles that had been reported missing were actually found. Simon protested again; he had not placed those articles there; he knew nothing about them. It must be a "plant." Some one was trying to "put him in bad." His employers had nothing but good to say of him. He had been an absolutely dependable mechanic, working in their shops for twenty years without a single black mark against his record. They could not understand his robberies. He had very good wages. He had no children. So far as was known, he did not gamble, was devoted to his wife, not interested in other women. "But that only shows," said his boss, "how you can be deceived in a man. Of course, we can't keep him on at the shop, even if he gets a light sentence. He'll probably get at least a year in jail. Although the value of the stolen articles doesn't seem to amount to more than fifty dollars." Mrs. Scales, convinced of her husband's guilt, besought him to plead

guilty, which he refused to do. He had done nothing wrong, he said. It was all a mistake. "Why," he said, "would I want to steal? And why steal two women's hatpins and a powder-puff, besides all the other stuff that was planted in our garret?" But Mrs. Scales could not believe him. She packed up and went home to her mother. Their little house, that had been almost paid for, was put up for sale, and Simon stayed in jail awaiting trial. Until I heard his story, I thought him merely an ordinary thief. But one day, while I was examining other cases at the jail, he buttonholed me in the corridor. He knew I was a "nut doctor." Would it be possible for a man to steal a lot of things at several different times and not know he had done it? That was the only possibility in his case. And if that were true, then he must be crazy. So I grew interested and then heard the whole tale. Ten years ago I should not have believed it. And surely it would never have been accepted then by even the most lenient judge. Yet, knowing what our modern alcohol can do, I laid the case before one of our judges. Simon was given a suspended sentence, allowed to go back to his job— which an enlightened boss restored to him after hearing my explanations. Curiously enough, all of Simon's troubles came from a simple thing. He had been changed from the day shift of mechanics on which he had always worked, to the night shift. On the day shift he knew all the men and they knew him. They knew that he didn't drink, that he went straight home from his work to his wife. But on the night shift, they didn't know him so well. It was a cold spring when he started on the new schedule, and he was not used to working at night, anyhow. After he had been working for a week, he made a new friend on the night shift. One cold morning, as he and his friend left the shops, this friend suggested a drink. Simon was not a drinking man, but he was tired and he felt that he had taken cold. He couldn't afford to get sick and be laid off. So he went into a speakeasy with his friend. Remember, he had been working all night, his powers of resistance were at their lowest ebb, and he had nothing in his stomach. He took one drink. It made him feel so much warmer that he took another. Then he started home. The next thing he remembered was waking up in his own bed at about three in the afternoon. He questioned his wife. She had noticed nothing wrong.

He had returned as usual from work, only a little later than was his custom, and had had his breakfast and gone to bed. The only unusual thing he had done was to go up to the garret. He had said that he wanted to look at a bad place in the roof. So Simon put the whole thing out of his mind. Ten days later, after the work of the night shift, Simon's friend persuaded him to have another drink. The same thing happened. Later on, it happened again. But by that time, Simon had begun to feel that something was wrong. Three times he had come home without remembering how he had got there. He went up into the garret, but found nothing there, nothing unusual so far as he could see. But he was frightened. And for a month he refused to drink after the night's work. But at last, he yielded once more to his friend's suggestion, only this time he tried, as best he could, to keep his wits about him. But the alcohol clouded his consciousness. On his way home, he found himself almost compelled to peer into the backyard of a quiet house, in which the family was still asleep. He pulled himself together and went home. But he did not know that a policeman had followed, or that this same officer had recognized him as a man seen several weeks before, coming out of a neighboring house. At that time, the policeman had not stopped him. The officer was sorry for this, when the people of that same house reported a theft that same day. But since that time, the policeman had been on the look-out, and at last his patience had been rewarded. Simon was sitting at his breakfast when the policeman came. The experiences of the past mornings had made him feel self-conscious and not sure of himself. He submitted willingly to being searched. Nothing was found on him. But the policeman was a thorough official, and searched the house. In an old trunk in the garret he found what he was looking for. There is no doubt in my mind, that on the morning of Simon's first drink, he had, on his way home, quietly walked into the first house he came to, picked up anything that took his fancy; and on arriving home hid the stolen articles in his garret, had his breakfast, and slept and on waking had forgotten absolutely what he had done. That he should have done this same thing three times before he was discovered seems hard to believe. It may be that he was lying about his complete loss of memory for the second or third theft. But I felt sure that his amnesia for the first offense was a real one. Moreover, his previous spotless record and the comparatively small value of the articles stolen helped his case a great deal. He had a severe lesson. He will not take another drink of immatured or synthetic spirits on an empty stomach, or I imagine, on any kind of a stomach. That a man should do such things under the influence of alcohol is no new matter; but that he should have a complete amnesia, after taking so small an amount of alcohol, is another proof, if proof were needed, of the dangers involved in an indiscriminate use of our modern types of alcoholic liquids.

(3) Still more tragic is the story of a young sailor whom I saw on one of my visits to our jail, sitting in his cell, with his head buried in his hands, a picture of despair. A splendid type of humanity; a sailor with an excellent record. Kind-hearted, but stronger physically than he realized. I supposed that he was an "ordinary drunk and disorderly case." I sat down on the bed beside him in the dark cell. "What are you here for?" That is the opening gambit of all such conversations. To my surprise he lifted to me a face distorted by mental agony and wet with tears. "Murder," he said. "And Doctor, as sure as I'm alive and in jail, I don't remember a single thing about it." He said: "I came ashore on an evening's leave. I was with two other men from my ship. We didn't have much money, but with what we did have, we bought two or three drinks. We had to buy cheap stuff. I don't know what happened soon after that. The policeman says that I went up to a stranger who was coming along the street and asked him for fifty cents, so that we could get one more drink apiece before we went back to the ship. And he says that, when the stranger refused, I got angry and hit him. He fell over backwards and struck his head on the curbstone and got—got killed. He must have hit his head; I couldn't have hit him hard enough to kill him—but perhaps I did. If I can't remember hitting him at all, how do I know how hard I hit him? And I'll be tried for murder—a murder that I don't remember anything about at all."

B. Narcotics and "Medicine Habits."

(1) Morris Kildare was charged with having snatched a

purse from a woman on the street. He did it very clumsily and was soon caught. On arrest, he was found to be intensely nervous, agitated, unable to eat or sleep and apparently in great mental and physical agony. Both his arms were covered with the healed pin-pricks of hypodermic needles and with the scars of old abscesses, the results of unsterilized injections. He was not known as a "user" to the narcotic officers, and no narcotic drugs were found in his possession. He had an excellent record as a clerk in the office of a large manufacturing company; was unmarried, lived a very quiet, eminently respectable life, and was much beloved by a large group of friends. He had no vices; he did not drink, and had no promiscuous sex relationships. His story was as follows. He had acquired a habit of using morphine many years ago, before the passage of the Anti-Narcotic Act, when it was possible to obtain supplies at almost any drug-store. He had learned the use of morphine from a friend of those early days, who had himself acquired it after a very painful attack of inflammatory rheumatism. At the time, Kildare had had a bad bout of sciatica, but had to keep on working in order to support his mother. The morphine made it possible for him to sleep at night and to get through his day's work. After a while, his friend moved to another city, his own sciatica got well, the old mother died—but the habit remained. The dose, for the past fifteen years, had never been increased. Since the passage of the Anti-Narcotic Act, Kildare had been forced to get his supplies from drug peddlers, who charged enormous prices. He used about four grains a day, and his supplies, bought from peddlers, cost him from five to ten dollars a week. Naturally, he had no money for amusements, or for holidays. As he said: "I could go without food, if necessary. I could go without clothes. But there was one thing that I could not go without, and still keep working and earning my living. That one thing I *had* to have." For more than fifteen years he went on in this way, doing his work well, respected by every one. And then, through no fault of his own, he lost his job. It was only a temporary setback. He knew that in a few months he would be able to get another one, for he had excellent references. His company would take him on again "as soon as business conditions" improved. He had never been able to save. The money that he might have put into the bank had to go to the drug peddlers. For, as he said, he could get along almost without food, but there was always one thing that he *must* have, and that thing cost money. He did not dare go to any one with the true story of his trouble. People would think he was "a dope fiend" and that would mean the end of ever getting work again. Gradually his supply of money and his supply of morphine dwindled. He was cutting his daily dose in half, not sleeping, unable to eat, growing weaker, and less and less able to think connectedly. Finally, when he was almost out of his mind, his former employers sent for him and told him that at the end of two weeks his old position would be open to him. He had to get through those two weeks. He soon exhausted his possibilities of borrowing. He had to eat a little. He had to keep himself in condition to take up his work again in the office, when the time came for him to present himself there. Finally, his last grain of morphine was gone. His money was gone too, and he still had three days to go before his work began. He could, he thought, have begged enough food to get him over those three days; but, if he went without morphine for that period, he would be a mental and physical wreck. In such a condition no one, not even his old employers, would take him on again. All he wanted was enough money to buy a few grains of a certain white powder. In a moment of dispair, he snatched at a woman's purse—and was caught. Cases of this type show one way—almost the only way— in which a drug addiction may lead directly to crime or delinquency. If Kildare had only realized that the Federal Narcotic officials are not hard-boiled, unsympathetic policemen, he might have found help by laying his case before them. But drug users of Kildare's type are afraid, constantly afraid of two things; first, that they may lose their source of supply, and second, that the secret of their addiction may become known. You and I, as physicians and pastors, and social workers, must delete the words "dope fiends" from our vocabularies and treat such unfortunate people not with abhorrence, but with kindness and sympathy.

(2) Michael Newman was a novice, or rather a postulant in a monastery. A very religious, able young man, introspective, fearful. He had been a "delicate child"; his mother had surrounded his

boyhood with an atmosphere of constant anxiety; and he had always had a "delicate digestion." His mother had always insisted on "the regularity of a daily evacuation"; no day passed without the mother asking whether or not a certain remote place had been successfully visited. When Michael went away to college, he carried these mental habits with him. He was studious, took little exercise, ate a good many sweets. Naturally, to speak euphuistically, "his intestinal reactions became costive." When his lower bowel did not act regularly, he was too lazy to take exercise, to eat less sweet stuff, and so to readjust the apparent difficulty. If things would not work of themselves, then he would make them work by "taking something." One year he depended on one type of laxative, another year on some other kind. He never travelled without an apparatus for enemata and internal irrigation. In this way, he gradually disturbed the muscular tone of his lower bowel. His enematical habits loosened things up too much; his use of purgatives, in order to make the lower end of it contract artificially, poisoned the entire intestinal tract and his constant fear of not being able to defecate, kept his rectal, especially his anal muscles tense and tight. By the time he finished college and came to live in a monastery as a postulant for the novitiate, he had developed certain definite habits of mind and of body. He set the clock of his day's happiness by the condition of his lower bowel. If it emptied itself, somehow, then the sun shone brightly, and all was for the best in the best of all worlds. If it did not, then the day was not only spoiled, but Michael's mind was filled with persistent fears. For, so he believed, if there is no movement, then there may be "stasis," and intestinal stasis leads to all sorts of terrible things—eventually to a "stoppage" that requires a surgical operation, which may come too late. Moreover, from habitual costiveness there flow a whole set of terrible things, beginning with dull headaches and running up or down to inoperable cancer. But so long as Newman had his purgatives and his enema-machines, he had a means of protecting himself from these fears. Now, after three months as a postulant, he was clothed as a novice; and a novice comes under the complete direction of the Father Novice Master. There is scarcely any mental relationship in the world that is so close and so intimate as that of the Master of Novices and the novices themselves. So dear, old Father Woods, who was Newman's Novice Master, came to hear of his spiritual son's dull headaches; of the peculiar apparatus that Newman had in his cell; and the purgatives. A novice has no money of his own, and after a while when Newman's supply of "medicine" was exhausted, he asked Father Woods for money to buy a fresh supply, which was refused. Newman was in a temporary panic. Why, a few days without his usual laxative and—he could not bear even to think of the possible consequences. So, one day he slipped into the village drug-store, asked for what he wanted and told the clerk to put it on the monastery's regular account. For a week, Newman was reassured. But one morning Father Woods appeared suddenly in the novice's cell. Newman had not expected this visit; in fact, at the moment of the Father's entrance, the novice was attempting to take an enema of cold water, there being no hot water available at that hour. It was very embarrassing for the novice, but Father Woods did not seem to mind at all. He demanded that Newman should open, one after another, the drawers of his small bureau and of his desk; he even looked under the novice's pillow; and he gathered together all the bottles and tubes —all the paraphernalia of laxation and purgation that he could lay his hands on. "Now," he said, "I am going to throw all these things out of the window. I've told the druggist not to allow novices to put anything on the community bill. Open the back window please." Newman was in agony. "But, Father," he pleaded, "you don't understand. If you take away those medicines of mine, I—I—shall die." Father Woods looked at him coldly. "Very well, then," he said, "Go ahead and die. You are in a state of grace, I take it." And having pitched Newman's medicines out of the window, he departed. Of course, he knew that he was acting for the best. The physician who looked after the physical health of the monastery had examined Newman, and had told the Novice Master that the withdrawal of laxatives would do no harm if Father Woods would keep a special eye on Newman for the next ten days. But neither the physician nor the Novice Master realized the tremendous power of a medicine-taking habit that is built up as a reaction to fear; for Newman left the monastery that night. In a panic of fear, he turned his back on a type of life that he had deliberately chosen of his own free will and that he believed to be the will of God Himself. One of the other novices, who was up late that night, said that he had seen a black-robed shadowy figure on its knees in the little garden outside the monastery. He believed that it was Newman trying to get into the monastery again because he repented. It was Newman. But he was not trying to get back into the monastery; he was hunting among the weeds of the garden for his lost purgatives.

CHAPTER V

MENTAL MALADJUSTMENTS

(CONTINUED)

PSYCHONEUROSES: HYSTERIA, PSYCHASTHENIA, PSYCHOGENIC STATES, PHOBIAS, INHIBITIONS AND OBSESSIONS. THE TECHNIQUE OF DEALING WITH FEARS AND ANXIETIES. SELF-FIXATION. BELIEVING AND DOING. CLINICAL MATERIAL

WE have dealt, in the last four chapters, with types of mental illness that we call psychoses. Now we must turn to a much more difficult field. Doctor White[1] describes this domain of mental difficulty as "borderland and episodic states" or "the psychoneuroses." Under this head he includes neurasthenia, hysteria, psychasthenia, compulsion and anxiety neuroses, hypochondria, psychopathic constitution and simulation. Here is a whole list of long words, with which I do not want to burden your memory. What I really want to do in this chapter is not to give you a schematized list of all accepted types of hysteria, neurasthenia or psychasthenia, but to set before you, in the form of definite examples, some of the ways in which our mental habits can interfere with the functioning of our bodies, and sometimes make our lives almost as intolerable to ourselves as they have become to others. Nevertheless, here again it is a question of learning at least some of the names of the chess-men before we attempt to make even the simplest opening gambit.

I have already told you that neurasthenia comes from two Greek words that mean a "weakness of the nerves." The manifestations of this particular condition are innumerable. But the most frequent symptoms are fatiguability and irritability. I explained that a psychoneurosis is a general term to denote

[1] *Op cit.*, pp. 306 f.

those conditions in which there is a physical and a mental element; that they are the results of the body's action on the mind, or of the mind's action on the body. This is, of course, a very unscientific way of expressing ourselves, for we have no right to speak of "mind" as an entity separate from another entity that we call body. It would therefore be more accurate to say that in a psychoneurotic state the reactions of conscious or subconscious thought in an integrated personality have formed certain habits that interlock with the conscious or unconscious reactions of a physical organism in such a way as to disturb the complete integration of that personality, or at least to make the general reaction of the whole personality toward its environment either difficult, or annoying, or impossible. One set of habitual reactions, the reactions of consciousness, do not fit in as they ought to do with another set of habitual reactions, those of biological existence, so that the personality itself suffers from a constant state of friction or of tension, a state that makes it difficult for that personality to adjust itself to its environment to its own best advantage or to the best advantage of the environment in which it exists and to which it reacts.

If one tries to define "happiness," from a purely pagan standpoint, one might say that it consists primarily in the automatic functioning of the whole personality. If your heart is in a healthy, "happy" state, you are not conscious of it. You may walk along a level or climb Pike's Peak; you may greet an old friend on the street or you may just save him from being run over by a motor car; and yet the action of your heart will not impose itself on your consciousness and force you to take notice of the fact of its beating fast or slowly. It is the same with our mental processes. We are most contented when the mind works automatically along the lines of our daily endeavors, as well as in the accomplishment of some great task. Now, whatever interferes with this automatic, almost unconscious activity, with this smoothness of efficient reaction, is like some faulty adjustment in complicated machinery that throws a piston rod off centre; that causes an element of friction, and gradually spreads through the whole mechanism a sense of effort, called forth by the presence of a foreign body, by failure of balance and automatic action. Examine that machinery. You will find that all the rods, all the pistons, all the screws are there. But in spite of this perfection, there is some source of maladjustment that, in spite of the perfection of rod and piston and screw, throws the *action* of the whole unity out of gear. The organism may accomplish its work; but it accomplishes it at the cost of an effort that should not be necessary.

This may make you understand a little more clearly what we mean by the mental maladjustments of a psychoneurotic individual. One of these maladjustments, I have just spoken of—neurasthenia. In neurasthenic individuals there is no definite mental disease; but there is so much imperfect adjustment that the individual functions at the cost of great effort, so that he or she is always tired and irritable. The cause of that maladjustment may be some domestic difficulty. So a woman who feels that she is losing her looks, that she is no longer physically attractive to her husband who has a roving eye, may refuse to accept the facts of the situation and may force herself to attempt to hold by physical means a husband who can no longer be held in that particular way. Such a woman, sooner or later, becomes neurasthenic.

The subject of hysteria is a tremendously difficult one. I do not think that you will meet it, at least not in its extreme forms. It has all sorts of physical symptoms that are all psychogenic, that is, are all mentally conditioned. Buried sexual complexes are often converted into physical symptoms. There are strange bodily postures, assumed for many hours, that you would not believe possible for a human body to endure. There are disturbances of bodily sensation; parts of the skin are without feeling; they may be pricked, cut, or burned, and the hysterical patient feels no pain. Those who have read Professor

Kittredge's famous book on witchcraft[2] will remember how the judicial examiners were always searching the witches' body for the "Devil's mark"—a part of the body that was insensible and could feel no pain. According to many of the old records, such places were actually found. Without doubt, the so-called witches were hysterical women who showed other psychogenic symptoms besides these anesthesias, and presented to the physicians and the judges of those days so peculiar a picture that it could not fail to be attributed to a direct intercourse with the powers of Evil.

Besides these psychogenic disturbances of sensation, there are disturbances of the muscular or motor apparatus; contractions, paralyses and the like. On the mental side, we find amnesias or losses of memory, and a marked emotional instability, with loss of will power and extreme suggestibility. Among the so-called hysterical types you will find also those disassociations of the integrated personality which have given rise to so much discussion—and incidentally to so many psychic novels—the double or multiple personalities.

I do not think that you, as pastors and social workers, will gain very much along the lines of practical experience by a more detailed study of "la grand hysterie," or even of the less marked types. The word "hysterical" should be deleted from our vocabularies. As you probably know, it is derived from the Greek word for "uterus," inasmuch as hysterical manifestations were originally supposed to be manifest only in women and especially during the time of their menstrual periods or at least in connection with a disturbance of these same functions. Inasmuch as there are plenty of "hysterical men," it is a misnomer to apply to the male a word that suggests his possession of a developed female organ of generation.[3] "Hysterical conditions" are psychoneuroses of a certain type, and it has been, I

[2]*Witchcraft in Old and New England.*

[3]The male possesses a rudimentary uterus, just as he has rudimentary mammae. These rudimentary sex organs are discussed on page 184.

believe, a mistake to attempt to create for them a definite mental disease entity. All hysterical manifestations are "psychogenic"; they come from the imperfect interaction of the physical and mental habits and conditionings of imperfectly integrated and emotionally unstable human personalities.[4]

Much more important for you are the mental states that are grouped together under the general head of psychasthenias. You know what a neurasthenia means; a weakness and imperfect *functioning* of the nervous system. A psychasthenia is a weakness or an imperfect functioning of the Psyche, of the mind. Such terms are very imperfect etymologically, they do not at all express what we really mean by them. Let us call, then, a psychasthenic state, a state of human consciousness in which a functional disturbance—*not* a psychosis—is caused by a disturbed balance of mental activity, by an over-emphasis on certain reactions, by the growth of mental habits that tend to upset the peacefulness of perfect automatic functioning. You will understand all this much better when I can give you definite examples. But first let me block out, roughly, the field of psychasthenia. I do not like the word, therefore I shall use it as seldom as possible.

Psychasthenic states are marked by certain types of mental habits: phobias or fears, obsessions, inhibitions, anxiety states and the like. Phobias, inhibitions, and obsessions are mental habits that are all closely associated with emotional panics or with frightened people; and in order to protect themselves from these panics such patients yield to the inhibition, to the obsession or to the phobia. Let me give you a bare outline of these matters, which we can fill in afterward.

A. Phobias: The fear of something, of some place or action. The fear thought throws the mind into an emotional panic; and this panic is controlled by doing something or avoiding something. We speak of "agoraphobia," a fear of crowds, of theatres, of any large group of people. This is a "stay at home"

[4]A. S. Placzek, *Das Geschlechtsleben der Hysterischen.*

habit of mind. Then there is "claustrophobia," the opposite reaction. A fear of being shut in. This is a "get out of the house"
reaction. People troubled with this fear cannot stay in a room
with the windows closed; they cannot sleep in a lower berth
on a sleeping-car; they cannot enter elevators, or any inclosed
space. To avoid the panic that comes with this fear of "being
shut in," they must open windows, sit up all night on the train,
climb up six flights of stairs instead of taking the lift. There
are many other such phobias; fear of high places, often called
aerophobia; and the fear of lightning and thunder, astraphobia.
They are all common enough. You have met with many of them
already, I am sure. A phobia or a fear, with its attendant emotional panic, either makes you do certain things, or it prevents
you from doing certain other things. When it forces you to *do*
something, in order to avoid the emotional panic, then the
thing that you are forced to do becomes an

B. Obsession: The Germans have a word that they apply to
such things, "Zwang." It means a force that absolutely impels
you to a certain line of action. You are *forced* to the doing or
to the not doing of some definite thing. We may distinguish
two types of obsessions.

1. Obsessions that lead to action. Such obsessions are those
habits of thought that impel people to stealing, and that used
to be called kleptomania. The word "mania" is entirely out of
place here. If another person is obsessed by a desire to start
fires, to see the engines come and to secure excitement in this
way, his state of mind used to be termed pyromania. "Pyr" is
the Greek word for fire. Then there is an obsession of words,
onomatamania, from the Greek "onoma," a word. People with
this obsession get a certain word or a sentence in their minds
and they simply cannot get it out again. Sometimes they have
to say the words aloud; and then we have an obsession—an
impulsion to talk to oneself aloud. There are many other
types; but all of them lead to action.

2. The intellectual obsessions do not lead to action. As pas-

tors you have surely had experiences with what moral theology calls scrupulosity; with people who are never sure whether they have said their prayers properly and who will say them ten and twelve times over; who are always doubting about the rightness or the wrongness of this or that. They go over one past sin at every confession, for fear that they have not adequately explained it. They torment themselves, because at the moment of making their communion they fear that they *may* have committed some mortal sin, and may therefore, in communicating, be "eating and drinking damnation to themselves." Obsessions of evil, of blasphemous thoughts belong here.

When a fear *prevents* you from doing something, then it may become

C. An Inhibition: An inhibition is an inability to do a certain thing. Your fear has put a taboo on some form of action or some form of words. You have learned, as a child, that to go under a ladder means bad luck. You grow afraid to go under a ladder. After awhile, you become so inhibited that you will go all the way around the block in order to avoid passing beneath one. You are so inhibited, that if you do go under one by mistake, you are pursued all day long by the idea that something unlucky is going to happen to you.

Before I go on to discuss these various reactions in detail, let me mention one other classification of mental maladjustment that you may meet with occasionally; that is, psychopathic personality or psychopathic constitution. Now this expression is a kind of psychiatric waste-basket. If we are dealing with a patient who shows no symptoms of any mental disease, no psychosis, who seems fairly well adjusted to life, and yet, who is somehow not "just right," we call him a psychopathic personality, because we don't know what else to call him. You know that he is not mentally ill, that he is neither obsessed, inhibited nor afraid; nevertheless, his behavior, his mental reactions are peculiar, not logical, not exactly what you might reasonably expect from a man or a woman of his or her heredity, environment and training. There is something wrong, we know; but we are not able to say exactly what it is. The most careful examination of such a patient does not enable us to classify him according to any of our accepted classifications; his case does not fit into any one of our pigeon holes. Therefore, beside our desks with all their pigeon holes, we keep a large waste-basket, and label it "psychopathic personalities." Into it goes everything that we cannot find a place for on our orderly desk. You will have to deal with many people of this type. I can give you no general rules for helping them, as cases vary so greatly. The best way is to treat them as if they were perfectly normal, while you recognize their weak points and do not, therefore, expect too much of them or grow too depressed when they act in an entirely unexpected manner.

Let us devote the rest of this chapter to a more detailed consideration of phobias, inhibitions and obsessions.[5]

I must limit myself here to one or two fundamental facts.[6]

Fear, or anxiety, is one of the commonest emotions of our modern life. There are hundreds of thousands of people in our own country belonging to what we call "the employed class," who go to bed every night with fear in their minds, a fear of "losing their job," for that loss may strike them at any time. They do not "own" their jobs. By the decision of some one man, whose name they do not even know, but in whose hands their very existence lies, they may find almost any morning that "the force is being cut down" and that they themselves are "out of work." Most of you have not the faintest conception of what it means "to lose your job," not through any fault of your own, but merely because of conditions over which you have no control and which ¬ou do not even understand. Especially

[5]Examples of these states of mind will be found in the Clinical Material at the end of this chapter.

[6]More about fears and phobias has been set down in my book, *Fear* (Macmillan, 1927).

during the recent financial depression, the mass amount of fear has been tremendously increased in homes all over the country. To be dependent for your daily bread on work that is not yours, but that is given to you by some one else who really owns "the job," to know that it may be taken from you at almost any time; never to lie down at night with the absolute reassurance that the job will still be lent to you until the end of another week; all that makes fear. And fear is a poisonous emotion; poisonous to the body as well as to the mind.

Amidst all the hurry and strain of our modern life, fear walks behind almost every one. Not the *atra cura* of Horace that rides behind the horseman; that *cura* was a romantic figure, merely an uneasy sense of the shortness of life, an impulse to make the most of the good things of to-day. Our modern fear is a very plebeian companion. He does not ride on horseback; he walks, not behind us, but before us and at our side. A great deal of our successful modern advertising is built on the motive of fear. Who would buy a certain pharmaceutical preparation, a disinfectant that bears the name of the first great discoverer of aseptic surgery, if advertisements had not put into people's hearts the fearful thought that their greatest enemy may lurk in their very breath? The mind that is filled with fear never attains the happy automatic functioning that gives the individual his greatest power to help himself and to be of use in the world.

I have already spoken about "emotional panics." Do you know what I mean by the words? If you have never experienced such an emotional upset, you are fortunate indeed. Fear, when it floods the mind, is an overpowering reaction. You might have seen excellent specimens of its work during these past months, if you had stood beside one of those infernal ticker machines that carry the latest quotations of the stock market, and if you could have watched the men who gathered around it, picking up the white tape, glancing at a line of figures, and then turning away with white face and shaking hands and hurrying, whistling breath. We talk of "stock exchange panics," of "industrial panics"; how about the hundreds of thousands of individual panics in the tortured human hearts of men? And, remember, you can react as intensely to a mere fear of an imaginary infection, as you can to the loss of your fortune on Wall Street. You can become as acutely panicky in the shut-in space of an elevator and can suffer quite as acutely as if you had just received the news of the dangerous illness of your only son.

The picture is always, more or less, the same. The fear, the thought of certain possibilities connected with fear, suddenly rises to the surface of your consciousness. And you begin at once to react to it physically. The blood seems to drain away from your brain; you break out in a sudden sweat; your knees grow weak; you cannot think straight; and at the very pit of your stomach there is a sensation of emptiness, of agony, as if some one had suddenly struck you near the solar plexus and knocked the wind out of you. Your heart begins to race. Then, it seems to stop for a moment, as if it did not intend to go on beating again. Your throat is constricted; you cannot swallow; you feel as if your throat were filled with a great choking mass, that was growing bigger and bigger every moment. And when the acute panic is past, then comes a still worse experience; for your mind is flooded with fear thoughts; you cannot turn your attention to anything else; and the same fear associations go round and round in your mind until it seems that something must snap in order to stop the intolerable tension. You sit and stew in your fear.

No wonder that people dread experiences of this kind; no wonder they do their best to avoid them. They know that certain things bring on the panic; then, one must avoid these same things. Or there are certain actions that keep the panic from developing, and so these actions are performed over and over again. They become a kind of protective ritual, by means of which the panic is counteracted.

Let me cite here one example. You will find many others in the clinical notes at the end of this chapter.

One of your parishioners—the father of a family, a good, steady workman, comes to you in despair. He tells you that he must get a divorce. He simply cannot get along with his wife any longer. She cannot manage the home or the three small children. Breakfast is late; everything is late. And yet she is not lazy. She is apparently always in a tearing hurry. Overactive; wearing herself out. The husband has to go to work without proper food. The children are late for school. When he comes home in the evening, dinner is not ready. Everything is at sixes and sevens. And he "just can't go on like that any longer." He loves his wife. But of late she has become careless about her personal appearance. The house is dirty. So are the children. He has come to the end of his patience.

If you are wise, you will not attempt to help this man until you have seen the wife and won her confidence. When you call at the house, you may notice that during your call she dashes out of the room once or twice, and that her hands look very red and swollen. But you will have to make her realize that you do not only sympathize, but can also understand her difficulties, before she will be willing to tell you what these difficulties really are.

She has developed an obsession of infection, a fear of "microbes," as she calls them. This type of obsession is more common among women than men. And one finds it among women of education and ability also. In our particular case, one of the woman's children developed infantile paralysis and nearly died. She read in the papers a great deal about "infection" and "invisible microbes." At the hospital to which she took her child, she heard still more about mysterious diseases that come either "out of the air" or "from dirt" or "from touching some source of infection." She read, also, about "germ carriers." So she tried to learn how she could protect herself and her children. She must "disinfect" things. As her sick child grew better, she was in constant fear for the others. She kept them at home. But she herself had to go out into the "microbe infested" world. Might she not bring back some sickness with her—on her hands? For it was only with her hands that she seemed to come into contact with "sources of infection." She bought herself a cake of blue "disinfecting soap," and began to try to "keep her hands clean." The mere thought of any possible infection, of another case of infantile paralysis in the family, throws her into an acute panic of fear. But, since her hands are the only possible source of infection, she can quiet this panic by disinfecting her hands. By the time that you, as her pastor, or social worker, come to see her, she is probably disinfecting her hands twenty to thirty times a day. No wonder she is always late.

Breakfast is on the stove. But, in going out into the back-yard to throw away some dish-water, she touches the side of the refuse-can. The "swill-man's" hands have been on it. And he is so dirty. The can must be covered with microbes. She becomes panicky. In order to calm the panic and make it possible to go on with her work, she has to stop preparing breakfast, and go off somewhere to disinfect her hands. That takes her at least ten minutes. Of course, breakfast is late. She starts down to market, after getting the children off late for school. In getting on a bus or street-car, she takes hold of the long, iron hand-bar, by means of which people lift themselves up the high step. That dirty handle-bar! It must be soiled with a thousand filthy microbe-laden hands. Panic starts up in her mind. Off the car she gets, goes all the way back home, and disinfects her hands. When she does start for market, she is already an hour late. At the market, her first purchase amounts to forty cents. She gives a five-dollar bill and is given some loose change and four one-dollar notes. As she picks up these notes, the old fear-thought raises its head again. Through how many filthy hands must these same bills have passed! Perhaps they have come from a home in which there has been an infantile paralysis case. Another moment of panic. She asks the market man to stuff the four bills into her pocket; she does not want to touch them. But her hands must be already covered with microbes. Her marketing is not half done. Nevertheless, off she must go; she must hurry home and get her hands disinfected again at once. If, after this disinfection, she does go down all the way to the market again—and she may be obliged to do so—then she is several hours behind time. The children have come back from school for their mid-day meal, and there was no food ready for them. And so it goes. The woman is not a slattern, not a bad housekeeper. She is in the grip of an overpowering obsession.

You can easily see how the protective ritual works in this case. The ritual is the hand-washing or disinfection. The woman has formed such a protective habit that the hand-washing is the only thing that completely reassures her, and that quiets her panic at once. Moreover, the habit has become so strong that at the first suggestion of fear of infection, she simply *must* hurry off some place where she can go through the elaborate ritual of disinfecting her hands. She has washed her hands red and raw, and she has nearly driven her husband into the divorce court.

French writers call this obsession the *manie de toucher*. It has a negative and a positive side. In some cases the patient is *afraid* of touching something, so afraid, for example, of infection, that he or she will not touch the handle of an ordinary door without first putting on a glove or protecting the hand with a bit of paper; in others, the patient is afraid of *not* touching. You will remember the famous case of Doctor Samuel Johnson, who was often in wretched health and who was afraid of sickness and of death, just as most of us are. When he walked down Pall Mall in the morning, he used to touch with his open hand the row of posts that bordered the pavement. If, by any chance, he missed touching a post, he would stop in his walk, go all the way back, and touch the post that he had missed. This was his protective ritual. If he touched all the posts in the regular way, that reassured him for the day; gave him a sense of protection from sickness, from discomfort. If he missed a post, then the protection was nil. In order to regain it, he had to go back and complete the ritual in the proper manner. You can easily understand how mental habits of these types, although apparently harmless in themselves, may throw a whole life out of gear. There are thousands of individual phobias and obsessions. I am sure that every one of you can discover one or more in his or her own life.

Obsessions are tormenting things. A patient may become so obsessed by some hideous sexual or sacrilegious thought that he is unable to think of anything else. The harder he tries to put these tormenting thoughts out of his mind, the closer they stick. After awhile, he may become so disturbed and distressed that he cannot concentrate, and will have to give up work. Such obsessive thoughts often centre upon God—upon the Person of Our Lord; or upon the patient's own father or mother. This makes them all the more appalling. Other patients have obsessions about places; they cannot drive through a certain street; they cannot visit a certain spot. I remember one patient who simply could not pronounce the name of a certain American city. She had been unhappy there; and she was obsessed by the fear that if she did pronounce the city's name, unhappiness would come upon her again.

Inhibitions and obsessions are often the complements or the opposites of each other. If you put a taboo on anything and tell people that they *must not* do it, these people often develop an obsessive desire to do just exactly that thing. Take, for example, the extreme inhibition of all sex matters that was the fashion in Victorian times. Sex and all its connotations were taboo. As a result you find that people of our present day and age have acquired an *obsession* of sex. They cannot talk or write about anything else. They are reacting naturally enough. They are obsessed by the very thing that was formerly tabooed and inhibited. Because I realize all this, I do not worry very much about the extreme emphasis on sex interests among the young people of to-day. They are merely developing from inhibition into obsession. They are inheriting the mistakes of their grandfathers.

Let me also point out the only way with which to deal with all these things, for that is what you really ought to know. What advice to give to the people who come to you tormented with obsessions and tortured by phobias. The general rule is simple enough, but you will have a hard time to make people follow it.

If you have a phobia—a fear—do not be afraid of it. Do not try to keep it out of your mind. Do not be always on the look-out for it, always expecting to see it sticking its head in to your consciousness. *Accept it.* You *cannot* keep it out, no matter how hard you try. Therefore, give up that useless struggle. Say to your fear thought: "I am not afraid of you. I know that I cannot keep you out. So come along in. You are not a very pleasant guest. But I know you. I've had you as a guest before. And I know that you cannot do me any real harm—unless you stir me up and make me angry and afraid." *To be able to feel or to experience fear without being afraid:* that, in a few words, is the rule of victory. ·

Accept your obsession; make a friend of it; be able to talk about it. You will rob it of its power. If, for instance, you are afraid of railway journeys and have to force yourself to make them, the next time you get into a train, go into the smoking-compartment and sit down by the first man who looks as if he would like to talk. Say to him, quite simply: "You know, I'm scared to death of travelling by rail. I don't know why. But you can see now how my hand is shaking and how I'm perspiring. It's an unpleasant sort of thing. But there's nothing dangerous about it. And, after all, every man has some kind of a handicap. This is mine. But I shall get over it in time. Especially now that I am no longer afraid of being afraid."

One may deal in the same manner with all these obsessive difficulties. If a woman comes to you in agony of mind, tormented beyond control by obsessive sex thoughts or sacrilegious mental pictures connected with those she loves, with her father, even with her God—mental pictures that intrude upon her even at the most sacred moments of her religious life, during her prayers, at her communions, until she is struggling so hard to keep these thoughts out of her mind that she can think of nothing else, make her sit down beside you and relax as much as possible; or, if you are near your church, take her into it and kneel down at her side facing the altar. If you can take her to Our Lord's own covenanted Presence in the Reserved Sacrament, all the better. Then tell her to open her mind, not to the evil thought, but to the sense of God's love. Say to her: "You belong to God. Your mind is His as much as your body. If your body were invaded by some sickness, by some tormenting pain, you could learn to bear the pain all the better by offering it up to Him. Now offer Him your mind. If He allows these tormenting pictures to enter your mind, do not bother about them. Accept them. Do not try to keep them out, for, try as you may, you cannot keep them out. But let the sense of God's Presence and of His love enter your thoughts at the same time. Keep yourself emotionally calm. Do not react with horror or disgust to the obsessive thoughts. Let them pass in and *out* of your mind, without being able to stir you up. When you can do that, they will begin to lose their hold."

For, after all, this is the end for which such a patient must strive; any patient with fears or obsessions. The fear, the obsession, does you harm and upsets you only in so far as you react to it emotionally. As soon as you cease to react, the phobia loses its power to harm. So, when the fear-thought with all its old habitual associations presents itself to your mind, do not get panicky, do not say to yourself: "Oh, how terrible! Here is this old fear again. I must try to push it out, to hold it off. But it is getting its old hold on me. How appalling it is. My heart is beginning to thump; my breath to come short. And I have a weak heart. This strain and stress may make it stop suddenly. Oh what shall I do? What *shall* I do?" Well, don't do any of the things you usually do under such circumstances. *Make friends* with your fear, with your obsession. When it presents itself, look at it kindly; say to it: "Well, here you are again. I know that I can't keep you out, so I shall not waste my energy in trying to do so. But I know you of old. I've experienced you before. I know that you can't kill me, or make me lose my mind. I know that you are not a symptom of any mental illness. I know that you are nothing more than a bad mental habit, that has become, in some way, linked up with the emotion of fear. Whenever you come into my mind, you bring fear with you. Bring it then. I am not afraid of you or of the fear either. And because I am not afraid, therefore you shall not stir me up. You may make my heart beat faster, you may make my knees feel wobbly, but you cannot stir me up emotionally, make me panicky and force me to do a lot of things that I have learned to do in order to make myself believe that you aren't here. In trying to defend myself against you in the wrong way, I've built up a lot of defenses; habits of washing my hands, of counting certain numbers,[7] of touching certain things, of going through a long complicated ritual. Now I am going to throw all these defences down. I'm not going to try to protect myself against you any longer. The gate is open. Come along inside. I know that I can keep you out only at the expense of a lot of energy, at the cost of going through an unnecessary ritual. And even then I don't really keep you out. So I let you in, because then I can look you straight in the eye. Do your worst; and to prove that I'm not afraid of you any longer, I can talk about you with other people. I'm not hiding you any longer as some sort of a ghastly secret. I'm accepting you as a sort of temporary handicap. And I know that there is

[7]See Case 2 under section *B* in the Clinical Material.

no handicap that cannot be made into an achievement simply by accepting it and by losing one's fear of it."

In dealing with patients who suffer from obsessive sex or sacrilegious thoughts, it is often well-nigh impossible to get them to put these thoughts into words, especially if the patient be a reserved and shy woman. For she is appalled at the very words in which she must express her obsessive thoughts. She would not like any one to know that she had ever heard such words as these. And yet, if you can persuade her to say the words that are so intimately associated with reactions of disgust and shame, you will have helped her a great deal.

Let me illustrate this obsessive power of words by a definite case.[8]

A Protestant minister, about forty years old, comes to you in absolute despair. Let us suppose that you are, at the time, the rector of a country parish, and that this minister, Methodist, Congregational or Presbyterian, has a church in an adjacent village. He comes to tell you that he is resigning his pastorate, that he is giving up his life work, while he is yet at the height of his usefulness. He has found that he simply cannot preach any longer. And a Protestant minister who cannot preach or make extempore prayers is not of much value to his congregation. If you merely tell him how sorry you are that he is resigning; if you do not take enough interest in him to ask him *why* he cannot preach, you will have missed a great opportunity. But if you are able to establish between him and yourself a "rapport" of sympathy and understanding, he may tell you what has happened to him. His entire ministerial life is being made impossible by a "word obsession."

His congregation is a very stiff, very conservative group of "fundamentalists"; people who believe what they do believe with absolute sincerity and who are remorselessly logical in their attitude toward what they regard as "sin." In this congregation, there is a small group of very zealous people who

[8]Similar cases are given in the Clinical Material at the end of this chapter.

have banded themselves together in a campaign against "swearing" and "foul language." The head of this same group is the senior deacon of the little church, and on Sundays he always sits directly under the pulpit where he can follow every word of the preacher. He is something of a "heresy hound," a "sin hunter." He is the minister's most outspoken critic. And, moreover, he is the richest man in the congregation. Five years ago, the minister, your friend, came to this particular church. For three years he preached acceptably, with only one or two adverse comments from the senior deacon. But about two years ago, one Sunday morning, as the minister was getting up into the pulpit, this same minister looked down at the hard expectant face of his senior deacon, and had a momentary fear-thought. He said to himself: "I am not feeling very well to-day. I had indigestion all night, and I'm a little confused in mind this morning. Not quite so sure of myself as usual. Suppose that in the middle of my sermon I should, for just a moment, lose control of myself and say a swear word, say 'damn' or 'hell,' or something still worse. What a terrible thing that would be! There sits my senior deacon, who is so strongly opposed even to 'darns' and 'the devils.' What would he say if my self-control should slip? Why, I should be ruined. I should have to leave the parish. He would write to the presiding elder, or to the bishop. I should be condemned as a 'man of unclean lips.'" Such was the content of that first fear-thought. It was a mere temporary reaction. But, from that Sunday on, the minister never got up into this pulpit without that thought in his mind. After a while, preaching became more and more difficult. As soon as he was through with his sermon on Sunday evening, he would be mentally at peace, until the next Friday when he would have to begin to think about next Sunday's discourse. The same obsession began to extend to his extempore prayer. What, oh what would happen if, in the middle of an impassioned prayer, he should suddenly stop, "slip a mental cog" somewhere, and say aloud, one of those "smutty words" that he had learned in his youth from whispered conversations with bad boys behind his father's barn. The mere thought of such a possibility was appalling. Yet, it was always in his mind the moment that he said, "Let us unite in prayer." Sunday after Sunday, his sermons cost him more and more mental effort. Then the Scripture lessons began to bother him. In the Bible there were words like "damnation" and "hell." He deliberately chose scripture lessons that did not contain such expressions. After awhile, whenever he got up to preach, he had to force himself into the pulpit. His breath would come fast, he would sweat profusely, his knees would knock together. It required all his strength and determination to make himself even begin his sermon. He grew thin; his digestion gave out; he could not sleep; he was irritable at home, unkind to his wife and cross with his children. Finally, he could not stand it any longer. He was going to give up his ministry. That was the only way out of his difficulties.

This is not an imaginary case. Here is a useful career cut short by a bad mental habit. If this minister, in his distress, comes to you, and if you can get from him the real story of his trouble, I hope that you will persuade him to take a walk with you into the country. When you get him into some lonely district, and if you see, anywhere near, some shade-giving tree with cool green grass beneath it, point out that spot to your tormented friend and tell him this. "You see that tree over there, and the cool shade beneath it. It is miles from any house. You are out of earshot of your senior deacon as well as the smallest child in your congregation. Now go and walk up and down under that tree. I shall stay here, where I can see you, but where I cannot catch a single syllable of what you say. As you walk, *swear out loud*. Say distinctly, over and over again, every swear word that you know. Enunciate clearly every 'smutty' expression that you ever learned behind the barn. Say them all over and over again. Say them until the word 'damn' becomes merely a sound, expressed by four casual letters; until the sound of it and the look of it lose all fear associations. Spell out, one by one, all the nasty names of your boyish vocabulary; reduce them to their lowest form of vowels and consonants. Make yourself so familiar with the sound of them, that they become merely sounds and no longer spell horror and disaster and disgrace."

If your patient will follow your advice, you may watch him from a distance, pacing up and down, his lips moving and his shoulders growing less bent, less discouraged looking, as he walks and talks—and swears. He will come back to you, relieved, but utterly ashamed of himself. "I did not know," he will say, "that I remembered such a lot of vile words." And you must answer: "Now that you do know, now that you have accepted into your conscious mind a lot of unpleasant material that was always surging up from your subconsciousness, you will begin to get some relief from your obsession. But don't be ashamed. No one could hear you there, walking up and down under the apple tree. No one, except God—and I am sure that He is not at all like your senior deacon. He knows that it is more important that you should go on working for Him than that you should be afraid to pronounce a few Anglo-Saxon words of four letters." Keep up this treatment. Take your friend for several walks. And if you can show him how to deal with his obsession by getting the fear elements out of it, you will have given him back something that was more precious to him than life itself—his ministry—new power to work for God.

There is an easy way and a difficult way of dealing with phobias and obsessions. And, as is usual, the easy way becomes the most difficult way in the end; if not for the pastor or social worker, at least for the patient who asks your help. Suppose you have to deal with a case of claustrophobia; a patient who develops a mental panic if he or she has to be "shut in" anywhere—in a lower berth, an elevator, in a room with closed windows. The easy way to deal with such a case is to say: "You are afraid of using elevators; very well, then, don't use them. Climb the stairs. If you get panicky in a closed room, open the window. If you are afraid of certain things, avoid them. Then you will be quite all right." Many people are able to get along in life with a mild phobia or two. I freely admit, in my own case, that I am afraid of passing under a ladder. I will take a lot of trouble to avoid ladders, or to have them moved before I pass beneath them. If I force myself to go under, I am pursued all day by an uneasy feeling that hinders complete concentration. So I do not go under ladders. *But* if I were a painter or a carpenter; if my life were closely connected with ladders; then I should have to cure myself, for my avoidance of ladders would make my life much more inefficient than if I went under one occasionally. As a matter of fact, I do not run across a ladder once a month. I can accept my foolish obsession without upsetting my life. It all depends on the importance that the obsession gradually attains. Perhaps, some day, when I have time and when my life is cast among ladders, it will pay me to cure myself. Up to the present, I accept my little obsession. I am not even ashamed to speak of it openly. The hard way, and the best way, however, is to teach the patient how to weaken gradually the power of the obsession, until it either disappears or else becomes of no importance. I have tried to show you how that may be achieved.

Perhaps I have not sufficiently emphasized the important results of chronic fear and anxiety. The physical results can be and have been measured by laboratory tests.[9] And these results are always toxic, poisonous to the human organism. But even more important is what we call the lowering of the level of consciousness as a result of fear.[10] When you are anxious

[9]See Dr. George W. Crile's work, especially *The Origin and Nature of Emotions*, 1915; and Walter B. Cannon's, *Bodily Changes in Pain, Hunger, Fear and Rage*, 1915.

[10]See *Fear*, pp. 230–235.

about your heart action and get your fear-laden mind concentrated on its activity, you will become conscious of a great many sensations connected with your heart beats that you were never conscious of before. The biological reactions, of which you become conscious, are perfectly normal, they have been going on all the time; but hitherto they have never reached the threshold of your consciousness. Now that you are afraid, now that the level of consciousness has been lowered, you "feel" them. And the more you "feel" them, the more frightened you become; while the more scared you get, the more definitely do you experience these disturbing sensations. You are caught in a vicious circle.

So much unnecessary unhappiness is caused by self-fixation. The focus of your mind is intended to be a constantly shifting one. If you are climbing a difficult pebble-strewn path, your mind is of necessity fixed on your feet; but if you still keep on thinking of your feet days after you have come down from the mountain, you will soon become so "foot-conscious" that you cannot walk at all. No patient goes through greater mental torments than he or she whose mind has lost its power of easily changing focus. The focusing machinery gets stuck, and the lens is permanently focused on the patient's self; on his heart, on his business troubles; on his wife; even on his religion. Such a cramp in the focusing machinery is often very difficult to break. If you can persuade such a patient to do something for another person; to do it, not for any self-regarding reason, but simply for the love of God, or even as a mere mental medicine, then you will have begun to loosen the mental cramp that is ruining the patient's entire power of happiness and usefulness.

Doubtless, you may feel that in attempting to show you how to help obsessed or inhibited patients, I have not touched at all on the help that may come from religious activity and belief. But I have been trying to show you merely the machinery of helpfulness; merely the shifts in mental attitude that will lead to the defeat of a tormenting obsession. I have not touched on the sources of supernatural strength that will give the patient power to maintain the shift; I have not spoken of the Power House that will keep the readjusted machinery going during the difficult period of its new redirected activity. You and I know what that Power House is. But let me merely point out, that in all kinds of power houses the things that you *do* are more important sometimes than the things that you believe. Of course. you ought to know something about the laws of electricity, by which the great dynamos are governed, so that you may aviod dangerous short-circuits that may suddenly shut off the current. But, even if you know nothing about electricity, you can always turn on the current, if you push the right handle, if you *do* the right thing. I am always recalling the thoughts of my own church people to their confirmation vow, in which they promised to "believe and to *do*" the things that their sponsors undertook for them once in Holy Baptism. I like to put the emphasis on the *"do,"* as even more important sometimes than the "believe." For in ecclesiastical processions, the most important person comes last.

Very often your depressed, your obsessed or fearful patients will tell you that they have lost their faith, that they are mentally confused and cannot get any "comfort out of their prayers." If their powers to "believe" are inhibited, surely there is no reason for stopping the "doing" part of their confirmation promise. Even if they cannot think clearly, their legs still function; and their legs can bear them to mass on Sundays, to their confession and to their communions. These same legs can bear them to a "doing" of something, however little, for other people. If the eye of their mind grows dim, their bodily eye can still read the Psalms, their Bible, their St. Thomas à Kempis. They may not "get anything out of it." They may not find any "emotional satisfaction"[11] in their religion. Never

[11]What Aldous Huxley calls "a pleasant sensation in the pit of the stomach."

mind. They can still "practice" it. If the joints of their minds are stiff, their knees can still bend, they can get down on their knees and put themselves in the attitude of prayer. They can lift their hands to make the sign of the Cross, even though their minds are too clouded to understand the Doctrine of the Atonement. No matter how helplessly bound in misery and iron their mental processes may seem, they can still genuflect; they can still adore with the bodies that "do" the adoring and the genuflecting. Keep them "practicing" with their bodies. Never let them imagine that because they cannot "believe" —and by believing they usually mean feeling weepy and exalted when they sing some favorite hymn, or hear some moving preacher, or see the moon in some shadowy, beautifully appointed church—they cannot "do," and do well and acceptably to God.

The way in which you apply your own knowledge and experience of our Blessed Lord to the lives of those who seek your help; that I must leave to you. And I am sure that the extent of your power to help will depend, not on your knowledge of psychiatry or even of dogmatic or moral theology, but upon the assurance you bring to human souls that "you yourself have been with Jesus." In a later chapter I hope to say something about Our Lord as the Great Physician of Souls. Here I am speaking of Him as the source of your power to help. And, believe me, the troubled, anxious human being that seeks you out in the midst of his torment and that stretches toward you hands that seem to cry out for help, will often prove the best test of the reality of your own spiritual life. People, unhappy, anxious, self-tormented people, are drawn toward real holiness as moths are drawn to a candle. The brighter the candle, the wider the ring of its light, the greater the number of hurrying, blinded, flying things that gravitate toward it. And if the candle is not lighted at all, it will not attract even the dullest, most blundering moth. For it is still true, that "ye are the light of the world." Your light—the light of your own spiritual life—may not shine very brightly before men; you may not be over-anxious that "men should see your good works"; but when the anxious, fearful moths of this human world, who have singed their wings in so many different devouring flames, are brought within sight of it, they will recognize it at once as a source of healing and of help, because the light that you give comes from the same source that set glowing the live coal that once touched Isaiah's lips—the altar of the One Perfect Sacrifice once offered for the sins of the whole world. Yes, they will really test you, these people who come to you for help. And the world will judge you by your influence upon them.

Years ago, when I was a resident physician in a large mental clinic, I used to watch, on visitors' day, the groups of people who came to see our patients. I was especially interested in our clerical visitors, although in those days I knew scarcely any of them. Such "pastoral visits" were not popular among my medical colleagues. "Those parsons" were supposed to "upset the patients" and "make trouble in the wards." And very often that was exactly what they did do. I would see a very prominent ecclesiastic coming along the hall, a man of learning, doubtless, the head of a large parish, with all the *savoir-faire* of a long experience with souls. He would look into my little office for a second, ask about some patient, talk pleasantly a little about politics, a little about the latest important book, and then move on toward the wards. And I knew that in the afternoon when I went into the room of the patient whom he had visited, I should find this same patient upset, anxious, fussed, and retarded in his convalescence. At other times I would notice a scrubby, unkempt little parson, whose voice grated on my ear, who had no small talk, who seemed dumber than the beasts that perish; who would slink into the ward as if he were apologizing for his very existence; and after his visit, I would find the patient quieter, perhaps less depressed or less agitated—at any rate, all the better for what that strange, little man had said or done. Finally, there was one class of "parsons" that I always saw with a feeling of perfect reassurance. They did not come often. There were few of our patients well enough to see them. But they never stopped in my office. They held their hands clasped on their breasts, and went directly into the ward. I knew what they were carrying. I am ashamed to say that, in those days, I was unwilling to fall on my own knees as they passed by. For, when I saw later on the patients to whom they had brought their communions, I knew that those visitors had not come alone. Some one had been with them, Some One whose presence had left traces that even I could recognize in the heart of some strangely quieted and peaceful patient in the bare silent ward.

If that Some One walks with you as you go about your work in hospitals and outside them, and if you walk with Him, then you need not worry much as to your knowledge or your lack of knowledge, as to your grasp on theology or psychiatry, or on any of the so-called wisdoms of this world; for you will carry with you the only unfailing medicine for the sickness and the sorrow of our hungry human hearts.

CLINICAL MATERIAL

A. Hysterical or Psychogenic Conditions:

In the preceding chapter I have said that in so-called hysterical individuals, buried sexual complexes or repressed sexual desires are sometimes converted into physical symptoms. The physical elements in these converted desires may not be prominent. The hysterical condition may turn out to be a frustrated sex desire made objective and accepted by the patient as a definite fact of her experience.

All physicians, pastors and social workers are exposed to real danger from this type of individual. The history of our courts is full of cases of alleged rape, based on the definite accusations of emotionally unstable women. Respectable dentists have been ruined by extracting a tooth under "laughing gas" without a

witness, without a third person being present during the operation. An unbalanced woman, who may show no signs of mental
illness, recovers consciousness and goes from the dentist's office to
her lawyer or to the police station with a story of attempted rape.
Or, if she does not go to the police, she informs the unhappy
dentist of what she thinks he has done, and agrees to keep his
secret for a price, the price of his love, and of the physical satis-
fying of her repressed sex desires. In these days, dental surgeons
extract no teeth under an anesthetic without the assistance of some
nurse or attendant. The same thing is true of the physician in
general practice. If he has to make a physical examination of a
female patient, it is wiser to have his nurse or his stenographer
present. The secretary is supposed to be there in order to take
down the dictated details of the examination; but she fulfils also
the rôle of a protective witness. The psychiatrist is placed in a
difficult position. In order to establish the necessary rapport of
sympathy with his patient, he must see that patient alone. Even
the suspected presence of a nurse or a stenographer, concealed
somewhere about the office, acts like a snuffer on the dimly burning candle of a patient's confidence. Moreover, the concept of
"transference" in psychoanalysis often proves dangerous. The pure
Freudian procedure assumes that the patient has some sex fixation,
that is, his or her sex desires are unconsciously fixed on a father
or mother, or some one with whom sexual relations are hideous
or impossible. In order to dissolve this fixation, the psychoanalyst
must achieve "a transference" to himself of the patient's desires.
After having done this, he must do another transfer, and hitch
up the patient's sex wishes with some attainable object. But sometimes I fear that this does not prove easy. If the achieved transference to the physician sticks there and refuses to be retrans-
ferred, then I pity the psychiatrist. And this is one reason why I,
myself, in my own practice, have never used psychoanalytic methods. When I have a patient who I know would be helped by a
detailed psychoanalysis, I send her to one of my colleagues who
is cleverer than I and who is not so afraid of "sticky transferences."
    The pastor is often exposed to the same dangers. Even extreme
Protestants are coming to realize the practical usefulness of the
machinery of the confessional, as compared with individual con-

ferences with penitents in an office, the doors and windows of which may be closed. In the confessional, the penitent is separated from the priest by a wall that has only one small opening. Moreover, the penitent is on his knees. And it is not easy to indulge in sexual wish-fulfilments while you are in that position. But the pastor who does his duty has to make parish visits. And he has to learn to be very cautious. He is fairly safe, if he makes no purely "social calls," if he comes always as the pastor, as the priest, whose chief interest is the religious life of his parishioner. If he can keep persistently on religious subjects; if his interest in the parishioner is evidently and primarily the development of her spiritual life, he may avoid many pitfalls. Yet there are cases, tragic cases, in which some hysterical woman, without any real intention of evil, has absolutely ruined a valuable life. I give the following case as a warning.

The Reverend Francis Smith was a good and a faithful priest, about forty years old. He was happily married to a woman who was devoted to him. Both he and she were devout Catholic Christians. He had a small parish in the suburbs of a large city. He was not, I believe, a particularly attractive man to women. He did not have much of what is to-day commonly called "sex appeal." And it never for one moment occurred to him that one of the married women in his small congregation was emotionally interested in him. This woman had a quiet, hard-working husband, a man with a one-track mind. She had, if I remember correctly, no children. Unfortunately, there was never any examination made of the woman as a mental case. No one ever knew the real truth about her married life. Her husband may have been a frigid type, who could not give her the satisfaction that she craved. Perhaps she demanded more than he could give. At any rate, there was lying loose in her subconsciousness a whole mass of dammed up sexual desire, that could find no outlet. That was not her fault. One does not know whether or not she deliberately allowed herself to indulge in sexual imaginations that centred upon her parish priest. If she did, the priest knew nothing about it. He called upon her about once a month, usually coming in the afternoon, when her husband was away, as that was the priest's regular time for making his parish visits. One afternoon, he went to see her as usual. Just exactly what happened on that afternoon, one can only conjecture. She may have made some harmless advances; she may have told her visitor that she was "not happy" with her husband. But whatever slight advances she did make, fell on deaf ears. The Reverend Francis Smith did not understand or react to them. He did not recognize them as advances. At any rate, he made his call, and went back to his little rectory and to his wife. Meanwhile, the woman began to develop a psychogenic condition of confusion. One cannot tell whether she consciously and with complete determination upset a chair in her parlor, disordered the couch, and then tore her own dress and mussed up her hair. But in this condition her husband found her when he returned, about an hour after the priest had left. She threw herself on his breast, and sobbed out a detailed story of unprovoked assault, of attempted rape. She pointed to the disordered room; to her own torn gown. Naturally, her husband believed her. He went up to his room, got a loaded revolver, and went out onto the street. He was determined to take vengeance on the scoundrel who had "ruined his home." If he had only killed the Reverend Francis it would not have been so bad, for Francis, anyway. But the husband was not a very good shot. When he met the priest, he drew his revolver and fired. The bullet struck the priest on the left side of his face, put out one eye, broke his nose and seriously injured the other eye as well. You can imagine the hideous scandal; for the outraged husband surrendered at once to the police. At first, public opinion heaped abuse on poor Francis, while he lay blinded in a hospital. But he had a wife in ten thousand, who loved him and believed in him. When he could walk about again, feeling his way with a stick, the whole case came before the courts. And there, under the cross-examination of the Reverend Francis' lawyer, the "assaulted woman" admitted that no assault had ever taken place. She was, in a sense, almost as tragic a figure as Francis or his wife. For although she confessed that she had told her husband lies, she insisted that, at the time of telling them, she herself had firmly believed in the truth of her statements. I do not know what happened to her or to her husband. They passed out of the picture. I think that I am more sorry for the husband than for any of the other actors in that hideous tragedy of errors. But the Reverend Francis remained completely blind in one eye, almost blind in the other, his face scarred and broken, his parish gone, his ability to do his work gone also. For more than ten years after these happenings, he "carried on," he and his brave, devoted wife, taking such clerical work as he could find to do; never complaining, never even mentioning the tragic past. Perhaps, if he had not suffered as he did, he might not have been the example of suffering bravely born that he was to those who knew him, during so many years of weakness and a partially crippled life. But, why did it have to happen at all? That is a useless question. It did happen. And I have told the story here as a good example of the things that *can* happen when an emotionally unstable woman "converts buried sexual complexes into physical symptoms," or tries to turn "repressed sexual desires into objective realities."[12]

B. Phobias, Obsessions and Inhibitions:

I could give endless cases of these types. I am choosing a few from a mass of clinical material, hoping that they will illustrate what I have tried to say in the preceding chapter.

(1) Here is an example of a "conversion psychoneurosis," that is, a case in which some distressing repressed event becomes such a disturbing element in the personality that it has a direct objective physical result on the body.

During the last years of the war there was a soldier in a British hospital whose case puzzled all the physicians. His right leg, from the hip downwards, appeared to be paralyzed. He could not move it. The skin sensation was impaired, you could stick pins into it, and the patient felt nothing. Moreover, even the muscles of this leg were wasting away, when compared with the muscles of the other leg. The surgeons had examined the man, and could find nothing wrong with the anatomical apparatus of the useless limb. X-ray pictures were made; the neurologists, the nerve-men, were called in. They could find nothing wrong with the nerves of the leg itself. At last, in despair, the case was turned over, as hopeless, to the psychiatrists, to the poor despised "nut doctors." They worked on it for several months. At last, one of them, while turn-

[12]For similar cases see Dr. S. Placzek, *Das Geschlechtsleben der Hysterischen*.

ing out every corner in the most dusty garret of the patient's memory, came across a statement—a half-retained memory of something that had happened to the soldier during the first year of his military service. He had completely forgotten it. Little by little, he dug it up from his memory. Finally, the story was complete. He had been a very sensitive, rather introspective youth, afraid of pain, and easily upset by the sight of pain in others. He had, nevertheless, enlisted in a moment of enthusiasm, without knowing much about the horrors of war. He went through a rapid training, and soon found himself in the trenches. Then came his first experience of real fighting. His company was to make a night-raid on a German trench; a bayonet attack. He stood shivering in the trenches, until the signal came to go over the top. With bayonet fixed, he dashed off. Flares went up from the German trenches. And in this sudden, clear light, he saw a German soldier coming at him, a young fellow apparently not much older than himself. The British soldier bayonetted the German through the throat, with such force that the bayonet went straight through the German's neck; and as the latter fell, the British soldier's bayonet and gun were wrenched out of his hands. There was not a moment to lose. The British soldier had to get his rifle again. But the German had fallen on his back, and the bayonet protruding from the back of his neck had become fastened into the hard ground. The German's face was upturned in the light of the bright flare; the British soldier could see the staring, filming eyes; the slightly moving lips. Not quite dead yet. But the attack was moving on. So the British soldier, in order to recover his rifle and bayonet, had to put his hob-nailed shoe on the face of the dying German boy; had to lean down, grasp the end of the rifle, and tug the bayonet out of the German's throat. He said that, even through the thickness of his leather sole, he felt the yielding softness of the German boy's lips and nose as they were crushed beneath the impact of his shoe. What happened afterwards, during that attack, is of no importance. When the British soldier got back to the trenches, it was soon found that he was unfit for duty because his right leg was paralyzed. After countless examinations and all sorts of unpleasant tests to rule out malingering, he was sent back to England. And when the "nut doctors" got at him, he had been in the hospital for two years, a hopeless case. You can easily understand what he had done. The horror of the experience that I have described was so intense that the young man *mentally amputated his right leg*. He said to himself, "This leg that has had these hideous sensations, that has felt beneath it the yielding crunch of that dying boy's face, shall never feel anything ever again." He could not bear to think that any future sensation in that leg might ever recall the awful experiences that he had determined to eliminate from his consciousness altogether. So, bit by bit, the story came out. He was made to tell it over and over again. Made to *accept* it as part of his conscious memories. He was told: "Yes, war is a hideous thing. Such appalling experiences as yours do happen. But in your case, they happened years ago. The horror, the pain, is all over and done with. Accept the memory of it, and your leg will get well." And the leg did get well.

(2) Many obsessions have to do with numbers. Most of us have some number that we consider especially lucky, and that we like to see. Few people are absolutely neutral in their reaction to thirteen, and especially when the 13th falls on a Friday. It is curious, is it not, how powerful still is the thought of the first Good Friday, for it obsesses even the most unchristian mind still? The following case was told me by the patient himself, long after he had learned how to deal with his own obsession. He had cured himself.

He was a priest about thirty-five years old. And during the past ten years of his life he realized that he was becoming more and more obsessed by certain numbers. Whenever he saw an automobile license, he had to count up the numbers on it. The same thing happened with numbers on freight-cars, while he was travelling; or on trolley-cars; on the pages of a book; numbers anywhere. But his obsession was not a general one. He was apparently always on the look-out for two numbers, four and six. He always had to look for "four" first. If he saw "four," or if the number that he saw added to a multiple of four, he had an acute sensation of apprehension, a mild emotional panic. But he could cure this panic at once if he could see anywhere the number "six" or a multiple of it. This obsession began after a while to affect his efficiency. If he were driving in his car, and there was a car ahead of him, he had to keep his eye on the license number, until he could assure himself that it contained no fours or multiples of four. If it did, then he could not put his mind on his driving until he had seen a six or a multiple of six somewhere. So it went. He began to worry about his mental condition. If he were reading a book, and got to page 44, he had to turn backwards to page 6, or to 18, or turn ahead to 66, in order to be able to go on with his reading. It was the same thing with the numbers of hymns, when he gave them out in church, or saw them set up on the hymn board. If he could possibly help it, he would not give out a hymn that had a four in it. I do not know how he got at the basis of his obsession; but as soon as he did understand its genesis, as soon as he accepted it, could talk about it, could get away from his fear of it, the obsession began to loosen its hold on his mental processes. This was the explanation, and it illustrates better than any case of my own how fear and anxiety reactions can become closely associated with signs or symbols or numbers. This friend of mine was born, I think, in Wales. His father was a worker in a large coal mine. The entrance to this mine was an old-fashioned shaft, going down into the earth. Day by day, the boy saw people disappear into the shaft, and in the evening he saw them come up again. Close to the shaft there was a great bell that used to ring when the men went to work or returned in the evening. But sometimes—suddenly in the middle of the morning, or long before work in the mine was over—this same bell would ring in a different way. If it rang *four* times, that meant disaster in the mine. There had been an explosion, some of the gangs had been caught in a caved-in tunnel. "Four" spelled danger, fear, anxiety. Then the rescue gangs would go down. After awhile, the bell would ring again, six times. And six meant, "all clear," everybody is out, the danger is passed. Now, my friend, in his boyhood, had a friend of his own age, a miner's son also. One morning, against the rules, this boy's father allowed the boy to go down into the mine with him. My friend saw him go, and envied him, because his own father would not permit such an exciting adventure. So my friend hung about the entrance to the shaft waiting for his companion to reappear. While he waited, the bell rang—"four times." That meant danger, death perhaps. And his little friend was down there in the very midst of it. The rescue gang went down. My friend hung about the mouth of the pit for hours. At last the bell rang again, six times. All safe. And in a few more minutes his little friend was standing by his side, telling him of his exciting adventures. After he had been ordained, this clerical friend of mine came to America and became a useful priest. After two years of unusual mental stress and strain he began to be tormented by his "number obsession." You can easily see and understand how it developed.

(3) Here is a case of fear-induced scrupulosity that forced a priest to stop saying mass for a year. He was by nature an habitual worrier, but not excessively so. He had overcome endless obstacles in order to study for Holy Orders. At last he reached his goal. He was ordained. He said his first mass. But he began to be very particular about the ablutions. He would look and look at the corporal, from all angles, from fear that there might be on it some tiny particle of the Consecrated Host. He wiped and pollished the chalice until he wore out one purificator after another, and rubbed off the gilt on the chalice rim. The old ladies who came to daily mass complained that it took Father X three-quarters of an hour to get through the service. Still, if he was very, very careful, he *could* get through. One day, after the ablutions, he noticed hanging to one corner of the slightly broken nail of his forefinger, a tiny white particle. It was probably a bit of thread rubbed from the purificator. He thought it a particle of the Host. He consumed it at once. But now, after every consecration, he went over the nails of both hands, putting each finger into his mouth, and then starting all over again on the same process. Even after mass, he was constantly looking at his nails. Suppose that, in spite of all his care, there were concealed somewhere under the corner of one nail, a tiny particle of the Consecrated Host! How terrible! There was our Lord's covenanted Presence being carried about without due reverence. And then, think of the various, the horrid ways, a man—even a priest—had to use his hands during each day. It was intolerable. When he was especially anxious, he would hold his hands for an hour under running water, and then wash them while on his knees, so that he might at least pay due reverence to any unseen particle that might have escaped his notice. He genuflected to his fingers. Fortunately,

he had a very sensible spiritual director. He was forbidden to say mass at all for six months. Even then the obsession had not entirely disappeared. It was a year before he could say mass again.

(4) The way in which fear becomes associated with certain words, I can illustrate by telling a story on myself. During the past four years it has been my great privilege every Sunday to sing the High Mass at eleven o'clock in our parish church. Sometimes, especially during the hot weather, the long fast is difficult for a man of my age. One Sunday, about a year ago, a very hot Sunday in late September, I had finished the first part of the Canon; the Sanctus Bell had been rung for the Elevation, and as I rose from my knees after the first genuflections and after covering the chalice, I felt a wave of dizziness, of faintness sweep over me. My heart began to race, my knees to shake, my voice to wobble. I had the long prayer of Oblation to say. "I'll never get through it," I thought. "Especially those two long words, 'inestimable benefits.' I always have trouble with them, anyway. But I'm going to faint. And how appalling that will be. I have already consecrated. The Blessed Sacrament lies here before me. There is no other priest in church who might consume it and end the mass somehow. I'm getting more and more dizzy. If I faint, who will pick me up? There will be a terrible excitement. All the dear old ladies in the front seats will come running up, the choir boys will drop their hymn books, and in this quiet conservative church there will be confusion worse confounded." In other words, I was in the grip of an acute emotional panic. How I ever got through those words, "inestimable benefits," I don't know. Well, I didn't faint. I finished the mass without any one noticing my trouble. *But,* when next Sunday came, when I had consecrated and when my eye looked along in the Prayer of Oblation to those "inestimable benefits," I began to get dizzy once more, my voice grew weak, I started to perspire, my knees knocked. The same thing all over again. The same anxiety about the old ladies in the front seats, about the choir, about everything. "Inestimable benefits" became an obsession. Every Sunday, when I saw them coming, I developed not *mental* symptoms, but actual *physical* symptoms. Once I got through those words, I felt a little better. So it went on for two months. Then, I said, "Physician heal thyself." Therefore,

next Sunday, when I saw "inestimable benefits" coming along, when I began to feel dizzy and felt sure I was going to faint, I said to myself, "Very well, then, go on and faint. If you do faint, some one will pick you up. The stars in their courses won't fall out of the sky if there is a slight confusion during mass at Mount Calvary Parish in Baltimore. I do feel dizzy and weak. But I'm not afraid of feeling that way. Come on, "inestimable benefits." If I can't say you clearly, I can mumble you somehow. And the Lord won't mind. So faint, John, if you want to. Only, until you do faint, go on with the mass." From that Sunday on, I had less and less trouble with "inestimable benefits." I still stumble a little over the words. But they can no longer make me afraid, afraid of something that has, as yet, never happened, and that, even if it did happen, wouldn't make much difference anyhow.

(5) Few people realize how thoroughly a life may be thrown out of gear by a single obsession. A prominent public accountant had always been noted for his punctuality. About a year ago, he began being late at the office in the morning, he was late in coming back after luncheon. If he made an important appointment, he often kept people waiting so long that they gave him up and went away. His friends began to whisper. Something must be going fundamentally wrong. Was he "drinking in secret"? If people don't know what is the matter with a man, they say "he must be drinking." If they are puzzled by the unusual behavior of a woman, they say she must be having "an affair." But in this case, such criticism was serious. The man's career depended a great deal on people's unshaken confidence in him and in his integrity. One day, he called me on the telephone. He wanted to see me about some business matter. "Come to my rooms at once," I said, "I'll be here for half an hour. And, if you're phoning from your office, you can't be more than ten minutes away. So get into your car and come along." He mumbled something I did not catch. I waited ten minutes, then twenty, then half an hour. I was just ready to give him up when he appeared, hurrying, breathless. "Where have you been?" I asked. "Did you have a break down?" "Oh, no," he answered, "I came straight to you from my office." "But that is impossible," said I. "It doesn't take the slowest driver more than ten minutes to get from your office to my rooms."

"Well," he said, "it takes me half an hour." And then, gradually, he told me of his obsession. He was a reserved, but a very kind-hearted man, with a great love for children. He has done more for orphaned babies, has helped more boys and girls through school and college than any man I know. One morning, about a year before our conversation, he drove rather rapidly round a street corner. A child had dashed out into the street after a strayed baseball, my friend had pulled up and had *just* missed striking the child, who made a long nose at my friend and disappeared. But my friend kept thinking, "Suppose I *had* struck that child. I might have struck it without realizing what I had done. Had I hit a child and then driven on, in complete ignorance, some persons might have seen the accident; they would get my license number, and then, later in the day, I should be arrested and jailed as a "hit and run driver"—"a man who runs down little children and then drives on." To this thought, to this panicky idea, he began to yield little by little. If it came into his mind as he drove through a street, he would stop his car, turn around and drive back along that street in order to reassure himself of the fact that he had *not* run into any one. When he came to me, he was so obsessed by this fear that he would drive three or four times up and down each street through which he passed. When he got to the end of one street or block, he would say to himself, "Did I strike any one as I drove along here? I don't think that I did. But I might have done so. In order to quiet my fear, I'll turn around and go back and assure myself that I've not unintentionally hurt a child." Of course, he was late to all his engagements. It took him an hour to drive a distance in the city that should not have needed more than fifteen minutes. And, of course, he thought he was "losing his mind," "going crazy." After I had taught him the technique of accepting his obsession, taught him to talk about it, to make a little fun of it, not to be afraid of it, he soon shook it off, and began to keep his appointments punctually again. But that same obsession, if unchecked, might have had a very serious effect on a valuable career.

(6) There are some men who, after putting their cars into the garage and turning off the ignition, have to go out to the garage three and four times before they go to bed, in order to reassure

themselves of the fact that they *have* turned off the ignition. A man who is a little worried about burglars, goes down to the front door before he undresses, and locks it. When he gets to his bedroom and is taking off his coat, he asks himself, "Did I lock the front door? I think I did. But—well, I'll go down and lock it again." Back he comes once more. His wife calls him from the other room, "James, did you lock the front door? There were burglars in the next block last week." Again, he says, "Yes, I locked it." But—well, perhaps he did not lock it after all, perhaps the key slipped. Better go all the way downstairs again and be sure. I know a woman who has an electric iron. She turns it off, puts on her hat and starts off downtown. Half way down, she stops suddenly, "Did I turn off that electric iron? I think I did. But it might blow out the switch; it might set the house on fire." And so back she goes all the way, only to find the iron turned off. Such cases might be indefinitely multiplied.

(7) Some people cannot go to bed and to sleep unless their clothes are arranged in a certain way, or unless the light by their bed stands in a certain position. One man, whom I knew, could not go to sleep unless he turned off or blew out the light in one definite way. If it was a candle, he had to blow at it six times and then blow it off on the seventh blow. If it was an electric light, he had to turn it off and on six times, and at the seventh time, leave it turned off. Such procedures are often protective rituals. The man in question developed his in the following manner.

Years before, he and I had been taking a walking trip in the mountains of Tyrol. We had had a very hard, exhausting day and at night had just managed to reach a mountain hut. Here, my friend, who was tired out, ate too rapidly of rough food. He fell asleep, and at twelve waked with an attack of arrested digestion. He thought he was dying. His heart seemed suddenly to stop, he could not breathe, and he was frightened nearly to death. Of course, in an hour, the attack passed. The following morning we went on to the next hut, where we slept that night. My friend was rather afraid of going to sleep; he might have another attack during the night. He had a candle by his bed. As he blew it out, he happened to blow crookedly. He had to blow some six or

seven times before putting the candle out. Well, that night he did
not have an attack. So the next night, as he prepared for sleep
and started to blow out the light, he thought, "If I blow it out
just as I blew it out last night, it will be a good omen. Perhaps
to-night I shall not have an attack either." He had no further attacks for a week. Then, one night when we were at a small hotel
in a Tyrolese village, he forgot about the candle, he blew it out
with one puff. After that, he lay uneasily in bed, wondering
whether or not he ought not to light the candle again and blow it
out in the usual manner. But he told himself "not to be a fool,"
and went to sleep. He woke after a few hours, feeling sure that
he was *going* to have another attack. He did not have it, but his
night was an uneasy one. After that he surrendered to his protective ritual. It became a mental habit. If he tried to break it, if
he puffed out the candle at one blow, or shut off the electric light
with one snap, he would lie awake for hours unable to sleep,
until he got up, lit the light again and put it out in the proper
ritual manner. Here, then, was a mental habit that produced for
years definite physical results. The doing of the prescribed time-
honored rite had power over his night's rest. But it was not an
important obsession. It did not interfere with his efficiency. Later
in life he fought his way back to an acceptance of the Christian
religion, he became a devout Catholic, he learned how to pray,
he learned how to practice the habit of the Presence of God. His
candle-blowing habit disappeared gradually, without his becoming aware of its disappearance. For in the place of one mental
habit, he had put a stronger mental habit—the habit of surrender
to God's will.

(8) One peculiar obsession, that is not as uncommon as one
might think, is a fear of fatness. In the more expansive Victorian
days of billowy busts, this fear was doubtless infrequent. In our
own time, such insistence is laid by convention on "straight fronts"
and "boyish figures," that the possibility of spoiling such beauty
lines by "flesh" becomes a "fear-thought" indeed. In old books on
æsthetics and art, you will read that "the line of beauty is a curve."
Mais nous avons changé tout cela. The line of modern beauty is
straight and flat. Bulges are not permitted. It is only the beauty
specialist, or sometimes the physician, who knows how positively

terrifying to feminine ears the word "fat" may become. I remember one case in which it became such an obsession that the mere mention of the word brought on an acute panic that could only be quieted if the patient, when she looked at herself in the glass after her bath, could see her ribs; or if she could slip her hand inside her dress and feel them. She got intense pleasure from dancing with a man who held her so tight that she could feel his hand on these same ribs of hers. Moreover, she starved herself. She became positively afraid of food. She made out tables of fatty and non-fatty food-stuffs. The mere sight of a potato upset her. And as she was a very able young woman, holding a rather important clerical position, this obsession of hers began to interfere very seriously with her efficiency. I never had an opportunity to trace the obsession back to its source. It began, I believe, from the patient's contact with a very fat woman, whom the patient hated and who had been cruel to her. I tried to show her how to deal with the obsession, but I did not have sufficient opportunity to help her very much; and she needed help very badly ineed.

(9) I must include here a word or two on obsessions of stealing and of starting fires, which are wrongly called "manias." Kleptomania as we have pointed out above is a term that one no longer uses. If one has had close contact with cases of shop-lifting, with women who are anxious to dub themselves "kleptomaniacs," one will be very soon assured that the great majority of these cases is plain larceny. Shop-lifting does not increase because women are becoming more kleptomaniacal than usual; it increases because the temptations are becoming constantly greater, harder to resist. The tempting displays of the big shops, the lack of saleswomen, or the anxiety of good saleswomen not to lose a possible customer by appearing to keep too close an eye on her potential purchases—all these things create an atmosphere of temptation that it is bitterly hard to resist. I am not surprised that there is so much shop-lifting. I am very much surprised that there is not much more of it. And I am inclined to have little sympathy with the large shops when some unfortunate mother of a family, whose children need underclothes, is caught by the store detective with a pair of boy's drawers stuffed into a hole in the lining of her skirt. The shops deliberately tempt people to buy; and if

you have no money to buy, the temptation to take is always present. There may be women who have acquired habits of petty
thievery from childhood onwards, habits that are very difficult to
resist. But I am inclined to doubt the existence of an objective
kleptomania, an obsession to steal that is so strong that the stealer
does not know what she is doing and is not responsible for her
actions. The same thing is true of pyromania, the habit of setting
things afire. This is a very dangerous type of reaction. Just why
it is that children love to "play with fire," I must leave to the
psychoanalysts. Most pyromaniacs are men and women who are
childish in more ways than one. They set fire to things not because they are attacked by some mental illness called pyromania,
but because they are either deficient in intelligence, imbeciles or
morons, or are still in many respects childlike in their mental
reactions because they still love "to play with fire." From such
cases one must distinguish the man who sends in false fire-
alarms; such a man may be intellectually deficient or at least mentally retarded. Just as the boy loves to see the fire-engines come,
so this man, with the intelligence of a ten-year-old child, loves to
see the same thing. And in order to get what he loves, all he has
to do is to break a little pane of glass and pull down a hook.
Other men who torment the fire department in this way are obsessed with a sense of inferiority. No one pays any attention to
them, they are zeros in the sum of the world's interest. But they
can put themselves in the centre of the stage by imagining a little
smoke and then sending in a fire-alarm. They can do the same
thing even more successfully if they start a little fire themselves,
in their garret or their cellar, and then rush off to the fire-alarm
box. In such cases, the motive scarcely lies in an obsession. The
man is not forced into action by a definite mental habit of fear;
he deliberately chooses a certain line of action because he wants
to produce results that give him satisfaction.

Chapter VI

SEXUAL FACTORS

SEXUAL COMPONENTS IN MENTAL MALADJUSTMENTS. THE PROPER
APPROACH TO THE WHOLE QUESTION OF SEX REACTIONS. EXPLANA-
TION OF TERMINOLOGY. AUTOEROTISM, HETEROEROTIC REACTIONS,
BUNDLING, BIRTH CONTROL. CLINICAL MATERIAL

In the preceding chapter we have studied various types of
definite mental illness, psychoses and we have tried to understand some of the commonest kinds of functional mental difficulty, those mental maladjustments that arise from fears, inhibitions and obsessions from different sources and of varying
strength.

You have at least heard the name of Professor Sigmund
Freud of Vienna. While I myself was spending a medical
summer semester in Vienna many years ago, Dr. Freud was
only just becoming known. He was, at that time, an associate
or assistant professor in the Department of Psychiatry, and the
lectures that he gave on his new conceptions of the psychoneuroses had not roused much strictly academic interest among
medical students. To-day, Freud is much more than a name;
he is a system. He has written his name across the background
of modern psychiatry in such huge letters that no sensible
man can fail to read those letters, even though he does not
like or approve of the things that they spell. No matter what
your personal attitude may be toward the whole system of
Freudian psychoanalysis, you cannot ignore Freud's theories,
any more than you can ignore the work of Darwin in modern biology. You may be a bitter enemy of the whole theory
of Evolution, but you will be more than a fat-headed fool if
you try to pretend that there never was a Darwin at all. For

we can no more speak in terms of modern biology without making use of Darwin's work and concepts than we can speak of modern psychiatry without recognizing Freud's achievements and making use of his terminology.

Most people give a little unpleasant shudder whenever Freud is mentioned and they will tell you that "sex" is the foundation of all his theories, of all his teaching. That is a very exaggerated statement. One of Freud's fundamental concepts is based on the manifold manner in which *unexpressed* sex wishes, or repressed sex desires, may manifest themselves in our mental and physical reactions. His teaching is not a huge pornographic collection of the horrible things that sexually uncontrolled people *do;* it is a study of what people do and think who have not been able to express themselves sexually at all. It is the things that people want to do, half consciously perhaps, the things that they cannot or will not do, in which Freud is chiefly interested. And no matter what your reaction may be to this whole matter of *sex,* you must admit that Freud and his pupils have done us all a great service in making it possible, nowadays, to discuss matters of great importance to humanity, openly and cleanly, instead of pushing these same matters into a dusty, shadowy corner, relegating them to "medical books," and putting such a general taboo upon them that their very existence was almost denied. Had it not been for the freedom of discussion induced by the Freudian theories, the sex inhibitions of the early sixties and seventies would have resulted to-day in an obsession of sex even greater, even more appalling than the obsession from which we are still suffering.

Freud emphasizes the fact that the sex life does not begin with adolescence, that the baby, the child, has sex experiences, sex desires also. Fifty years ago, when people turned with horror from such a concept, many were the children whose entire future happiness was imperilled by the grown-up men and women who fondled and caressed them as if they were dolls

or toys without sensation and without power to react to
stimuli of sexual excitement.

I speak of all this as a sort of introduction to the next two
chapters in which we must turn our attention to the influences
of sexual desires, thoughts or acts upon the development of
our personalities. I suppose that I might have dealt with the
subject in a more strictly Freudian manner. In discussing psychoses, I might have brought out the sexual elements in each
mental illness. I might have dissected the "love lives" of the
alcoholics, of the drug or medicine users. I could have mapped
out the importance of sex repressions in the development of
phobias and obsessions. But rather than flavor the whole mass
of my subject with the one pervading condiment of sex—
like a whiff of garlic in so many different Italian dishes—I
prefer to attempt to isolate the condiment, to remove it from
its complicated combinations with other material and present
it to you in a sort of concentrated form. If you do not like this
particular condiment—just as if you do not like garlic—then
anything that it is mingled with is unpleasant to your taste.
And so if you simply *must* experiment with it, it is less
troublesome to take it in bulk—separate from other things—
and to get the disagreeable task over as soon as possible. I
sincerely trust however that there are few readers who will
react in this way.

In entering this whole domain, let me beg you to leave certain things outside the door. Take off your shuddering of
horror or your disgust when you take off your hat. Put aside,
together with your coat, your tormenting curiosity, the natural
eagerness to get just a few more shocking details. And put
on, if you please, the white duck clothes of a laboratory
worker, clean, disinfected aprons or tunics. Clothe your mind
in these, for you are entering a laboratory of human reactions.

If you visited, for example, a histological laboratory, and
were shown certain pathological specimens under a microscope, you would not draw back in distress from a section of

cancerous tissue, or be unable to gaze with equanimity upon another preparation of the adrenal glands. I want you to maintain here this attitude of objective interest. If I show you an example of sadism, I want you to consider it as coolly and as objectively as you would have studied the cancerous tissue under the microscope in the histological laboratory. For just as truly as the cancerous tissue was once part of a human being like yourself, so are the reactions that I shall try to describe the actions of human beings, who are much more like yourself than you probably imagine. Unless you can achieve this detached attitude of mind—unless you will keep close to Our Lord's command "Judge not"—I cannot put my material simply and clearly before you. For your reactions of shame, of outraged modesty, of hectic curiosity will inhibit me. I shall not be ashamed of what I have to tell you; I shall not be ashamed of the types of sexual behavior that I want to describe; but I shall be ashamed of you.

As I write, a picture comes to my mind, the memory of a crowded lecture-room in a seminary—crowded with men in cassocks, all preparing for Holy Orders, all gathered there to hear, from a learned Jesuit professor, a lecture on moral theology. The lectures have at last reached that dreaded subject "de Sexto," on the sixth commandment. You will remember that our seventh commandment, "Thou shalt not commit adultery," is the sixth according to Roman tradition. All the men in that room have been living for many years a celibate life, a life of repressed sexuality; and now the professor is to lecture, during the next two months, on the most intimate details of the physical activities that these men have been fighting and repressing and ignoring. They dread it. The eyes of some of them are fixed on the ground, the hands of others are tightly clasped together, on some cheeks there is a slight flush or a few drops of glistening sweat. And the Jesuit begins his lecture. He speaks in Latin, which is the *lingua franca* of all these seminarians of varying nationalities; they can take notes in it as easily as in their own language. The professor speaks very distinctly, very slowly; and he has not been lecturing for five minutes before the tension in the room subsides. The uneasy light of a morbid curiosity dies out in the eyes of one man, another student's tightly clasped hands are loosened, the hot flush disappears from another's cheeks. Yet the dreaded material of the lecture "de Sexto" is all there. The professor, who knows the very latest book of Freud's as well as his St. Thomas Aquinas, omits nothing. But his tone—his mental attitude—is that of an objective scientist lecturing in his laboratory.

And so, whenever I know that I must face the discussion of sexual reactions and of all that they involve, I send up a hasty prayer for help, asking that, somehow, I may catch the atmosphere of that lecture-room, so far off among the mountains of my beloved Tyrol—the atmosphere that, in spite of the subject of the lectures, made that lecture-room a place of scientific interest, of learning, and of peace, while Pater H. Noldin, S. J., held forth to us "de Sexto," so many years ago.

No matter how much you may resent the legalistic, hair splitting tone of Roman moral theology, there is one glory of which you cannot rob it. For during centuries of taboo on sex matters, the Roman moralists kept on with their calm objective discussions of these same matters, because they realized that men were still men and women still women. Old treatises on morals, such as the books of Sanchez and Suarez,[1] are the only books of their age that contain any scientific analysis of the sexual life of their times.

In all general discussions of the sexual life, one fact is frequently either overlooked or forgotten. It is an anatomical, or rather an embryological fact. *There is no such thing as an absolute male human being. There is no such thing as a*

[1]Tomás Sanchez (*b.* 1551, *d.* 1610), *Opus morale in decalogum. De matrimonio.* Francisco Suarez (*b.* 1548, *d.* 1617), *Vir fundatissimae scientiae et profundae humilitatis.* Published 23 works.

human being absolutely female. Never forget this. And there is no such thing as a combination of both sexes in one personality. Hermaphrodites, as antiquity imagined them, do not exist. There may be malformation of the genital organs. But no matter how the *external* organs of an individual may look, the person in question is a man, because somewhere there are testicles; and because there are ovaries hidden away somewhere, the person is a woman.[2] These malformations of the external genital organs sometimes deceive the mid-wife; although in our modern lying-in hospitals, mistakes of a baby's sex are usually impossible. In the country, however, it happens, not infrequently, that a child brought up as a girl, because it "looked like a girl" to mother or mid-wife, turns out, later in life, to be a boy, or else goes through life with apparently inverted sexual desires, while as a matter of fact, it is a perfectly ordinary woman-loving man, and not really a homoerotic woman-loving woman.

Let me repeat, absolute male and absolute female types do not exist. Every male has rudimentary female characteristics; every woman has rudimentary characteristics of the man. Every man has rudimentary breasts; you are so used to them that you forget their very existence. You may be forgiven for not knowing that you possess, near the inner mouth of the bladder, a rudimentary uterus.[3] It is the same way with the female. She has rudimentary male organs. And why? Because while the baby is developing in the mother's womb, the child is bi-sexual until the fourth month. Or to speak more accurately, it has the rudimentary organs of both sexes. Then the development proceeds toward the final male or female type. But—and here is the important point—just as each sex has in

---

[2] For a description of the anatomical conditions and of the embryological developments, etc. . . . see *Anatomy, Descriptive and Surgical,* by Henry Gray. 13th ed. 1893 (London: Longmans), p. 1014, "uterus masculinus"; and Rauber's *Lehrbuch der Anatomie des Menschen,* edited by Köpsch. 8th ed. (Leipzig: George Thieme, 1909), Abteilung 4. Eingeweide pp. 376–386, especially pp. 380–386. Plates 441–451, especially Plates 434, 450.

[3] See Gray *loc. cit.* and Rauber-Köpsch, *loc. cit.* in note 2.

it the rudimentary physical remains of the other, so in the mental sphere,—in the reactions of the integrated personality, there is no human personality that, in its characteristics, is purely and exclusively male or female. Otto Weiniger, a distinguished Viennese biologist, who died before he was thirty,[4] attempted to establish these facts on solid scientific ground. He drew somewhat fanciful conclusions, however. He held that the ordinary male is about 80 per cent male and 20 per cent female. The average female 80 per cent female and 20 per cent male. Between these extreme groups are all sorts of varying states. Men who are 40 per cent female and only 60 per cent male. Women who may be 50 per cent male and 50 per cent female. Of course, these percentages refer to the *general characteristics of the whole personality*. Most of you have, I am sure, seen women who have very marked masculine characteristics, both of mind and of body. And the same thing is true of effeminate-looking men. I want you to keep these facts clearly in mind. They will help you in understanding many of the complex sexual types.

One more word of general introduction: a word about the names of the counters, of the cards, the chessmen in the game. In times past, people used the word "homosexual" to denote women who were only sexually attracted to women, or men who were only attracted to men. Now "homosexual" is bad etymology; it is a half-breed word. One half, "homo," is Greek; sexual, is Latin. Nowadays, we use a thoroughbred word that is all Greek. We say "homoerotic." You know who

---

[4]Otto Weiniger, *Geschlecht und Charakter*. The book was translated into English with the title *Sex and Character*. It is of very great value still. Weininger, a talented young Jew, committed suicide in a period of mental depression just after finishing this book. Especially valuable are his statements about the periodicity of the male and female sex life (see German ed., p. 509. Also notes in Appendix to p. 65) and the connections between the nose and the female sex organs (*ibid*.). See also Wilhelm Fliess, *Die Beziehungen zwischen Nase und weiblichen Geschlechtsorganen in ihrer biologischen Bedeutung dargestellt*. Also by the same author, *Der Ablauf des Lebens*.

"Eros" was, the God of Love. And "erotic" means, "having to do with love" or "loving." Now, taking "erotic" as the end word, we tack on to it three words, which taken together cover the various types of sex reaction. First, we speak of "auto-erotic" reactions. You recognize the "auto" in "automobile," a thing that moves by itself. "Autos" means self. So "autoerotic" is a self-loving sex reaction, a love reaction that has self for its object. Classicists used to call it "Narcissism," from Narcissus, who fell in love with the image of his own body reflected in a quiet brook. But, in our ordinary meaning of the word "auto-erotism," we include much more than a mere looking at oneself in a glass. By autoerotic acts we mean sexual actions that may be consummated without the presence of a sex part-ner, actions that were once spoken of with bated breath, our very names for them reflecting our misconceptions of their nature. "Masturbation" is a word like "syphilis." It has become associated in our minds with "hidden horrors," with "secret, solitary sin." If we are to consider these very common auto-erotic habits from an objective scientific standpoint, we must get away from the old emotional reaction of disgust, which is still evoked by the very names that people once gave to them. So we will forget that word "masturbation," we will blot out of our vocabularies expressions like "self-abuse." We shall call all these habits of mind and body "autoerotic reactions."

Secondy, we speak of "heteroerotic reactions." These form the great majority of all sex activities and expressions. We have the same ending, "erotic," and we tack on to it a word, "hetero," that comes from the Greek adjective "heteros," "the other." So that a heteroerotic reaction is a sex activity that takes place between two persons of the opposite sex—of "the other" sex, between man and woman, or woman and man. Under this head come all the sex activities of married life, all the sex relationships of a casual nature, between men and women, from the "necking" of two adolescents down to the most complicated, perverted acts of a prostitute and her temporary partner: all extramarital, promiscuous sex intercourse in which the actors are of opposite sexes.

Thirdly, there is another large and important classification of sexual activities that we call "homoerotic." The Greek word "homoios" mean "the same." A homoerotic relationship therefore is a sexual relationship between two people of "the same" sex; between women and women, and between men and men. As a matter of fact, most of us live a "homoerotic" life. We men spend most of our time with members of our own sex. Very often the influence of our men friends, our business associates, is more powerful than the influence of our wives, mothers, or sisters. If there were not a marked homoerotic element in all of us males, there would be no clubs, no secret orders, no Y. M. C. A's, etc. If women lacked this same element, they would be impelled to make all their social contacts with men. And as you know, a woman who has no intimate friends of her own sex is an anomaly, and is often criticised as a man-hunter. As Weiniger pointed out,[5] we are none of us completely heteroerotic—none of us entirely woman-loving men, or man-loving women. We carry in ourselves the possibilities of all types of sexual expression, autoerotic, heteroerotic and homoerotic.

Some investigators have a theory of sex development that I must mention here. They believe that every individual passes normally through all three stages of sex development. The child, the pre-adolescent, who has no means of finding some sexual partner, is autoerotic. It seeks its sexual satisfaction within itself and expresses it by actions performed by itself on its own body. During adolescence the first wide social contacts are made, usually at school. This is the homoerotic period, the second stage, the period of intense emotional friendships of boys with boys or with older men, of girls with girls or with older women. The period of hero-worship. The days of school-girl "crushes"—of intense boyish admirations for

[5]Cf. Weiniger, *op. cit.*

some older school-fellow or for one of the younger masters. At the close of adolescence, when social contacts broaden still more and when the sexes are no longer segregated at schools or colleges, then the ordinary individual passes out of the homoerotic stage and becomes heteroerotic, the girl-loving girl becoming a boy lover, and *vice versa*. But, in the course of this development, from autoerotism through homoerotism to heteroerotism, certain sex experiences, or some mysterious element in the personality itself, may prevent or hold up this regular process. Some people stick fast in the autoerotic period; others never get beyond the homoerotic stage. And these auto-erotic and homoerotic sex types become permanent. This is a very ingenious theory. Unfortunately, I have not found that it is born out by actual experience; for I have never come across a man or a woman, congenitally homoerotic, who could ever be made by any process into a heteroerotic personality. However, I shall try to explain this more fully later on.

Now that I have given you this etymological introduction, we may pass on to a more detailed description of these three classifications. Inasmuch as "autoerotism" is the least highly dif-ferentiated type of reaction, the most immature, we may begin with that.

Of all the sad chapters in the sex history of modern life, no chapter is so sad, so full of tragic misunderstandings, so haunted by the ghosts of remorse as the chapter of auto-erotism. I do not need to go into details as to the physical vari-ations of the actions by which the individual who is tormented by a sexual tension for which he or she can find no outlet, procures for himself or herself a kind of "self-relief"—a relief that is associated with a certain amount of pleasurable sensa-tion. What we are most interested in is the *reaction on the individual* of acts or of habits of this type. There are many boys and girls who develop autoerotic habits, who find in them a temporary relief and satisfaction, but who never worry about them and who discard them easily, as soon as they find opportunities for the expression of their homo- or heteroerotic desires. But there is another class whose lives are distorted, whose happiness is poisoned and whose future is often threatened by their wrong adjustment to their autoerotic temptations and activities. In this class there are more men than women. It is an unusual thing to come across a woman who has worried very much about her autoerotic practices.[6] Women are as a rule more sensible than men in their adjustments to their sex lives. But the reason why men worry more about autoerotism than women do is easy enough to understand. The woman who has yielded to an autoerotic urge has not "lost anything."[7] The man, on the other hand, has lost something that he believes to be "life" or "strength." Any authority on anthropology or on primitive medicine can tell you of the "magic" that is associated by primitive peoples with all excretions of the body.[8] But of all bodily excretions, the most mysterious, the most potent is that fluid which is, even to the most primitive mind, closely associated with the begetting of children. That is, "life giving"; it contains "the very essence of life"; it is "life itself." This age-long superstition still persists even in modern minds.[9] And so the boy or the man who has yielded to his autoerotic desires, imagines himself depleted, weakened, degraded, un-manned. Now this conception, this inheritance from primitive civilizations, has many dangerous consequences. And these consequences are constantly reinforced by the still active traditions of our grandfathers, a

[6]Cf. Katherine Bement Davis, *Factors in the Sex Life of 2200 Women* (New York: Harpers, 1929), chaps. VI and VII, "Some Autoerotic Practices," pp. 91–187.

[7]I.e., she has no seminal emission.

[8]I.e., with sputum, urine, feces, semen.

[9]Married men will tell you that after marital intercourse they always feel "weakened," they often avoid intercourse because it "saps their strength." This is the antithesis of the truth. Sexual intercourse is intended by nature to be a source of new strength, of refreshment, of complete relaxation and repose.

belief that autoerotism always ended in complete physical and mental disaster.

As parish priests, as ministers or as social workers you will be constantly brought into contact with sex conflicts that arise on the basis of imperfectly understood autoerotic habits. If you tell me that the boys of your parish are all "clean boys," that you have never heard of such habits from any of them, then I can only reply that, if this be so, your boys do not trust you, and you are not giving them the help that they so often bitterly need. For in all my experience I have not met with more than a dozen men whom I could implicitly believe when they told me that they had passed through boyhood without any personal experience of autoerotism. And among that dozen, there were at least five who were sexually frigid, who, when they married, were unable to beget children. No, the normal healthy boy, with a normal genital apparatus, always has some autoerotic experiences. And such authorities as Dr. Bement Davis[10] assures us that among women autoerotism is as prevalent as among men, if not more so.

If an ordinary boy of from fourteen to eighteen comes to you for his confessions and he never mentions sins of this kind, you will do well to question him a little. He may be so inhibited by false information that he is afraid to mention the one sin that is tormenting him the most. He will be grateful to you all his life if you can break down his inhibition and make him tell you—and God—the truth. There are more imperfect confessions than you realize; confessions made deficient and so blocking the grace of absolution; confessions that are made in the same imperfect way, by some penitent, month after month, because there is one "sin" that he imagines to be so heinous that he is afraid even to mention it.

Let me take an ordinary case. Let me try to show you the intensity of the conflict, the depths of mental suffering that may go on for years in the mind of some young man or boy who finds his whole life ruined by one persistent spectre.

[10]Cf. *op. cit.*

One of the boys in your parish, or in your particular social group—one of the very finest of the lot, a very fair scholar, a good athlete, a cheerful, happy-minded fellow, begins to show poor results in school. He does not mix as well with others as he used to do. You catch him sometimes staring at you with a question in his eyes; but as soon as you look at him, he turns his eyes away. There are no definite symptoms of any mental trouble. And yet you know that the boy is unhappy, that something is wrong somewhere. Or, he may be able to keep up a cheerful exterior, and you may not even guess the conflict that is going on beneath the surface happiness of his life. Yet you ought to be able to sense it. Well, suppose that you do sense it; suppose that you do notice the slight changes in his behavior, and that you are at last able to gain his confidence. You need not wait until he gets as far as an actual confession of his autoerotic habits. Say to him, "I don't know whether you realize it, but there are certain sex habits which are often greatly exaggerated so far as their evil results are concerned, and you ought to know the truth about them. I dare say that you may not have any anxieties of this kind, but at least let me set you straight in this one matter."

Usually you will not have said two of these last sentences before you will see his eyes glance up into your face with a look of startled happiness, as if he had just heard something so important that he could scarcely as yet believe it to be true. It may be that even after you have explained matters to him, he will not admit that he has any real need of your advice. But nevertheless you may have lifted from him a persistent cloud of despair, you may have taken his feet out of the mire and clay and set them permanently on a rock. Here is the story he would tell you if he could. Here is the story that another boy less inhibited can tell you if he will.

When he was about ten or eleven, he acquired a certain amount of sex information from other boys, in the usual furtive, smutty manner. With this information came knowledge of a certain kind of bodily pleasure that could be gained by doing certain things. Perhaps one of his older companions showed him just how these things were done. Very often, a boy discovers them himself, without the necessity of any teaching. Many a boy, many a girl, has learned the secret of auto-erotic sex stimulation from climbing trees, from riding a bicycle, from jumping up and down on a see-saw and in a thousand other ways. Life—every-day life—teaches them, if there are no friends "behind the barn" to give the necessary information. So your boy acquires a certain habit. At first, he gets little satisfaction out of it. But, with adolescence, the satisfaction becomes much more dominating, and he begins to associate this same satisfaction with thoughts and dreams "about girls." By the time that he is fifteen the habit is well established; but it has given him no trouble, there seems nothing in it to worry about.

And then he goes to a lecture or he reads a book. He goes to a so-called "purity talk" for men and boys only. Or he picks up somewhere a little pamphlet "What boys should know." And after hearing the lecture, or reading the pamphlet, his whole life is suddenly changed. For he has learned for the first time that his "habit" is something hideously wrong. Even the name of it is so terrible that it has to be called "the solitary vice." And worst of all, it is "an abuse," a "self-abuse." Moreover, its results are appalling. Boys who "do that" get softening of the brain, their spinal cord disintegrates, they have blue lines under their eyes, and they have pimples on the face and they can't look a real man straight in the face. If they persist in their wickedness, they are lost beyond hope, lost not only in the next world, but in this world also. For all boys who "masturbate" go crazy. The insane asylums are filled with them. And "that is where you are going, my young friend, if you persist in this vile habit."

Such knowledge, coming suddenly into an adolescent mind,

is a serious mental "trauma," a mental wounding, a shock. It leaves permanent traces. For now the conflict begins. The boy, terrified by what he has read, has at least one ray of hope. He can stop. He *must* stop. Perhaps it is not too late yet. And so this lad, with his immature judgment, his undisciplined will, enters the arena of conflict to fight with the strongest emotional urge known to man. He squares his shoulders. He has made up his mind. He is never going to do "that" again. Never, never.

Of course, he does it again. Habits are not broken in a moment. He makes new resolutions, he breaks them. He falls. He picks himself up in an agony of shame, goes on for a few weeks, then he falls again. And often when he does fall, he is so discouraged that for a few days he lets himself go in a complete orgy of self-indulgence.

Of all the pitiful documents that I have ever seen—and I have seen a great many—the most pitiful was an "Oath" written in red ink, by a fifteen-year-old boy—an oath sworn to Almighty God, signed in the boy's own blood, and signed on his knees. The oath, God, the red ink, the blood, the kneeling —all to make the thing more impressive, to make it stick, so that the signer would never do "that" again. Poor child! I found the paper among his things, after he had made a half-hearted attempt at suicide, "because," as he wrote to his mother, trying to deceive her to the last, "because he feared he was going to fail in his school examinations." Thank God, the conflict does not drive many boys as far as that. But it does something to them that is sometimes almost as bad, for the marks of it persist all through life.

Look for a moment into the mind of the boy who has fought this particular habit, fought and failed, fought and failed. What is happening in that tormented mind of his? Just this. The physical act of autoerotism does him no harm. To quote a recent book, "It is merely an imperfect form of experiencing a certain amount of sexual satisfaction." It never made any one crazy, nor did any one any physical harm. But, in the case of this boy of yours, it is doing him irreparable harm. It is not sapping his brain, or making soft his spinal cord. The act itself is doing nothing to him at all. It is his adjustment, or attempted adjustment to the habit that is harming him a great deal. After every fall, he promises himself, solemnly in the sight of God, perhaps with blood and red ink and all the rest, that he will never do a certain thing again. He does do it again. So gradually he comes to realize that there is a power in his life that he cannot control. It is stronger than he. So what is the good of fighting any more? He is headed straight for the insane asylum. He looks at himself in the glass at every available opportunity. Yes, he has black lines under his eyes, and there is another pimple on his chin. He practices trying to look people straight in the face. But when it comes to a test, his own eyes turn away. Why? Because he knows that the other people see the black lines, see the pimples, and must know exactly what kind of a boy he is, just what he is doing, just what his secret habits are. He can almost see their knowledge in their eyes; so he begins to avoid people. Better not let them see him, especially when the lines under the eyes are very black or a new pimple has appeared; so he loses hope, he loses interest in life; his mind turns in on itself.

But even if he does not go quite as deep down as this into Hell, the danger to his future is always present. Every time he drops back into his old habits, what is he doing? Physically he is doing nothing harmful. But from a mental standpoint he is constantly breaking his word to himself. He is doing something that he promised, that he resolved, not to do. Naturally this undermines one of youth's most precious possessions, his self-confidence. Little by little he loses his sense of self-confidence—that power to direct his own life, which is such a necessity for the young man in his early manhood. Robbed of it, he begins to develop one of the most poisonous, one of the most handicapping mental habits in existence, a sense of inferiority. And this habitual sense of inferiority is ten thousand times more serious than all the autoerotic habits in the world. It will follow him through life, will make him shy, self-conscious, distrustful of himself, envious of others. It may make a complete failure out of a life that should have been successful and valuable. These are the real dangers of auto-erotism.

What help, then, can you give to the boy who comes to you in the midst of such a sexual conflict, already discouraged by his own constant falls, and with an incipient obsession about his inferiority, about his loss "of manhood"? You can put your advice in a few words. "First of all, don't think of yourself as an exception. These habits that bother you are very common. Scarcely any boy gets through his adolescence without some experience of them. So get out of your mind the *fear* of them. There is nothing to be afraid of. The book that you read, or the lecture that you heard, was based on the imperfect perverted ideas of an age long since past. There is no physical danger in autoerotic habits. You see, in times past, people, especially physicians, reasoned in the wrong way. In the awful insane asylums of a hundred years ago, they saw that mentally diseased patients lost all sense of modesty, and were constantly stimulating themselves sexually even in public; so they thought that these patients had become insane because they had practiced this stimulation to excess. In reality, it was the other way round. The excessive autoerotism of these patients was not the *cause* of the mental illness; it was only a *result,* a symptom of their loss of control. So remember that, as far as medical science goes, this habit of yours carries with it no physical danger. Of course you may practice it to excess, and all excess is harmful. If a man should keep himself so constantly stimulated that he sought satisfaction with a woman three or four times every day, he would do himself harm. But if with your habit, you exercise reasonable control; if you do not intentionally create the mental atmosphere that leads to temptation; if you do not yield to the sexual tension more than three or four times a month then you may rest assured that the habit will do you no physical injury. However, do not misunderstand me. I am not trying to palliate sin; not trying to lower your ideals or standards. Our ideal *must* be complete continence—continence until you are married. Such continence is possible, and in spite of what many people say, it is not physically harmful. That is the ideal. But in trying to attain it, you are involved in a struggle with the strongest force in human life. And you yourself have already weakened your power of resistance by acquiring a habit of yielding. It may take you years to build up a counter-habit of complete resistance. So, do not be afraid and do not be discouraged. Do the best you can. Let there be at least two temptations that you successfully resist for every temptation to which you yield. And when you do fall, don't stew over it, and throw stones at yourself and imagine that you have lost your manhood or have ruined your body by abuse. You have done none of these things. You have done something in the stress of temptation that cannot harm your body, but that may harm your soul. God's law says that such an act is sinful. Very well, then. If you commit it, see to it that you make an act of contrition; that you are sorry for it and resolve to do a little better, to resist a little longer the next time. And go to your confessions. Get the grace and the help of absolution and spiritual counsel. Above all, keep on with the fight. After all, the Christian life does not consist of one undeviating upward progress in spiritual living. The Christian life is a falling down, and getting up again, asking for and obtaining God's forgiveness and the strength to do better; going on again and perhaps falling down again also, but still picking yourself up, still going on. Above all things, don't get your mind so concentrated on this one habit that you measure your own advance in your religious life merely by the number of times that

you have fallen into this particular sin. *There are other sins.*
Suppose you turn your mind to your sins of unkindness, of
lying, of gossiping unfairly about others. Get something
else done in your religious life. Don't allow one sin to
dominate the entire picture. Finally, feel quite free to come to
me at any time when you are especially tempted. Come and
tell me about it. And remember that, strange as it may appear,
I was once a young man of your age myself. I had exactly the
same temptations. And I dare say that I did not fight them
half as successfully as you have fought. Now, kneel down and
I'll give you my blessing."

You will, of course, fill out this outline for yourself in order
to meet special cases. But one of the best pieces of practical
advice, in dealing with all sex temptations, is summed up in
the two Latin words "obsta principiis." Look out for the beginnings, avoid the situations—the primary conditionings that
make the final act not only a possibility, but almost a determined necessity. If you play with the "beginnings" of autoerotism—of adultery, of any kind of sexual intercourse—you
will soon find yourself engulfed by a stream of emotional
urge too powerful to resist. To say, "I'll go so far, and no
further," is always a mistake. If you get "so far," you've *got*
to go farther, because you have put yourself in the grip of a
power that very few men or women are able to dominate.

I know that some modern moral theologians feel that, when
we have to deal with autoerotic habits of long standing, we are
dealing with actions so predestined by past yieldings and so
dominated by the power of sexual urge, that they scarcely have
the "nature of mortal sin." In your moral theology books you
will find that mortal sin, which extinguishes the life of grace*
in the soul, requires a clear and deliberate choice by which
the sinner, intentionally and with unclouded judgment, turns
his back upon God. If this definition is pushed to extremes,
there must be comparatively few mortal sins among ordinary
practicing Catholic Christians. But I feel somewhat disinclined

to deny to autoerotic indulgence the nature of mortal sin, and to make of it merely a sort of venial offense. Here again, one must discriminate between individuals. I can imagine that a person would commit mortal sin, who, *without any previous habit of autoerotism,* deliberately chose to indulge himself or herself in that particular manner, knowing that it is an offense against God's law. On the other hand, a person tormented by sexual tension and with years of autoerotic habits behind him, has really so little chance of clear-headed choice in the matter, that the offense must be judged in a much more lenient way.

One other practical point. People are more obsessed by the sinfulness of sexual indulgence than by the wickedness of any other types of sin. This, I suppose, is the result of the sex repressions of our forefathers, of the Puritan domination, of the accursed New England conscience. You do not find it in the Middle Ages. If you will read some of the mediæval collections of religious tales, such as the *Dialogus miraculorum* of Cæsarius of Heisterbach,[11] you will find that sins of sexual expression were not then placed in a category of their own. And I believe that the theologians of those ages were nearer the concept of the Gospels than we are, for, during Our Lord's earthly ministry, there was surely one class of sinners to whom he was especially gracious and forgiving. The Pharisees, whom He so bitterly criticized, were doubtless not troubled with erotic temptations of any type. But because of our Puritan forebears, people even to-day are more ashamed of an autoerotic act of their own than of all their evil lying, slandering and uncharitableness put together. I have known devout people to be kept away from the Sacrament of Penance for months because they were ashamed to confess—not that they had slandered their neighbor, not that they had

[11]*Cæsarii Heisterbachiensis monachi ordinis Cisterciensis dialogus miraculorum textum, edidit Josephus Strange* (Coloniae, 1851). Cf. *Medicine from the Standpoint of History,* by John Rathbone Oliver, pp. 27–28.

lied or stolen or given needless pain to those that loved them, but that they had "been guilty of an act of impurity by themselves—once." There are others who measure their entire growth in holiness by the number of times that they commit or do not commit this one particular sin. I repeat, there are other things in life besides sexual interests and reactions. There are other sins besides the unrestrained activities of our human bodies. Sometimes it seems to me as if the persistent misunderstandings about autoerotism were more powerful for harm in individual lives than many definite clear-cut acts of self-indulgence or of intentional evil.

You will occasionally read in the newspaper about some apparently happy bridegroom who left his bride waiting for him at the altar and disappeared forever; or a community may be appalled by an unexpected suicide, the self-destruction of a young man the night before his wedding day. But the newspapers keep no record of the men who might have been happily married, but who have been afraid to marry. Such a man may have been attentive to some one girl who returns his love, a girl who is constantly expecting that the young man will, at last, ask her to marry him, and who is as constantly disappointed of her hope. He may be the one real love of her life. He may be deeply, irrevocably in love with her. But between them stands a barrier—a ghost from which the young man cannot escape. The primary cause of all these tragic happenings is often a misunderstanding of autoerotism.

A young man, engaged, ready to be married on a certain day, is obsessed by sexual fears. As a boy he formed autoerotic habits. They may still persist, especially if he has tried to live a continent life and to keep away from promiscuous sexual intercourse with chance women. He has been taught that one of the permanent results of this habit is "loss of manhood." He has read little pamphlets about it, he has seen in the newspapers advertisements of "physicians" who treat this same "loss of manhood." He is sure that he will "inherit the sins of his youth"; then, when he marries, he will be what he calls "impotent." On his wedding night he will be unable to function "like a man." This failure will debase him forever in his bride's eyes. She will suspect—she will guess the reason for it. And, it will not only kill her love, it will do something that the young man dreads still more—it will humiliate his manhood in the sight of the woman he loves. Men are so self-centred, especially in sexual matters. They are so prone to confuse love with sexual activity. But our particular young man, with his wedding coming nearer every day, gets into a panic. He does not realize that the woman whom he is to marry will not care at all what happens or what does not happen on the first night of her married life. If she loves him, nothing that he can do or fail to do, will affect her love, so long as it does not involve any treachery to that love itself. Yet, he wants to impress her, not as the man who loves her, who will go on loving her so long as they both shall live, but as a dominant male animal. And his panic may become so intolerable that on his wedding day he may yield to it, may disappear and leave his bride waiting at the altar, may expose her to all the notoriety and ridicule of a deserted bride, and all this because he is still dominated by the fear of his boyhood's sex habits. If he loves her enough to be unwilling to expose her to ridicule, he will think that he does her a service by shooting himself the night before his wedding day.

These are no fanciful imaginings, but facts of experience. And many are the men who have drawn back from marriage, who have been afraid to marry because they feared to inherit the sins of their youth in the shape of impotency, a loss of manhood. There are unhappy married men and women who have no children, who have never been able to achieve satisfactory marital intercourse, because on their wedding night the bridegroom was obsessed by a fear of impotency and *was* impotent. And that first failure has poisoned all their attempted acts of intercourse. Impotency demands a discussion of its own and such a discussion belongs under the heading of heteroerotic reactions. But I mention it here because it has a very real connection with autoerotism and all the misunderstandings connected with it. Nothing defeats the end of nature in sexual intercourse more than the emotion of fear, fear of impotency, fear of impregnating the wife because the husband wants no children—fears of all kinds. And one of the strongest, the most devastating of these fears is the fear of "lost manhood." That kind of manhood, sexual potency, is never lost unless there is some definite disease or pathological condition of the sexual organs. If a man, physically perfect, is impotent, then he is either obsessed by some fear, or else the woman with whom he is seeking intercourse is not to him what we call an "adequate sexual object." Many married men who are impotent with their wives because these wives have lost their physical attractions in doing household work and in bearing children, would be potent enough with some more attractive partner.

However, when all is said and done, autoerotic habits are sterile reactions. There is no love element connected with them, except those pale images of so-called love with which the autoerotic strives to fill his imagination in his effort to turn a solitary activity into an imaginary partnership. This "mental erotism," what the moral theologians call *morosa delectatio,* is a bad form of mental amusement. Apparently those men and women adjust themselves most satisfactorily to autoerotic habits who regard the act itself as a kind of "self-relief" from uncomfortable tormenting sexual tension, and not as an element in a complicated sexual debauch of the imagination.

Moreover, autoerotic activity is so easy, and therein lie both its danger of excess and the power of its temptation. A man may yield to a desire for heteroerotic intercourse, but between his yielding to the idea and the accomplishment of his desire, there is a series of actions that must be performed. He must have a human partner, he must have a proper place,

and a proper time. In finding one or the other of these neces-
sities, he may lose his desire, and so he falls into no sin; he has
been protected by circumstances. The autoerotic boy or girl
has no such difficulties. Very little is required for satisfaction,
except privacy of a certain kind, for a boy may sleep in the
same bed with his father and indulge in autoerotic acts without his father being any the wiser. This simpleness of circumstances makes autoerotism too easy for the weak-willed, and it
increases the power of the temptation even for the bravest
struggler.

At the best, it is a love-less activity. Love-less in the right
sense of love. And here, let me beg you to make some sort of
fight to bring people's minds back to the proper conception of
that small word of four letters, for it seems to me that we have
debased our sense of the word until it has come to mean nothing except sexual intercourse. Whenever we speak of "love,"
there lies at the back of our minds another short word, the
word "bed." I knew a woman once who would not have a bed
in her house, for she said that all the evil in the world came
from beds; so she had couches and sofas instead. I do not think
that she kept much evil out of the world. But we must
clean up our associations with the word "love." We must recognize that, among the human ways of expressing love, there
are certain physical actions that we call "sexual" and which nature has hitched-up with the procreation of the species. But we
must constantly keep before our eyes the fact that love, in its
best sense, can exist without sexual expression; that there may
be sexual expression without love; and that any sexual activity
must be measured by its love-content. A sexual relationship between two human beings that is devoid of love in its highest
sense, becomes a mere physical reaction, like eating or drinking or other even less beautiful bodily functions. On the other
hand, the presence of a real love element is able to ennoble
and to give constructive significance to a physical relationship
that may in itself be illicit or positively wrong.

Here, again, in our dealing with sex difficulties and relationships we must individualize. An extramarital relationship between A and B may have quite different sources, quite different motives for each of the partners in the same action. To B, the sexual act may be the only thing of any value or importance. To A, the same act may be only a secondary thing—a thing not desired of itself—perhaps a thing deeply regretted—but a thing that has happened in the course of a lasting self-sacrificing love—which is the only element in the whole situation that A really desires. Keep these principles in mind; they will teach you how to tax justly the real objective ethical values of many a sex relationship.

We can now pass on to a consideration of the great majority of all sexual activities, those sexual reactions that we have called heteroerotic, the relationship between husband and wife, between man and woman. As this is a tremendous field of human activity, I can only touch on a few outstanding questions that arise within it.

Older people are constantly told that modern youth has shaken off the shackles of sexual repression and given free rein to all its sexual desires. There is no doubt that the young people of to-day have freed themselves from a great many unnecessary inhibitions. It is a good thing that they are able to talk openly about matters that used to be only whispered in closets and written down in Latin in the footnotes of medical books, published "for the profession only." It is always good to let fresh air into a stuffy darkened room. The air may blow a bit too roughly, and may disturb the antimacassar of Great-grandmother Snooks or tip over the wax flowers created by Great-aunt Maria. You can always put the antimacassar back again in its place, if you still insist on finding any beauty in antimacassars. Most of us are grateful to the rowdy wind that has disturbed these relics, when it freshened the general atmosphere of the closed room. In the domain of human behavior that lies beyond speech, where speech spills over into action, here our young people do go farther; they act more freely than was once considered·"decent." But most of the things that they do are nothing new. They were done even in the most proper Victorian times, although not so openly. And they will always be done so long as there are young people in the world, who insist on doing things that older people would probably like to do themselves, if they could. *Si jeûnesse savait; si vieillesse pouvait.*

The forms of behavior that are more openly permitted among our young people of to-day may be classed, from the sexual standpoint, among what are usually called "the forepleasures," the "introductory rites of the service of Aphrodite," as a Frenchman might express it: all those physical acts that precede and are meant to lead up to the definite act of heterosexual intercourse. Whether or not actual acts of intercourse are more common to-day among young people than they were fifty years ago, I shall not attempt to decide. Here I am dealing with the "pre-requisites," the *principia,* with which sex activity usually begins. I mean the touchings, the kissings, the closeness of one body to another, the stimulation that comes through the organs of touch in the fingers, and through the sensitive mucous membrane of the mouth and lips. I believe that modern people sum up all their "pre-pleasures" in the words "necking" and "petting." They are as good words as any. I am surprised that we physicians have not already coined some Greek words for them.

At any rate, this preliminary sex activity is commonly practiced nowadays. We are interested in it only in so far as it has certain definite mental and physical results on the young people who are committed to our charge. In the first place, our young "neckers and petters" are doing something that almost deserves the word "unnatural." Of course, there is, in reality, no such thing as an "unnatural act." Everything that is, is natural. If it were not natural it could not be. But it is surely a sort of artificial reversal of the order of nature to take certain sensations and the means of producing them, sensations which are by nature intended to lead up to one definite act—to take them and to make of them an act in itself, or to let them lead up to nothing at all. To side-track them, to treat them like a motor-car that has been run off the road into the shadow where it is no longer getting anywhere, but just standing still with the engine running at top speed. That is a mistake, I am sure. And you can easily see how bad the results are. I have watched some of my own young men go jauntily out on what they call a "petting party" and return after two or three hours of such "exercise" so tired and drooping with tense, exhausted bodies, and nervous twitching faces, that they might have been playing two football games or three lacrosse matches, instead of having been "making whoopee."

This is a perfectly natural result. They have been stimulating themselves, their bodies and their minds along one line of excitement that is intended by nature to lead up to an act in which the stimulation ceases, the tension is smoothed out and the entire human organism is rested and refreshed. But at this last act, the "petting pair" must stop. And one cannot help being sorry for them. I do not know how the girl looks when she gets home. I know how the man looks, and he has often told me how he feels and where. I know, too, that such a "party" leads necessarily to autoerotism. It must. And in a sense, such petting parties are merely a new type of autoerotic acts, accomplished by two persons in one another's presence. Moreover, both man and woman are using up certain sources of pleasure and of stimulation that they will need later on in life. If they use up and exhaust all the fore-pleasures of sex activity, make them so common that they react normally to them no longer, what will the marriages of the future be? Young people who, before marriage, have had a long and detailed petting experience will have nothing left to experience except the sexual act itself.

To the historian there is nothing strikingly new in what is to-day called "necking" or "petting." During the first part of the nineteenth century there was a similar social habit, called "bundling."[12] The following passage from the *History and Genealogies of Ancient Windsor, Connecticut*,[13] sounds as if it might have been written to-day by some *laudator temporis acti*, some bitter critic of "modern youth" and its depravity. "Then came the war[14] and young New England brought from the long Canadian campaigns stores of loose camp vices and recklessness, which soon flooded the land with immorality and infidelity. The church was neglected, drunkenness fearfully increased and social life was sadly corrupted. "Bundling," the ridiculous and pernicious custom which prevailed among the young to a degree that we can scarcely credit, sapped the foundations of morality and tarnished the escutcheons of thousands of families." Webster's dictionary defines "bundling" as follows: "To sleep together with the clothes on." Ministers railed against the custom, but it persisted. Unmarried young men and women would spend hours together in bed with their clothes on. Just how many garments were to be worn seems to have varied with each bundler. Let me quote the words of the Reverend Samuel Peters[15] who rather defends the practice. He says: "Bundling is certainly innocent, virtuous and prudent or the Puritans would not have permitted it to prevail among their offspring. People who are influenced more by lust than a serious faith in God, ought never to bundle. I have daughters and speak from nearly forty years' experience. Bundling takes place only in cold seasons of the year. *The sofa in summer is more dangerous than the bed in winter.* In 1776, a clergyman went into the country and preached against the unchristian custom of young men and maidens lying together in bed. He was no sooner out of the church than he was attacked by a shoal of good women, with

---

[12]Cf. H. R. Stiles, *Bundling: Its Origin, Progress and Decline in America.*
[13]Published in 1859 and quoted in Stiles' Introduction to *Bundling.*
[14]I.e., the French wars in Canada and the War of 1812.
[15]Cf. Stiles, *op. cit.*, pp. 54–56.

'Sir, do you think we and our daughters are naughty because we allow bundling?' 'You lead yourselves into temptation by it,' he replied. The women all answered at once, 'Sir, have you been told thus, or has experience taught it you?' The priest admitted that he had been told so. The ladies then bawled out, 'Your informants, sir, we conclude, are those city ladies who prefer a *sofa* to a *bed*. We advise you to alter your sermon by substituting the word sofa for bundling—for a sofa is more dangerous than a bed.'"

The parallels between the "bundling" of the nineteenth century and the necking or petting of the twentieth are so striking that I advise any one, who is disturbed about the "immorality of modern youth," to comfort him or herself by reading a little about the former custom. The young people of the eighteenth and nineteenth centuries survived the evils of bundling. They became the progenitors of our early Victorian sexually repressed ancestors. No doubt, the young people of to-day who give so much apparent cause for scandal and criticism will in time become more repressed than the Victorians, more "pure" than the Puritans themselves.

In the "bundling" days there were doubtless plenty of people to point out that "the youth" was exhausting all the "fore-pleasures" of marriage, that actual sexual intercourse was much more frequent than it had ever been before among unmarried young men and women. As a matter of fact I do not imagine that such acts are more frequent to-day than they were in this parallel period of bundling a hundred odd years ago. If they are, it is not because of "petting"; it is because our modern "civilization" has made fornication easy and safe. In the "bundling period" there was at least the fear of pregnancy to act as some sort of restraint. But, *nous avons changé tout cela.* Thanks to the thing that we call. "birth control."

It may seem to you that I could more properly discuss this particular matter in connection with the heteroerotic reactions of married life. If I wished to speak of it in that connection I should not use the words "birth control," but "contraceptive methods," two other words which have come to mean quite a different thing.

We Americans are often the slaves of a catch phrase. We create an expression, which at the time of its creation means one and only one definite series of facts or concepts. Then, as the expression or the phrase becomes popular, it is twisted, by constant use, out of all likeness to its original meaning, It comes to connote things that were never imagined by the original coiners of the expression. We are a wonderful people in the way we give the wrong names to the right thing, or express wrong things by right names. Or else, we give a new name to an old thing, and think that we have made a new and startling discovery. Ever since marriage became an accepted relationship in human society, there have been men and women who have wanted to live together without getting married, without submitting to the restrictions involved in the concept of monogamy. Such men and women *have* lived together, and the extramarital relationship has been called by various names. But why call that old relationship "companionate marriage" when it is not a marriage at all, and why pat ourselves on the back because we have discovered a new kind of marriage, a new type of social relationship? We let ourselves become obsessed by names. For instance, that apparently harmless word "Prohibition." At the mere sound of it, certain people prick up their ears and paw the ground and "smell the battle afar off."

It is the same thing with birth control. Those two words have come to have a meaning altogether different from the signification that was originally attached to them. To one woman, worn out by bearing too many children and afraid of another pregnancy, they may mean scientific "contraceptive methods." But to thousands and ten thousands of other men and women, to the every-day man in the street or the woman in the house, they mean something entirely different. They mean, the way to make promiscuous sex relationships easy. They mean, how to make fornication safe for everybody. Thanks to all this modern agitation about contraceptive methods—which in themselves are at least debatable—any young girl or young man can buy in the nearest drug-store a "safe preparation" or instrument that will not "control birth," but that will make it possible for them to indulge their sexual desires in complete disregard for any physical consequences of an unpleasant kind. Thanks, partially at least, to the hesitating approval that our own Communion has extended—blessing birth control with the little finger of the left hand—our country, although it may not have been made entirely safe for democracy, is rapidly being made safe for fornication.

Believe me, I do not overstate the case. In discussing the subject, you must not let yourself wander into loose definitions of your terms. Contraceptive methods are one thing. Every physician recognizes situations in which it is necessary to interrupt a pregnancy. But even he will not take upon himself to interrupt it without protecting himself by securing the opinion of some colleague. And I have no quarrel with the activity of reputable Bureaus for Contraceptive Advice.[16] The women who go to such a bureau are in the hands of able obstetricians; they are carefully examined; they are protected from their own ignorance, and all the results of the advice given are carefully tabulated and published. Here is no question of making fornication easy and safe. You may or you may not believe in the right of the individual to interrupt a pregnancy under any circumstances, but if there be any circumstances under which such an interruption is permissible, then a reputable bureau or clinic administered by sensible and well-trained physicians is surely the best means of determining when a pregnancy is to be interrupted or prevented altogether. Taking into consideration the attitude of the Roman Church toward this

[16]See *Third Report of the Bureau for Contraceptive Advice,* 1028 South Broadway, Baltimore, Md., 1931.

whole matter, it is enlightening to read in the report of one of these bureaus or clinics, that out of 183 women who came to the clinc for contraceptive advice, 36, or 19 per cent were Roman Catholics. As the Lord Bishop of Birmingham said at Lambeth, "In questions of birth control the Church of Rome maintains a very high ideal, but a very accommodating practice."

But birth control does not mean contraceptive clinics to the average man or woman of to-day. It means, as I have already said, certain definite medicinal preparations, certain manufactured articles that are on sale openly in drug-stores, and that are as openly advertised. I have collected a great many of these advertisements. They appear in publications that pride themselves on their "high moral standards."[17] And every physician's mail is filled with new suggestions about "feminine hygiene." Not long ago, in a big medical clinic, I was looking through some of the new "literature" that had come in and that dealt with birth control. A colleague of mine knew that I was collecting choice specimens. He told me that he had saved an especially choice one for me. But he could not find it. One of his assistants, when asked where this printed matter was, said: "Oh, it was so filthy, that I simply couldn't stand it, wouldn't have it on my desk. I threw it into the waste-basket." Physicians are not especially queasy, nor are they supposed to be easily shocked. And yet this man was so offended by the tone of the matter of an advertisement of "feminine hygiene" that he would not allow it near him.

The development of feminine hygiene still goes on. I suppose that, within a few years, when a young man and his adored one start out for an evening's entertainment, they will stop at a drug store on their way, where she will get something

---

[17]E.g. "Some women wonder, while others find out. What to do about this vital matter. Our preparation is safe and powerful. The newest knowledge of feminine hygiene." That is the catch word now. We are covering up all the unpleasant connotations of the words birth control by talking about "feminine hygiene."

that she can drink in a glass of soda water, while he will buy something else that he can put in his bill-fold, and then they will be able to go on their way completely happy, and completely safe. Safe, thanks to birth control.

If you think that I am overstating the case, ask some mothers what unexpected objects they have sometimes found in the purses or handbags of their eighteen-year-old daughters. Better still, ask some of the girls themselves. They will often admit quite freely their more or less promiscuous sex relationships, which are all the more promiscuous because nowadays "the woman is protected." If you say, "Yes, but you intend to marry some day, do you not? You look forward to a devoted husband, to children?" The girl will answer: "Of course I intend to be married. And I want children too. But when I marry, I shall really *give* myself to my husband." That is the outstanding element in all the temporary sex relationships of so many young people. None of these relationships are perfect. The woman holds something back, so does the man. And an intimate relationship in which there is always some sort of a wall between the two people who share it can have very little to do with love in its highest, most ideal and Christian sense. Because of this, I cannot but feel, as I have already said, that these sex relationships, made safe by birth control, are not heteroerotic reactions at all. They are merely a form of autoerotic satisfaction. The man is used by the woman as a mere temporary instrument in the attainment of certain physical sensations. When neither partner gives him or herself, but only uses the other as a physical machine for relaxing sexual tension, there can be no real unity, no sinking of both individuals in the creating of a new life.

The Roman Church is not far wrong when she calls all ordinary methods of birth control, *purus putus Onanismus*.[18] It does seem, not only unfair, but exegetically unsound to make poor old Onan responsible for all autoerotic reactions.

[18]Cf. Ferreres, *Compendium theologiae moralis*, sec. 1165, Vol. II, p. 645.

As I understand the story of Onan, he was punished, not because "he spilled his seed upon the ground," but because he did not love his brother or his brother's wife and did not want to "raise up seed" to that dead brother as the law of Moses compelled him to do. The incidental fact of his spilling his seed has for centuries unjustly made of Onan the founder of autoerotism. Indeed, autoerotism is still, in old medical and theological books, called Onanism. But if the decision of the Roman "Congregatio Pœnitentiæ," that I have quoted above, had said that most acts of "protected" sex intercourse were *purus putus autoerotismus,* nothing but simple, rotten masturbation (Forgive the word, this once), I should be inclined to agree.

Please do not misunderstand me. I know of very little good that I can say about feminine hygiene and birth control. Contraceptive methods are different matters. I recognize that there are difficult cases in married life requiring some contraceptive intervention that must be judged on their individual merits. They are often difficult. It is easy to say, be continent. Continence is the only sure and recognized method of contraception. But husband and wife may differ in their powers of continence. Continence may be easy for the husband. Yet the wife, if she be highly sexed, may suffer torments of repressed sexuality, and may be exposed to temptations to which she ought not to be exposed, inasmuch as she has a husband. If only that husband could give her the sexual satisfaction that she craves, and to which she has a right, without giving her at the same time another baby, then the conflict would cease, perhaps the home would be happier, the wife less cross and tense, the children less "picked on" and fussed over. Perhaps. Such cases are very hard to decide. It is so much easier to say, "No; such methods are *never* permissible among married Christians," than to try and decide each difficult case as it comes up, being willing sometimes to sacrifice a too rigid principle in order to gain a definite readjustment in a single situation. On the other hand, to concede the possibility of using contraceptive methods under certain circumstances is a kind of lowering of the flag, a loss or a partial loss of an ideal, a betrayal of all those really bravely continent men and women who for years of married life have subdued their own desires so that they might limit the number of their children by foregoing the physical satisfaction of matrimony, and who have won a glorious victory over themselves. Shall we say to people like that—"You were quite wrong. Your long years of struggle were quite unnecessary. How much easier it would have been if your wife had paid more attention to 'feminine hygiene'"? Still, if the modern exploitation of feminine hygiene continues at its present rate, if our Communion begins to bless birth control with more than one finger, then it will become unnecessary to worry about such continent married people, such unselfish fighters, such idealists—for there will not be any of them left.[19]

Heterosexual reactions may be roughly divided into two groups. First, those reactions that take place outside of marriage, and secondly those that take place between husband and wife. Under the first group belongs a discussion of prostitution. It may belong there, but I scarcely think that it belongs in this chapter. You can find many histories of prostitution that will give you the important facts. Here I can confine myself to a few statements. In prostitution, as in anything else, it is the demand that creates the supply. If the male sex were continent, there would be no brothels, at least not enough to make the business pay. The prostitute herself is usually not half as dangerous to the young man as the semi-prostitute. The prostitute knows that her body is her stock in trade; she does her best to

[19]"Problems of the Christian Conscience, III. "Marriage and Sex," by the Rev. S. A. McDowall. In the London *Spectator* for Oct. 24, 1931, pp. 519–520. "For healthy people in normal circumstances to marry with the intention of never having children is to deny instincts as deep rooted as the primary sexual instinct and to lose sight of the original purpose of mating. Instincts may be nobly transformed but they may not be thwarted without loss. The Christian who values the sacrament of intercourse cannot countenance indifference to the sacrament of the family." A very important new book is *Judgement on Birth Control*, by Raoul de Guchteneere.

keep it free from venereal disease. But the semi-prostitute, the girl who is employed and who wanders easily from one sex relationship to another, is often ignorant of danger, often becomes infected without knowing it, or if she does know it, is afraid to seek medical help. She poses as a *virgo intacta*. And many is the man who has found himself with a severe gonorrhœa after an experience with that same untouched virgin. But there is a mental danger to our young men both in semi-prostitutes and in prostitutes themselves. Often a young man who has had his first sexual experience in some brothel is so disgusted by the surroundings and the details of the act itself that he acquires a mental obsession, a fear of the act, a belief that it is always animal, dirty, bestial and utterly vile. When he meets, later on, a girl with whom he is truly in love, he may marry her and then find himself impotent, because the mere thought of his first sexual experiences rouses such memories of disgust that he cannot carry out with this woman, whom he adores, the natural physical actions which have become to him so odious and appalling. Young men who have their first experience with prostitutes often lose more than their virginity.

If, in your parishes, you ever have to deal with women who have been sexually promiscuous and who are fighting their way back to self-control, you will often be surprised by the ease with which they seem to resist what you would call "the temptations of the flesh." As a matter of fact, such a woman has seen so often the very vilest side of men, that when she does get away from her old life, she never wants to know a man intimately again. Or, if she does marry, the sexual relationship in marriage is never as important to her as her companionship with her husband. If she does not marry, her intimates will be members of her own sex. No one would blame her if she never wanted to have a man near her again. The same thing is noticeable among prostitutes while still living their ordinary lives. The loves of their lives, the really fine and splendid devotions of their existence, are hardly ever associated with any male animal. They love some member of their own sex. And when one considers what they have suffered at the hands of men, who shall be willing to cast the first stone?

But there are many extramarital heteroerotic relationships that have no contact with prostitution or semi-prostitution. And it is with such relationships that you, as parish priests, as ministers, or social workers will often have to deal. These are the sexual partnerships that develop between some young man and some young woman in your parish. They may be planning to marry later on. They may not be thinking of marriage at all, but there the sexual relationship is, and sometimes you will have to judge it; to try and cut out the bad elements in it and to keep the good ones.

I have already described what we may call the "loveless level" of sexual reaction; those relationships that are purely physical or animal without any intermixture of kindliness, of affection, of self-sacrifice, of love. For instance: a man of middle age is in town during the summer. His wife and children are away. It is hot; he has few relaxations. He begins to be tormented by sexual thoughts. At last he can stand it no longer. Some Saturday afternoon, he packs a small suit-case, slips off on the sly to some fairly distant city, where he is not known, goes to a strange hotel where he registers under an assumed name, gets a good dinner, walks the streets, picks up the first attractive looking woman he finds, and goes home with her. By Sunday morning the whole thing is over. His tension is relieved. He does not even know the woman's name; nor will he be able in a week to remember what she looked like. He has not exerted any influence on her life, except in so far as she has been of temporary use to him in one particular way. This level of sex reaction is the lowest level of all. Two personalities touch, then separate. Neither is the better for having known the other, neither is perhaps much the worse. There is very little to be said in defense of such relationships as this.

But the case may present a very different aspect when the actual sex activity is a secondary, a subservient thing. One of your young men is deeply, honestly in love with a girl. His only desire is to be of service to her, to give her everything in his power, to make her happy. And she reciprocates. Something prevents their immediate marriage. And then, in some moment of relaxation or excessive stimulation, some sex act occurs. It may occur fairly frequently. But it is never the *sine qua non* of the situation. Both he and she regret it, wish that it had not happened. They do not want it to happen again. This is a higher level of relationship. As a rule, you can judge of such relationships by the presence or the absence of the unselfish, constructive motive of love. If the young man is not seeking his own happiness, but the happiness of the girl; if the primary factor in their relationship is not physical, but mental, then you may be able to make something valuable out of this same relationship, no matter what the extramarital elements may have been. But do not make the mistake of *forcing* people into a "loveless marriage." If a man "gets a girl into trouble" not because he really loves her, but because he craved a certain physical satisfaction, then do not tell him that he must make an honest woman of her and give her child an honest name by making her his wife. He doesn't love her, he doesn't really want her. If you force him to marry her, he will be unhappy, so will she. And two wrongs never made a right yet. As for the girl, it is much better for her to have her baby in some hospital, and to adopt it afterward, to try and forget this first experience and go on with her life, than to tie herself permanently to a man who does not love her. I do not think that the unborn child will suffer very much if it does finally enter the world outside the holy estate of matrimony.[20]

The whole subject is far too wide for a satisfactory discussion in such a book as this. I can only throw out a suggestion here and there that may prove of help.

[20]Dr. Julia Deming, "Problems Presented by Children of Parents Forced to Marry." *The American Journal of Orthopsychiatry*, Vol. II, No. 1, pp. 70–82.

When we turn to the heteroerotic reactions of married life we enter a very complex field. For happiness in marriage depends on the power of two individuals to adjust themselves to each other, mentally, physically, spiritually. That is not an easy thing. It may take a life time to achieve. And if matrimony were not a sacrament, we should have to make it one, for two people who promise to live together for the rest of their lives need so much spiritual help, that they *must* fail in their attempts unless some source of supernatural aid can be given them. As pastors and social workers, you will frequently be called upon to smooth out marital difficulties, to keep some marriage from drifting into the divorce court. And you will have a very hard job indeed, unless you realize some of the fundamental reasons for those imperfect adjustments that so often separate man and wife.[21]

CLINICAL MATERIAL

A. Sex Difficulties in adolescence.

(1) One of your parishioners, a healthy boy of about sixteen, is in your confirmation class. You have been preparing him and others for their first confessions. And you are doing a part of this preparation with individuals, not with a group. You have been explaining to this boy the sins against "purity." After listening to you, he asks the following questions. He may not be able to put it into words as clearly as I am stating it here. But this is what will be in his mind; these are the questions he wants answered. He says: "I understand the things I ought not to do. And I'll try to avoid them all I can. But I want to understand the differences between some of them. Here is my difficulty. I am sixteen. Nature has already made me a man. I could have children now, if I wanted to. But you say that the only way to have children is in marriage. So your religion, or the thing you call the social order, works against nature. It says that I can't marry until I am older, until I can support a wife. You make it impossible for me to act

[21]Robert Daton Dickenson and Laura Beam, *A Thousand Marriages* (Baltimore: Williams and Wilkins, 1932).

in a natural way for a long time. I couldn't marry and support a wife until I'm twenty-one or two at the earliest. So I've got six years to go, then, before I can do what nature has made me able to do now. Very well. But how am I going to get through those six years? Nature, you know, isn't easy to work against. I shan't have an easy time. How shall I get through those six years and do the least harm to others and to myself? Some of my friends say, 'Go get a girl.' Well, there are two kinds of girls. I can go down into the Red Light part of our town. There's a house there that fellows have pointed out to me. And I could save up the money I earn out of school and go there once in awhile. But I don't want to do that. I've heard about the kind of diseases you get in those places. I'd be afraid to go there. The other kind of girl that I could get would be what we call 'a good girl.' But, if I did myself harm by going to the bad house, I'd do this good girl harm by going with her. If I did with her what seems natural for me to do, I might give her a baby; she would be disgraced and we'd both get into all sorts of trouble. So the girls are out of it. Some other fellows 'do things' together. I can't say that their way has ever attracted me much. But I've got two friends, intimate friends, fellows with whom I can discuss anything, fellows whom I trust. I might go and sleep with them sometimes. They wouldn't mind and I wouldn't mind. But, somehow, it doesn't seem exactly the right thing; although you don't get babies that way. Finally, there's the habit I learned when I was a boy of twelve. It helps a little. At night, when I can't sleep and my mind is full of thoughts about girls or actresses I've seen on the screen, and when I'm so tense and tormented that I just toss from one side of the bed to the other, then if I do fall back on the old habit, the thoughts go, and I get to sleep. That's the situation. I've got to face it for the next six years. What do you think I ought to do?"

These questions are in the minds, if not on the tongues, of hundreds of boys and young men who have some moral sense, and who are really trying to orient their lives by some definite ideal. From what I have said in the last chapter, you should be able to give a satisfactory answer. But emphasize the *ideal* of continence. Don't tell the boy that if he takes lots of exercise or cold baths he will stop his sexual activity. Excessive exercise, as well as cold water, can act as an excitement. But emphasize the mental side of resistance. Show the boy how he can put a clean non-sexual imagination in the place of the mental pictures that torment him.[22] And make him realize that if he does yield to the urge that torments him, he is safer, for himself and for others, in a reasonably restricted autoerotic activity. But do not let him supinely accept such habits as a kind of adolescent sexual life; as something that he has as much right to as a husband has to intercourse with his wife. Teach him to strive for self-restraint. If, however, his self-restraint wears thin, it had better wear thin along the edges of autoerotism than anywhere else.

B. Results of misunderstood autoerotic habits.

(1) John Sands, a healthy, respected but not over-bright man of twenty-five, has been arrested for stealing ten dollars from his employers. He has a good record; is a trusted employee. He collects small amounts from customers and always turns the money in without question. Every one was surprised when his collections were found to be ten dollars short. Other defalcations were suspected, but none were discovered. The employers would not have prosecuted, had they not feared that an unwillingness to prosecute might have a bad effect on their other employees and collectors. He was engaged to be married. In fact, the wedding day had been set. But when it came, John was in jail awaiting trial. I got his story only after many attempts.

There were no symptoms of any mental illness. No signs of psychoneurotic difficulties except autoerotism. John had fought bitterly hard and at eighteen had finally conquered his autoerotic habits. But he had always been afraid of the results of them; had felt that he ought never to marry because he had "lost his manhood." Finally he fell in love with a girl, who was sensible enough to do most of the love-making and most of the proposing herself. John found himself engaged to be married. Apparently he never thought of going back on his promise. But he cast about in his mind as to what he had best to do. In reading his paper one day, he came upon an advertisement: "Dr. X cures lost manhood, and the re-

[22]See L. D. Weatherhead, *Psychology in Service of the Soul*, pp. 175–185.

sults of early sexual errors by his newly patented electric belt."
John went to see Dr. X, who took specimens of John's blood and
of his urine; looked very anxious, and then told John that he
could cure him in three months. That, said John, would be no
good to him. He was to be married in a month, and he must
have his lost manhood back by that time. Dr. X, after consideration, thought that it might be done, if John would wear one of
the *strongest* of his electric belts, which cost usually fifty dollars,
but which the Doctor would give to John for forty because he
took a special interest in John's case. So John bought the belt on
the instalment plan. He paid down ten dollars and he agreed
to pay ten dollars each week. This was a strain on John's resources. After wearing the belt for two weeks, he felt very much
better, much more full of "manhood." It had given him confidence: it had inhibited some of his fears. But when the third
week came around, one of his colleagues who had borrowed five
dollars from the easy-going John failed to pay his debt. John had
only five of the necessary ten dollars for Dr. X's third payment.
Dr. X was adamant. If John could not pay the regular amount,
Dr. X would take back his belt. And if John would not give it
back, Dr. X would cut off the current from it, so that it would
not do John any good any longer. John was in agony of mind.
His wedding day was approaching. He *had* to have that belt.
Did he not *have* to wear it for four months in order to "regain
his manhood." He wasn't going to postpone the wedding either.
However, he had just collected fifty-odd dollars from customers.
Here was money in his hand. He took out what he needed and
a little more, paid Dr. X, and kept the belt, with the electric
current going. An understanding Judge, to whom I told the story,
released John on a short, suspended sentence. The only thing that
really troubled the Judge and myself was that we could not get
hold of Dr. X, try him, and *not* suspend sentence. Here in John's
case is an example of how ordinary misconceptions about autoerotism can almost ruin a useful life. I still wonder how John
explained the whole matter to his affianced bride. I hope that he
told her the truth, at least after the wedding.

C. Nocturnal Emissions.

(1) Often one of your young men will come to you in a per-

fect panic of fear. He will tell you that in early boyhood he acquired autoerotic habits. They did not bother him much, and he did not worry about them. He knew that other boys did the same thing; and he did not believe all "this stuff about it making you crazy." In fact he assumed towards his habit a very enlightened attitude, until one night, about a year ago (he was seventeen at the time), he woke up to find that he "had done it" in his sleep. This gave him a bad shock. He had probably acquired such a firm habit that he could not control it. He "did it" while unconscious of what he was doing. He had always held down his habit to very reasonable limits. But if he started doing it in his sleep, what control had he left? So he took his old skate straps and tied his hands together and fastened them to the iron bar at the top of the bed. In this way, he could not possibly get his hands lower than his shoulders. It was torment. He did not sleep much. And then, after about two weeks of this arrangement, the thing happened again. Although his hands were actually tied fast about his head, he had "done it again" and without knowing it. Then he became panicky in truth. It was not "his hands" that were performing habitual actions while he was asleep; it was something radically wrong with his sexual apparatus itself. Somehow, by his past autoerotism, he thought he had indeed "ruined himself." Something was broken inside the machinery somewhere. Doubtless it could never be repaired. There are thousands of boys and young men who react in this way to their first nocturnal emissions. You would not believe the history of self-torture that they go through in their efforts to keep themselves "from doing it" while they are asleep. Such a history reads like a chapter from a guide-book description of the Torture Chamber at Nuremberg. If only such boys and young men have sense enough to come to some one whom they trust. But so often they trust no one. And they are in for months or years of needless anxiety. Tell them that such emissions are perfectly natural. That they are not even sinful, so long as they are not provoked by an indulgence at night in sexual imaginings. Their frequency varies. Of course, if you get hold of a psychoneurotic type who is having emissions every or every other night, then you had best get him medical advice as soon as possible. But as a usual thing, you can reassure

your young friend, you can give him back courage and he will
be grateful to you all his life.

(Clinical material on heteroerotic difficulties will be found at
the end of Chapter VII.)

SEXUAL FACTORS

(CONTINUED)

VANISHING IDEALS OF HOME LIFE. SEXUAL MALADJUSTMENTS IN
MARRIAGE. FRIGIDITY. HOMOEROTISM. TYPES OF HOMOEROTIC
WOMEN AND MEN. MASOCHISM. SADISM. SENSE OF INFERIORITY.
CLINICAL MATERIAL

IN this chapter, we must consider the heteroerotic reactions
of married life, and then pass on to the question of homoerotism and finally to such other peculiar manifestations of the
sexual urge as may, at some time or other, come within the
sphere of your influence and of your power to help.

In our present state of civilization, there is at least one institution or traditional social arrangement that shows marked
signs of disintegration. I mean the social entity that we call
"the home." Looking back on the history of the development
of our American life, one feels that the very back-bone of our
national individuality has been what I venture to call "The
Middle-Class American Home." When I say "middle-class," I
speak in no disparaging terms of a class-conscious mind. The
term excludes the more or less luxurious houses of the very
rich as well as the wretched disorganized dwelling places of
the very poor. In America these two types are seldom permanent in the same group of individuals. A family that has been
rich in one generation becomes in the third or fourth generation a family of only moderate resources. For in America we
have no means of founding dynastic family fortunes that are
sure to persist for centuries from eldest son to eldest son. On
the other hand, we have little permanent poverty such as one
sees in cities like London, where the same family has been on

the border line of destitution from great-grandfather to great-grandson. With us a poor family, if it contains in it any power of achievement at all, is better off in the second generation than it was in the first. If, instead of rising in the economic scale it falls still lower, it generally disintegrates and ceases to be a family at all. Therefore the only type of "home" that persists, and that becomes a permanent factor in our national development, is the home of the moderately well-to-do, of the great "middle-class." The individuals that constitute this type of "home" have been the real creators of American life and of American achievement.

This "home of the great middle-class" is gradually disappearing. People of moderate means do not live in houses any longer, but in apartments. The female head of the house is no longer a house-wife; she often has not time to be a mother, and she grows easily tired even of being a wife. By a "home" I mean a protected social atmosphere, created gradually by two persons of opposite sexes who agree to live together for the extent of their natural lives, to bring children into the home, to give them a medium in which to develop and to watch over that development. In order to accomplish this, these two persons must learn, little by little, to adjust themselves, not only to one another, but also to the changing home conditions—to babyhood, to boyhood and girlhood, to adolescence, to daily work and daily play, to employment and non-employment, to hard times and to periods of success. All sorts of things will happen that will test the human material which binds wife, husband and children into the unity of the home. And the success or failure of the entire social achievement will depend on the stuff out of which this coalescing material is made.

Naturally, the very foundation of the whole thing is the union of man and woman in that social contract called marriage or matrimony. Hitherto, in America at least, this contract has been a contract of life-duration. So far as our experience can show us, we ought to know that a sound American home cannot be built on a temporary sexual alliance between a man and a woman; an alliance that may at any time, and for almost any cause, be terminated by the action of one or the other of the contracting parties. If our American homes are beginning to disintegrate, we may be sure that one of the chief causes of this disintegration is a loss of the old concept of the contract on which that home is founded.

Many people—many clergy—even many bishops are disturbed about "the evil of divorce." Personally, I am not half so troubled by the divorce evil as I am terrified by the utter loss of the Christian ideal of Holy matrimony. Divorces will go on indefinitely! Renos will flourish; and there will be quite socially respectable men and women who are legally married in one State and living in adultery in another—until we can revive among our people the fading conception of what Christian marriage really means. Believe me, you do not realize the situation. You would get some idea of it had you been associated as closely as I have been with courts of law and with prisons and prisoners.

One hears a great deal about "crime waves," about the appalling increase of delinquency, especially among younger people. There are no real crime waves; but there *is* a constantly increasing supply of young criminals who are the products of "broken homes." Ten years ago, if a "hold-up" case were being tried, you would see in the dock or on the bench reserved for the accused, hard-bitten, experienced law-breakers between thirty-five and fifty years of age. To-day, if some one is accused of "robbery under arms"—one of the most serious charges after murder in our code—you will soon discover that the accused persons are youths, anywhere from seventeen to twenty-one. Why, during the past ten years, has the age-limit of such offenders fallen from forty to twenty? The answer to this question can be given you by our "modern hold-up men" themselves, if you care to ask them. Of these immature boys, over seventy per cent—and that is a conservative estimate—come from "broken homes." While they were children, the father deserted the mother, leaving her to support the babies, to go out to work and to allow them to grow up on the streets and to learn how to evade the truant officer. Or the mother went off with another man, and the unfortunate father, who had to be at his work all day, could not overlook his children's development, and was so tired out when he came "home" at night that all he asked of them was "to keep quiet."

During the past ten or fifteen years, there has been an absolutely new development in legal or juristic history. An entirely new type of court has been invented. It had to be invented, and courts of this new type are very busy places. We call them "Domestic Relations Courts." And they had to be called into existence in order to force people, who would not stay married, to fulfil their duties as husbands and wives. Think what that means! If people lived up to the old Christian ideals of matrimony, there would be no need for domestic relations courts. Such "domestic" cases as did turn up could easily be heard by the regular judges. Never before in the whole course of legal history has it been necessary to create legal machinery that will *compel* two people to carry out the duties that they took upon themselves when they become man and wife.

If you think I am an alarmist, I should advise you to make friends with a probation officer who is attached to some court of domestic relations. Run over some of her routine cases; and remember that she gets only the cases in which there is some hope of patching up the marital relationship, some hope of "saving the home." Or spend an hour talking with the men and the women who are thronging the office of that same probation service. Ask them all one simple question, "Why did you marry your wife?" "Why did you choose your husband?" You will be surprised at the answers you receive. You know well enough what each of those people *ought* to say. "I

married him, because, first of all, I loved him. I married him
because I intended to spend the rest of my life going on loving
him. I wanted to bear him children; to make a home for him
and for them. I wanted to create a place where our love for
the children and for one another would make an atmosphere
of rest and refreshment; a place from which new lives could
go out to help in the world's work and finally to marry, as we
married, and to love and to work, as we have worked and
loved." You will not get that answer or even a part of it from
any of those people in the domestic relations court to-day.
"Why did I marry him? Well, I didn't like things at home.
Mother was cross, and I didn't get along with father. Besides,
neither of them paid much attention to me. Father was always
out in the evening at some sort of meeting. Mother was just
as bad. I was supposed to look after the baby, and I hate
babies. I just had to get away from home, and so I took Bill.
He was the nicest of my three beaux. Make a home for him?
Why no. I hate housework. A baby? No, thank you. I've got a
job in a store since I left Bill. If I'd had a baby while I was
living with him, I probably'd have spoiled my figure." And
the same answer or type of answer comes from the men. "Did
I love her? Well—sort of. I wanted to get her, and, of course,
I had to marry her for that. Home? With a lot of squalling
brats and diapers all over the place. No thanks. Besides I
don't think I'd ever have married anyway, if she and I hadn't
been out one night in my car, and I got sort of careless, so that
when she said, 'Let's get a license to-morrow and get married'
—I just did what she said."

Of matrimony as a lifelong contract, as a form of mental
discipline, as an achievement, as the foundation of a "home,"
there is not one trace, not one ideal. It is along this line, that
the ministers and social agencies must work to-day. They
must try to bring back among our young people the old Christian conception of Holy matrimony as a lifelong contract, a
sacrament, the essence of which is the mutual contract of two

baptized persons to function as man and wife according to God's law so long as they both shall live.

But even in the Christian homes that yet remain, there are difficulties of adjustment, which pastors and social workers must understand. And these same difficulties are very hard to get at. A distinguished Judge, who had heard thousands of divorce cases, once said; "The real reasons for the average divorce seldom, if ever, come out in court. For they are usually difficulties of sexual adjustment. Only the psychiatrist or the priest who has the confidence of his people or his patients can discover them."

I cannot go into the details of the various sexual acts which so often contribute to marital unhappiness or cause separation and divorces.[1] There is, however, plenty of "literature" on the subject. Books are published to-day which may possibly be of help to the unhappily married, but which are devoured by the adolescent and the undergraduate, and in comparison with which he finds the *Decameron* or Rabelais as tame as a temperance lecture or a pamphlet on home economics.[2] The basic

[1]One must not forget that almost every opening of the human body has a sexual significance. Excluding the openings of the ear, sexual activities may be associated not only with the vagina, but also with the mouth and the rectum. These things are so persistently concealed that they are seldom put into words. And yet these difficulties might be readjusted if people would only treat them as ordinary physical or mental symptoms.

[2]I possess a rather large collection of such publications, although I have never had time to read them. I collect them as specimens. The best-known is probably a translation from the German, *The Ideal Marriage: Its Physiology and Technique,* by Th. H. Van De Velde, M.D., translated by Stella Browne (N. Y.: Covici Friede, 1930). Less "stimulating" are the following: *Married Love: Or Love in Marriage,* by Marie C. Stopes (N. Y.: Putnam); *The Sexual Crisis: A Critique of our Sex Life,* by Grete Meisel-Hes, translated from the German. 3rd ed., 1932 (N. Y.: The Critic and Guide Co.); *Sexual Truths versus Sexual Lies: Misconceptions and Exaggerations,* edited by William J. Robinson, M.D. (Hoboken: The American Biological Society, 1919). This same Dr. Robinson has written at least thirty books on similar subjects, *Married Life and Happiness,* published by the same society, being the most popular. I believe that there is no doubt of Dr. Robinson's sincerity. His productions are much the best of their type, and are not to be confounded with other books on similar subjects which are written and printed merely to sell and not to instruct.

sexual difficulties of many couples lie in their different mental attitudes to the sexual act itself. Many women are "frigid," as the psychologists say; they have little or no sexual urge, yet they may love and desire children. When they marry, they find no physical satisfaction in marital relationships. The act, to them, is either definitely painful, or else disgusting—animal, degrading. If a healthy man, with a normal sex urge, mates with such a woman, he naturally finds her unresponsive, cold, unstimulating. She may love him devotedly; she may show her love by bearing him children, by caring for them and for him. But there is *one way* in which she cannot show her love at all. And for him this is the only way that he knows of showing love. There are many more frigid women in the world than we realize. These are the women who, when they determine to get married, have to pluck up all their courage and "take the jump" into matrimony. If their husbands happen to be rather brutal sexually, especially on the wedding night, such women may acquire from that first terrifying experience a definite inability ever to function as loving wives—at least in bed. The same thing happens when the rôles are reversed. There are plenty of frigid men, who from some early extra-marital sex experience have acquired a persistent obsession about the sexual act itself. To them it has always a suggestion of "the animal," of the barnyard or the stud-farm. They may, therefore, be more or less impotent, or if they do function normally, they always believe that sexual intercourse "saps their vitality."

Suppose a man of this type married to a woman with extreme sexual desires. Many more women than modern writers would have us believe go through their early lives without any sex experiences at all, even without autoerotic habits of relief. Their entire sex life has never been awakened. They have no conception of what the strength of the sexual urge may be, once it has been aroused. So they marry. And their husbands transform them from ignorant virgins into women with an entirely new set of physical needs. But the rather cold husband is absolutely unable to satisfy the desire that he has aroused. His wife lives continually in a state of sexual tension; stimulated persistently by her husband's presence, but never wholly satisfied. Her married life may become a perfect hell of starved desire; and she may look back upon her earlier sexless days as the sailor on a stormy sea glances back to the peace of the land from which he is separated. Either one of three things happens. Such a woman either develops, for the first time in her life, autoerotic habits as some sort of relief from constant tension; or she becomes irritable, unhappy, cross with the children, impossible as a mistress with her servants; or she may be exposed to some sudden temptation and may, in the extremity of her sexual need, seek relief in the arms of a man whom she does not love at all. In such marital situations, there is always the possibility of tragedy. And the situation can only be saved by a free and open acceptance of it; by an effort on the man's part to live up to his marital duties, and a determination on the part of the wife to teach herself the hard, hard lesson of sexual restraint, of the final domination of love over lust.

You must deal very gently, very circumspectly with situations of this kind. You must sense them, even before they are put into words.[3]

[3]See "Sexual Neurosis," by W. R. Reynell, M.D., in the *Proceedings of the Royal Soc. of Medicine*, Vol. XXIV, No. 7, May, 1931, pp. 827–836 (quoted with permission of the Royal Society of Medicine). "The aggressive instinct is masculine and the sexual act is essentially an act of aggression. To some men of gentle, sensitive and rather timid nature, aggression of all kinds is against their instincts. If such a man marries or is married by a dominating self-assertive woman, his wife will find submission as difficult as aggression is to him. Here the relationship is not seldom a cause of impotence. Such a man might be normally potent with a prostitute or a social inferior or perhaps with a woman of gentle and submissive nature. In normal sexual intercourse a man plays an active, a woman a passive rôle and to some women such a rôle is distinctly distasteful. Such women are usually self-willed, egotistic and often sadistic. Having acquired a husband of the type described, they humiliate him and render him impotent. Their domination

I cannot in the space of these chapters do more than point out some of the main elements in such situations, and to refer you to other sources for more detailed information. I commend to you the paper by Dr. Reynell, mentioned in the note above, and to another paper by Dr. George K. Pratt of the National Committee for Mental Hygiene in New York, entitled "Some of the Psychopathology of Marital Maladjustment."[4] Among the sources of marital maladjustment mentioned by Dr. Pratt are emotional immaturity, a mother or a father-fixation in husband or wife, various types of sadism,[5] homoerotic trends in one of the two partners,[6] frigidity in the wife, and a clash between two "wills to power." The emotionally immature person is an adult individual who "despite professional or business success has never grown up so far as his or her emotions are concerned. An emotionally immature husband married to an emotionally immature wife tends to create a family situation that for sheer childishness, for illogical and uncontrolled impulsiveness finds a parallel only in the sandbox squabblings of a pair of four-year-olds."[7] You know yourselves how tragic in matrimony a mother-fixation may be on the part of the wife. It is not a mere accident that there are so many bitter jokes about mothers-in-law. But fathers-in-law

is then complete. Such women are often the daughters of inferior, alcoholic or degenerate fathers, who have been bullied, managed, mothered or divorced by their wives. The daughter grows up without a father ideal (here again one sees the danger to the children of divorces, of broken homes), and has always looked on men as an inferior race. Such cases are difficult or impossible to cure. But success may be achieved when the patient and his wife have *gained insight into the cause of the disability* and are determined to do their utmost to overcome the psychological impasse." *Op. cit.*, p. 831. This entire paper contains material of great value. The *Proceedings of the Royal Society* may be found in any good medical library.

[4]Read at the 85th annual meeting of the American Psychiatric Association, Atlanta, Ga., May, 1929, and published in the *American Journal of Psychiatry*, Vol. 9, No. 5, March, 1930, pp. 861–870. This journal may be found in any good medical library.

[5]Sadism will be discussed later.

[6]See discussion below on homoerotism.

[7]Pratt, *op. cit.*, p. 863.

are often just as much to blame. The man with a mother-fixation is always more dominated by his mother than by his wife.[8] And many women make husbands unhappy by persistently comparing them, to their disadvantage, with fathers-in-law. It is a hard lesson for mothers and fathers to learn, but the best thing that they can do for their children, when they come to marriageable age, is to make them as mentally independent as possible of the home atmosphere and home influence. The little bird, if it is ever going to fly, has sometimes got to be *pushed* out of the nest.

Finally, the clashing of two wills to power is a source of endless marital friction. If the husband's will to power is not satisfactorily "drained off in business or professional associations," he will make trouble at home. The wife "should find her catharsis in household management, child training, in entertaining and in other social activities. If, however, the outlets of husband and wife chance to be cast in similar or identical activities, then rivalry enters and it is indeed a powerful marriage bond that will withstand the daily menace of competition at the very hearth stone."[9] On the other hand, "if husband and wife have traits and needs of equal power in *opposite* directions, then one set of personality equipments complements the other and the integrity of the family is welded centripetally."[10]

I hope that I have said enough to give you at least a few suggestions in dealing with your married people—with those

[8]Some of my readers may have seen that powerful play *The Silver Cord,* which describes the mother who keeps her son from marrying and the son who, because of his mother-fixation, is unable to marry or to stay happily married.

[9]Pratt, *op. cit.,* p. 865. Dr. Pratt adds: "Notorious, for example, are the marital infelicities of movie stars, where husband and wife are engaged in the same work. There are other situations in which identical traits may cause disharmony. A man with certain outstanding traits and needs marries a woman with identical traits and needs. No opportunity being provided for one of them to satisfy these needs in the other, there is recourse to bickering and misunderstanding."

[10]Pratt, *ibid.*

among them who seek your help because for some reason or other "they can't get along together." You will never go far wrong if you insist that an imperfectly adjusted couple should separate *for a time*. Never allow them to make any important decision as to their future until they have taken a holiday from one another. No one, even the most Job-like individual, can live in close contact with another individual, day in day out, for years, without rubbing himself or his partner mentally raw, and causing unnecessary friction and distortion of judgment. Make your disgruntled pairs get away from one another—for a month at least. Then, when they come together again, they will approach their problem from a new standpoint and with minds that are not clouded by present misunderstandings, bickerings and hurt-feelings.

You will have in your parish some married women who are more mothers than wives, some who are more wives than mothers. Unhappy, frequently, is the childless family. There, the wife has to spend all her maternal instincts on her husband; and that is not good for him, and is surely bad for her. Sooner or later, he will resent being mothered; or else he will become so used to it that he will lose his own power of individual judgment. If you have a childless pair to deal with, childless not because of any feminine hygiene, but because the woman never becomes pregnant, first be sure of your ground. Advise the woman to see a good gynecologist. Many a woman need never have been childless had she known that some slight operation might have made conception possible. But if your physician finds that the woman has normal organs, then do not let the reproach of sterility rest upon her. Get the husband to see a physician also. It may be that it is the man, who through no fault of his own is sterile. If you find, therefore, that medical science cannot give this pair a baby, then call in social science, and persuade them to adopt a child. People are so often chary of adoption. They want "one of their own blood." And they are afraid that "the child may turn out badly." Tell them that nowadays adoption is a scientifically managed matter. To-day we do not simply wander down to an orphan asylum and pick out a baby to adopt. We go to special agencies, that make adoption their business. And we learn what types of children—with what kinds of parents—are available. Do get your childless people to make a trial of it. I have seen an unhappy childless home turned into a new Garden of Eden by the presence of an adopted baby. At any rate, the experiment is always worth the making.

We must now turn to the difficult but very important subject of homoerotism; these sex reactions that take place between two people of the same sex. And let me exhort you once again to approach this topic in a scientific frame of mind. The historian is never tempted to despise the homoerotic man or woman. He knows how much these types have contributed to the happiness of the world, even if the modern world has allowed but little happiness to them.

Alexander the Great, Michael Angelo and hundreds of other important names belong among the homoerotics on the male side, while Rosa Bonheur, George Eliot, George Sand and hundreds of similar women, all with homoerotic traits, have been among the creative types—musicians, artists, writers. Nor does the psychologist despise this type any more than the historian. Unfortunately, however, he sees it, not in its unrestrained powers of creative activity, but hampered by convention, misjudged and often persecuted. He knows how many mental maladjustments, how many "nervous breakdowns" so-called, are the results of repressed or tabooed homoerotic desires. Indeed, there is a group of psychiatrists who are prone to attribute almost every mental difficulty, every phobia, every source of mental friction, to "suppressed homoerotic tendencies." The parish priest, who hears a good many confessions, knows also a great deal about the difficulties, the mental torments of the homoerotic man or woman. So does the judge. For our worn-out, antiquated laws

still stamp homoerotic relationships, between men at least, as
a crime. Fortunately, most modern judges are more enlightened than the law that they must apply. But the attitude of the
ordinary man or woman is still the attitude of the unchristian,
unscientific tradition, that we have inherited from centuries
of misunderstanding and persecution.

Just as poor Onan has been made responsible for the wickedness of autoerotism, so the inhabitants of the two cities of the
Plain, of Sodom and Gomorrah, have had the names of their
cities tacked on to a particular type of sexual reaction, because
the story of their destruction by fire and brimstone has been
misunderstood.

The people of Sodom were no more renowned for their
promiscuous sex activity than any of the many other nations
that, later on, were not entirely supplanted by the conquering
Hebrews, and which, during the times of the Judges and of the
Kings, maintained the habits of their forefathers, just as they
had maintained them during the days of Abraham. Eastern
peoples have a less restricted sexual life than we nations of
the West. But there is one thing, one social habit that among
eastern people has always been held in the deepest reverence:
the rights of guest-friendship—the protection given to the
traveller or the stranger and assured to him by his acceptance
of bread and salt at the hearth of his host. To outrage this is
indeed to be a sinner beyond all other men. Yet this is exactly
what the men of Sodom did. They were destroyed, not because
they were homoerotic debauchees, but because, when the
angels took refuge in Lot's house and had become guests of an
inhabitant of the city, they outraged the strangers' guest-rights
and denied them protection. Ask any non-Christian man of
the Far East to read the nineteenth chapter of Genesis. He
will be shocked, not at the sexual life of the men of Sodom,
but at their lack of respect for the fundamental law of guest
friendship and guest protection.

Nevertheless, like Onan, the Sodomites have been assigned

a sad rôle in our literature, our laws, even in our medical books. As you know, there was no antipathy against homoerotic relationships among the Greeks. To Plato,[11] the love of man and woman was a lower, more vulgar relationship than the love of the older man for the youth of his own sex. And "Platonic love," that people talk about to-day, does not mean the sexless attraction of man and woman, but a restrained disciplined affection of the younger man for an elder companion, who represents to him his highest ideal of complete manhood. Among the Romans it is true that homoerotic relationships lost the ideal beauty that had made them, among the Greeks, such a powerful social institution, powerful for the development of manliness, of athletic prowess, of all soldierly virtues. But they were no less common. No less accepted as a reaction of every-day life. Nietzsche says somewhere that "Christianity gave Eros poison to drink." At any rate, after the conversion of Constantine, and the legal reforms of Justinian, homoerotism became criminal. The Christian did not approve of the licentious life of the great Roman baths. So Christians did not bathe. Christians hated the great gladiatorial combats. So Christians did not take any part in games or athletics. And in the Code of Justinian, two crimes are punished by death by burning, not apparently because of their inherent wickedness, but because they are supposed to be especially hateful to God and to bring disasters, earthquakes,

[11]See Plato's *Symposium* and *Phædrus Symposium*: §178–180 c: and §181 c–e. English translation in the Loeb bilingual series of classical authors, *Plato*, Vol. V, 99–123 esp. 109–111. *Phædrus*, 32–38, §251 c–§256 e. In Loeb series, *Plato*, Vol. I, pp. 487–503. This last passage sets forth the highest Greek ideal of homoerotic love. For an able discussion of the entire subject, see *A Problem in Greek Ethics: Being an Inquiry into the Phenomenon of Sexual Inversion Addressed especially to Medical Psychologists and Jurists*, by John Addington Symonds; and especially *Sittengeschichte Griechenlands: Das Liebesleben der Griechen*, by Dr. Hans Licht (Dresden and Zurich: Paul Aretz Verlag, 1926). 3 Vols. See Vol. II, chap. 5, "Die männliche Homoerotic," pp. 117–210. Goethe says: "Die Knabenliebe ist so alt wie die Menschheit, und man kann daher sagen, sie liege in der Natur, ob sie gleich gegen die Natur ist."

famines upon any land that harbors them—witchcraft and homoerotism.

We no longer believe in witches. We would not burn them even if we did believe in them a little, but our laws are still full of punishments for the unhappy homoerotic man.

Nature, as I have said, does nothing *per saltum*. She makes no jumps. There are always connecting links between extremes. I told you that an absolute male personality does not exist; nor does an absolute female type exist either. And just as we all have, in our bodies, elements of both sexes, so in our sex reactions we have possibilities of sexual attraction to our own sex as well as to the opposite one. That is true of the great majority of us. But there are people who are predominantly homoerotic. How many of them are there?

Investigations of various types have been made in many countries along these lines. We may take it as generally accepted that in every hundred men, there is at least one definitely homoerotic personality; among every hundred women, at least one clean-cut homoerotic female. Take the population of an ordinary city and work out how many homoerotic types, among women and men, such a city must contain. Then there are transition-types that we may call "bierotic" for want of a better name. They are attracted to both sexes. Such women have homoerotic experiences, and yet marry and bear children. Such bi-erotic males may be good husbands, and yet be definitely attracted, now and then, by some member of their own sex. Of such types there are probably two in every hundred individuals. So you can see how great is the number of homoerotic men, to whom intercourse with a woman is as disgusting as intercourse with a man would be to the ordinary heteroerotic male: and how great the number of women who look upon intercourse with a man as disgusting and degrading, but who find their complete sexual satisfaction with some member of their own sex.[12]

[12]For the results of some of the investigations on the average numbers of

So much for numbers. Now how does it happen that homo-erotic men and women exist? Just how it happens—whether it is the result of some impeded development, like the mal-formation of the genital organs, or whether it is a natural variation of type, we do not know. But of one thing we may be sure: homoerotism is a *biological fact*. A woman is born with homoerotic desires. She is no more responsible for having them than she is responsible for having red hair instead of black. She is "born that way." She is not a pariah, not an out-cast; she has not "acquired" her type of reaction by evil sexual habits or by long periods of sexual excess. She may be the chastest of all chaste virgins; she may never have experienced any sexual reaction at all; but, until she dies, she will be, not man-loving, but woman-loving. That is the first thing that you must tell your homoerotic parishioners, patients or friends, when they come to you in great anguish of mind, terrified be-cause they are "not like other women," not "like other men." It is a terrible thing to realize that there is something, a very powerful something in your sex life, that is tabooed, perse-cuted, cursed by others as inherently evil and utterly disgusting. You must make such persons understand that they are neither outcasts nor debauchees; neither criminals nor pariahs. Make them realize that they are not responsible for their sexual desires; but that they *are* responsible for the way in which they allow these desires to translate themselves into action. Tell them that their type of love may be, if they will, just as high, just as ideal as the love of Dante for Beatrice, just as construc-tive in its results as the love of the noblest knight for the lady that he serves. It all lies with them, just as it does with all of us, for we are all responsible for what we create out of the rough material of our sexual desires. Above all, make them *accept* their type of reaction, their homoerotism. If they try to

homoerotics in various communities see *Jahrbuch für sexuelle Zwischenstufen, herausgegeben* von Dr. Magnus Hirschfeld (Leipzig: Max Spohr, 1898–1910), Vol. VI (1904), pp. 109–178. This series of "Year Books" contains invaluable material on the whole subject of homoerotism.

pretend that it is not there, if they attempt to push it into the background of their minds, then, later on in life, when some unexpected temptation comes, when their powers of resistance have been rubbed thin, the repressed urge may break out in almost irresistible force and may engulf them in some tragedy that will ruin their lives and cut them off from possible spheres of usefulness and of service. The only way to deal with homoerotism is to accept it; to look upon it, if you please, as a kind of handicap, and by God's help, to use it constructively, to make it into an achievement. It can be done. I have seen it done over and over again.[18]

Let us consider first the homoerotic woman. Among women of this type one finds all the variations between extreme male and feminine characteristics. It is quite wrong to imagine that the homoerotic woman is predominantly masculine, that she wears men's clothes and has a deep bass voice. Of course, there are many homoerotic women of this kind. But, on the other hand, a homoerotic woman may present all the ordinary feminine characteristics of the average heteroerotic female. In such cases, the homoerotism is not so noticeable in early childhood. On the other hand, if a girl during her early years is a tom-boy, if she loves to play boys' games, if all her early

[18]There is much misunderstanding about the nature of homoerotic acts. The activities of homoerotic women are a kind of mutual autoerotism, unless one of the homoerotic partners is very markedly male and copies the part of the male agent in sexual relations. Among men, most people understand by "Sodomy"—as the law and moral theology do, a "rectal coitus." This is quite inexact. The great majority of male homoerotic acts is a mutual masturbation; or a placing of the penis between the thighs or legs, *coitus inter femora.* Actual penetration of the rectum is rare; more rare than in ordinary heteroerotic *marital intercourse.* Oral coitus, i.e., the use of the mouth and lips, is no more common in homoerotic male intercourse than in the promiscuous intercourse of men and women. There is also a curious persistent obsession about the danger of all oral intercourse; it is supposed to sap vitality, to cause "locomotor ataxia," and general pre-senile decay. This is not correct. In general one may say, that in homoerotic intercourse the same variations of the sexual act are found as are found in heteroerotic activities. There are probably more husbands who use rectal coitus than there are homoerotic men who do the same thing.

emotional friendships are with girls; if she likes to play with boys but strikes them if they try to kiss her, then such symptoms do suggest homoerotism. Nevertheless, we have all known women who presented all these early characteristics, and who yet married and made excellent wives and mothers. One cannot always diagnose a homoerotic case entirely by such early symptoms as these.

I am sure that all of you have, at some time or other, met a happy homoerotic female pair. Very often, one of the partners is markedly feminine, while the other has evident masculine traits. In homoerotic slang, the female partner is called the "Margey," and the masculine partner, the "Collar and Tie." The world looks with amusement, but without criticism, on such pairs of so-called "old-maids." Not for a moment would I suggest that definite homoerotic acts take place between all the partners in such pairs. Far from it. But the motive power that holds them together is a sexual one—a homoerotic one—even though the two women may live together as chastely as two nuns. Their love may be as near a purely mental or spiritual relationship as is possible among human beings who have to live and express themselves in material bodies.[14]

Let me warn you here against one danger—against giving one kind of advice to homoerotic women, a kind of advice which, if followed, usually leads to unhappiness and tragedy. When a homoerotic woman seeks you out in her difficulties, do *not* say to her, "My dear, all you need is to get married. Overcome your imagined repugnance to the male, and plunge boldly into matrimony. Then, all these peculiar desires of yours will find a natural outlet." It is far easier for the homoerotic woman to follow this advice than it is for the homoerotic man. In marital intercourse, the rôle of the woman is a

[14]For the frequency of such female relationships and for the manner in which most women regard them, let me refer you again to Dr. Bement Davis, *op. cit.*, chap. X, "Homosexuality, the Unmarried College Women," and chap. XI, "Homosexuality, the Married Woman," pp. 238–239.

passive one. If she hates the act, she can at least be quiet and endure it. Far otherwise with the man. If he hates the act, he simply cannot perform it. He is impotent. Therefore, wrong advice in these matters has sent many a homoerotic woman plunging blindly into matrimony. She finds that she *can* submit to her husband, hideous though his presence may be. She finds that she *can* bear children; and she may become a good mother, especially to her daughters. As the mother of sons, she is usually a failure, unless she herself has so many male characteristics that she can sympathize with and understand her boys. But she can never understand, can never satisfy her husband and his love. And later in life, she may fall intensely in love with some woman. If she does, she will leave her husband, she will leave her children without a moment's hesitation, and will follow her "mate," the "only real love of her life." Many a marriage comes to an evil end in this way. Or else the wife's female friend comes to dominate her so completely that her own husband is no longer master in his own home. The "Collar and Tie" of a married "Margey" is infinitely worse than the most dominating mother-in-law.

Women are socially far freer in their homoerotic relationships than men. Society—the Law (except in Austria)—has always looked with a certain tolerance upon those friendships that are often called "Sapphic," because the great Greek poetess Sappho was herself renowned in her day as a homoerotic woman. Even in the etymology or the nomenclature of homoerotism, the women have always come out ahead of the men. Who would not prefer to be associated with the name of the greatest poetess of Greece rather than with the men of Sodom and Gomorrah? "Sapphist" or "Sapphic" has a not unpleasant sound. But "Sodomite," or "Sodomitic" sounds quite differently.[15] The difference between the male

[15]Many modern scholars have put themselves to infinite pains to prove that Sappho was a self-restrained virginal president of a sort of female Girton, or Barnard in the Island of Lesbos. To the psychologist such an assumption is not only ridiculous, it is humanly impossible. If Sappho was not a female

and the female homoerotic is best expressed by a quotation
from one of the cleverest of modern French women writers,
Collette Willy. In one of her novels,[16] her heroine, Claudine,
who has had an adolescent homoerotic experience, is talking
with her cousin, a clean-cut homoerotic boy. She tells him to
be careful about his amours. He replies that she herself is
having feminine amours of her own. "May be," Claudine
says; "but the things that I do are smiled upon as *jeux de jeunes
pensionaires,* while your form of amusement is *presque une
maladie.*"[17]

One important question, that applies to both male and
female homoerotics, had better be answered here. The average
man still has a great fear of homoerotism. To discover that he
has a homoerotic son or daughter would be to him a distinct
social disgrace. He distrusts all homoerotic women; he hates
and loathes all homoerotic men. He is really afraid of the
entire group. One of these "abnormal women" might get hold
of one of his daughters and make her as abnormal as herself.
Or one of these "debased men" might corrupt and ruin one of
his chaste sons. He does his best to be just. He may not want
all "decadent rotten men and women" put into jail. But he

homoerotic, then she did not write the verse that has always born her name.
One trouble with scholars and university professors is that they do not know
very much about the plain facts of human sex activity. For the Greek attitude toward Sapphic love, compare Lucian's *Dialogues of Courtesans* or *He-
tairae.* An English translation with the Greek text is published by the Athe-
nian Society in its volume of Lucian, pp. 100–105. See Teubner text of Lucian, Vol. III, pp. 243–244.

[16]*Claudine à l'ecole, Claudine à Paris, Claudine en menage, Claudine s'en
va,* by Collette Willy. New ed. published by Albin Michel, Paris, 1931. "Ces
petites amusettes-la (i.e., homoerotic relations between women and girls) ça
s'appelle pour les gamines 'jeux de pensionaires,' mais quand il s'agit de
garçons de dix-sept ans, c'est presque une maladie." *Claudine à Paris,* p. 61.

[17]Modern homoerotic woman is gradually emancipating herself more and
more from social taboos. Read for example such books as R. Hall, *The Well
of Loneliness.* The male homoerotic cannot make any such public campaign
for general recognition. His form of "love" is a crime on the Statute Book.
But the openness of modern discussion, especially among young people, is doing much to lift the old taboos.

does not want any of them around his home. He is afraid of
their power to corrupt, to contaminate.

For his comfort, it ought to be said that homoerotism is
like poets, it is born not made. If a girl is not biologically
homoerotic, no amount of homoerotic intercourse can make
her so. Any experienced teacher in a girls' school could tell
you the same thing. She sees, for example, one of her girls
who is always in love with some other girl; who has countless affairs of this kind, affairs that are definitely physical.
And during three or four years of such a girl's life at boarding school she is soaked in an atmosphere of homoerotism. But,
the moment that her school days are over, or even during her
holidays while still a school-girl, she turns with absolute cer-
tainty toward her normal sexual partner—toward the boy—
toward the man. All her homoerotic experience—the only
sex experience that she has had—has not been able to make
her homoerotic or to change the biological conditioning of her
heteroerotic nature. The same thing is true of boys or men.
Ask any master at some large boarding school. Or better yet,
ask the chaplain or the social worker in some large penitenti-
ary. In prison—where the men are all cut off from their normal intercourse with women—there is plenty of temporary
homoerotism, simply as a means of escape, an artificial outlet
for dammed-up sexual emotion. There are always certain
prisoners who are known to be sexually adventurous. The moment that some new prisoner appears, some good-looking
young fellow, these men are after him at once. And their
sex activity may go on for years, for all the long years
of their imprisonment. But, once their sentence has expired,
once they are free again to go where they please, their feet
carry them immediately, automatically toward the source of
their real desires—toward women. All those long years of
homoerotic activity and of intercourse were powerless to turn
them into artificial homoerotics.

So fathers and mothers, and school teachers too, need not be afraid of any "contamination" from homoerotic individuals. If a boy, after an homoerotic friendship, persists during the rest of his life as a homoerotic, he has not been made into a homoerotic by his experience. He was born a homoerotic. And he would have remained so, even if he had never had any sexual experience at all, or had known it in the lap of some chambermaid in his mother's home.

I realize that these statements may be challenged. I can only say that in my rather long experience I have never come across a homoerotic woman whose homoerotism was artifically created by some homoerotic experience. Or any boy, who after some homoerotic friendship, became homoerotic on that account. If one examines carefully the so-called cases of artificially induced homoerotism, one will always find, I believe, in the patient's early history, definite symptoms of homoerotism that were there, plain, for any one to see, long before the actual homoerotic experience which is erroneously supposed to be the real cause of the patient's present condition.

Our courts, or most of them, have come to the conclusion that it is unjust to punish a man who has had homoerotic relationships with several adolescent boys and to let the boys go free. For no one can force another to sexual intercourse unless he drug his victim or make him unconscious. Neither will a decent heteroerotic boy allow the advances of a homoerotic man. If he does allow them, if he submits— especially if he is only too willing to take in return presents or actual money—if the homoerotic act is a crime, then the boy deserves as much punishment as the man. Indeed, in our present days, the ideal of their son's "purity" that is cherished by so many mothers; the concept of their daughter's "perfect and unsoiled chastity" that is held by so many fathers; these ideals and concepts, however noble they may be, are not borne out by the actual facts that are established by the daily lives of these same sons and daughters. Give the boys and the girls a little credit for having sense enough to know more about life than we did at their age so many years ago.

Let me, however, guard against one misunderstanding. Sexual intercourse of *any* type with a *minor*—that is, with a boy or a girl who has not reached the "age of consent"— ought to be and is a crime in almost every modern country. This age of consent varies in different lands; and rightly so. For the Italian girl of fourteen develops more rapidly than her English sister of the same age. There are men who are only attracted to sex relations with children. Not old, worn-out roués either.[18] With older women they are impotent. One is intensely sorry for such people. But the children must be protected as much as possible from forcible sex experiences.[19] Therefore, both homoerotic and heteroerotic must not invade the rights of minors; of those who are not legallv able to consent to any sexual act.

While speaking of legal restrictions, it may be well to point out that the reaction of the Law to homoerotism is somewhat like that toward Divorce in the United States. It varies according to locality. The act that is a crime and punishable by five years' imprisonment in America, is not punished at all in France, Italy, Belgium, Germany, and most European countries. All European countries, in which the Code Napoleon is the basis of the criminal law, accept homoerotic intercourse between two adult persons as a normal reaction with which the law has no concern. It is well, therefore, to remember, when we are tempted to condemn some unfortunate homoerotic man who has got into trouble with the law, that his offense depends on the fact that he happens to be living in the United States instead of in Europe.

Before we begin the discussion of the various types of male

---

[18]I have known cases of fine athletic youths of eighteen to twenty-four who have been sent to jail repeatedly for so-called sexual assaults on minors. All that they did was to uncover the little girl's body, and press their own bodies against hers. They had absolutely no sex interest in mature women.

[19]Nevertheless, many men have had the experience of being followed in the streets by little girls of ten, who make definite sex suggestions and ask for ten cents.

homoerotic, it may be well to point out one frequently forgotten fact; namely, the strength of the homoerotic sexual
urge. The ordinary heteroerotic man and woman find, as a
usual thing, no reasons for trying to repress the expressions of
their sexual desires. If a man kisses a woman, no one thinks
much about it. But if a man kisses a younger man, or if an
older woman is constantly petting a younger one, then, at
once, there is suspicion and gossip—suspicion and gossip that
may be utterly without any real foundation. The homoerotic,
especially the homoerotic man, is forced, all his life, to wear
a mask. He must be constantly on his guard, lest some one
suspect the secret that he has trained himself to hide. He is
repressed and obstructed at every point, even in the most
harmless expressions of his sexual life. Now, as we have
already seen, emotional reactions that find no outlet do one
of two things. On the one hand, they may "go bad," like wine
that has been bottled up too long; and then they turn into
phobias and obsessions. That is why so many repressed homoerotics develop all kinds of mental maladjustments; that is
why they are so familiar to the practicing psychiatrist. They
come to him, not for their homoerotism—for that secret they
hope to keep even from their physician—but for some relief
from the torments of depression and of fear. Unless the
psychiatrist can get at the root of their trouble, he will
not be able to do them much permanent good. On the other
hand, repressed sex reactions, instead of transforming themselves into mental difficulties, may simply increase the sexual
tension, and grow in strength beneath the calm exterior of
the individual's life until they suddenly break out with overwhelming force. Some chance temptation may light the
train of powder that has been already laid to the magazine,
and there is an explosion, which may annihilate the individual's good name, ruin his career and make him really an out-
cast forever. When we hear of some man who has finally
yielded to his homoerotic urge, yielded in some way that was

so sure of detection as to seem utterly foolhardly, we must not forget that in his past life there have been thousands of temptations successfully resisted for the single temptation to which he has finally succumbed. There is no doubt that the homoerotic sexual urge, just because it is so often repressed, is much more powerful, much more difficult to resist than the heteroerotic impulses of the average man and woman.

Among homoerotic women, we have described the extreme masculine type and the intermediate types that run all the way from "Collar and Tie" to the most effeminate "Margey." The same thing is true among men. But the variations are much more noticeable.

At one end of the scale stands the homoerotic man who is so intensely and so completely masculine that he can find no place for women in his life at all. Women simply do not enter into his scheme of existence. Physically, he is the best type of male animal, often an athlete—almost always what is called a "man's man." He is looked up to by members of his own sex. And although the opposite sex look up to him in a somewhat different way, yet they have their trouble for their pains, and always imagine that "Mister so and so must have had an unfortunate love affair in his youth, because he has no interest in women." The average heteroerotic woman is the bitter irreconcilable enemy of the homoerotic man. For she resents intensely the fact that he is immune to feminine attractions. It has always seemed to me a remarkable fact that so many women utterly fail to understand the reason for such a man's coldness and lack of interest. One hears a great deal about feminine intuition. One meets with many curious examples of its power. But there seems to be one field of human life in which this boasted intuition does not work; the field of sexual relations. In this domain the woman's intuition seems to be inhibited by her unwillingness to believe that any man can possibly exist who is not susceptible to the charms of at least one woman. Often, one has to smile behind one's hand when a woman is seen pursuing with her well-meant attentions a homoerotic male of unusual physical attractions. She will never get any reaction out of him. And yet she goes on trying all the harder. Her feminine intuition ought to warn her instinctively that here is indeed a case of Love's Labor's Lost.

This extreme masculine homoerotic type may well be called the Greek type. For it embodies the best elements in that type of love, in the Heavenly Eros, that was the ideal of the young Plato. Such men are instinctively drawn to younger men; less frequently to men of their own age, or to the adolescent. Seldom, if ever, to immature boys.[20] And it must be admitted in their favor that mere sexual satisfaction is rarely the motive of their affairs of the heart. When they become interested in some younger male, their chief desire is to make him like themselves—to make his body strong—to train his mind—to make him a *man*. They want to be able to say to themselves: "Such and such a young fellow, who has been my intimate friend for the past two years, is now all the better for having known me, for having come under my influence. He is stronger, more self-reliant—more athletic—a better scholar—in every way more of a man. If, during our friendship, certain physical acts have taken place, I regret them, not because I think them wrong, but because they make our relationship fall somewhat short of the true Platonic ideal. They have been secondary reactions. Had they never taken place, we should still have been as close friends as ever. I do not love merely my friend's body. I love *him*. And I love his complete and perfect manhood of mind and body more than anything else."

So many people judge of homoerotism by their experiences with the effeminate homoerotic type. When a "real man" displays homoerotic tendencies, they are utterly puzzled. They think that he must be insane and not responsible.

[20]See *The Palatine Anthology, Musa Puerilis,* Book XII, passim.

This masculine type always plays the dominating rôle in any sex relationship. But such a man tries to dominate his younger friend because he wants to raise him to his own level of manhood. He is always the active agent, the educator, the leader, the captain. Out of such men really great teachers, really powerful leaders of youth are made. They are the men who gladly give their whole lives to youth, who remain as beloved masters in some great boarding-school, who spend their years as assistant deans of undergraduates, who squander all their free time on boys' clubs and other activities of a similar nature. All that they ask is an opportunity of serving youth somehow, and if ever they lose their touch with youth, they are unhappy, useless. Many men of this type pass their entire lives without ever experiencing any directly physical relationship with the young people whom they love and serve. Among all types of male homoerotics, they are the most continent, the least self-indulgent. Sometimes they come to tragic ends. Sometimes, after years of continent service, their self-control slips. And then some boy, who in reality would rather cut off his right hand than harm the man who has done so much for him, talks too freely, and unintentionally pulls down the roof over the head of his hero. Then, there is a "scandal." Then the unfortunate man has to disappear. And the one thing that breaks his heart is not so much the disgrace, as the fact that he has automatically cut himself off from doing the one kind of work in the world that he loves to do. He has cut himself off from Youth. Wise is the headmaster who, in spite of an occasional scandal, is willing and able to shut his eyes to the exceptional happening, to remember the man's powerful influence and leadership in the past, and to hang on to him somehow as a valuable factor in the school's future.

Naturally, no headmaster would wish to retain on his staff a self-indulgent homoerotic man, who is too much of a Greek and too little of a Christian. But there are Greek Christians aplenty among homoerotic males. And they are often too valuable to lose.

Next to this masculine type comes the mildly effeminate homoerotic. He does not always play a purely active rôle in his emotional relationships. He may have a certain amount of feminine passiveness. His friends are mostly men of his own age, but almost never men of his own sexual type. He is attracted to the normal heteroerotic male. During his early boyhood, he may have shown certain homoerotic symptoms. His mother may tell you that as a boy he always preferred to play with girls' to dress occasionally in girls' clothes, to play with dolls instead of with tin soldiers. Yet such symptoms do not always mean homoerotism. A very effeminate boy may develop into an effeminate man, and yet may marry a rather dominating woman and become a happy husband and a still happier father. However, such symptoms *suggest* a homoerotic conditioning, even if they do not always absolutely prove its existence.

Finally, there is the extreme type of effeminate homoerotic man. I must admit that, for myself, I find it often very hard to be just and sympathetic with such types. Yet, I blame myself bitterly for my lack of sympathy. For such men have just as much right to freedom, health and the pursuit of happiness as the most matter-of-fact heteroerotic human being. They often feel themselves to be women, they react like women, they want to be loved, as if they were women, by some rough, dominating male. Their rôle is always a passive one.[21] In the old days, when vaudeville had not been ruined by the moving-pictures, you would see in almost every "show" a female impersonator; that is, a man dressed as a woman, who would sing songs in a high soprano and who then, just before leaving the stage, would pull off a blond wig, expose a very masculine head, and bid the audience farewell in a deep bass voice. Such female impersonators are, so far as I know, all homoerotics of the effeminate type.[22]

[21]Almost all effeminate homoerotics desire and practice oral intercourse. To the masculine homoerotic oral intercourse is an abomination.
[22]A modern novel dealing with this type is *Strange Brother*, by Blair Niles

In your parishes and in your social agencies you will have to
deal with this type, and it may give you much more trouble
than the masculine homoerotic, who minds his own business,
who rarely gets into difficulties, and who, in his service and his
love of youth, finds a satisfactory motive for living. If you do
hear of his troubles, it will be only in the Tribunal of Penance. But the effeminate type often hangs around Catholic parishes, especially parishes in which there is a great deal of
showy colorful ritual and not much practice of the Catholic
religion—parishes in which there is a Solemn High Mass every
Sunday with a hundred or more people making their post-
breakfast communions—parishes in which there are plenty of
pretty processions, but no confessionals. I am willing to admit
that such parishes become fewer every year. But the effeminate
homoerotic loves them. He likes the bright colors, the ritual,
the bowings and the crossings. He does *not* like getting up
early and making his communion before breakfast, and surely
he does not want to go to confession. Sooner or later, he will
get into definite trouble. He may be arrested; he may be
cruelly "beaten up" by some blackmailer. He will come to you
for help. And whether you like him or not, he belongs to you;
he is a soul in distress; you must help him if possible. Such
men are often very difficult to help. They know all the modern quasi-scientific clap-trap talk about the ˙down-trodden
homoerotic. They know that they are not responsible for their
sexual desires. But they go a step farther and insist that they
are not responsible either for their sexual activities. "Society,"
they often say, owes them happiness—their own kind of happiness. They are doing no harm to any one. The older men, who
put up with their intimate company, go with them of their
own free will. And they demand that you should protect them

(a woman), (New York: Horace Liveright, 1931). See also two rather painful books, privately printed: *The Female Impersonators: An Autobiography,*
by Ralph Werther, or "Jennie June " (New York: The Medico-Legal Journal
Co., 1922), and by the same writer *The Autobiography of an Androgyne*
(same publishers, 1918).

from the results of their actions. They do not believe that it is possible or even healthy to learn continence. Why should not they "express themselves" in their own way? They take the attitude of the unjustly persecuted. And sometimes I feel that, in a sense, they are right. With them, the sexual urge seems so strong, that perhaps it *is* impossible for them to resist temptation. Only they go out to meet temptation. They make it for themselves. If they do not find it, they complain to you that they are lonely, that nobody loves them. I confess that I am often at a loss to help people of this kind. And yet I have known men of this type to take themselves sternly in hand and, little by little, to dominate their impulses. But before they can even begin to do this, you must entirely readjust their sense of values. You must make them see that the world does *"not* owe them sexual happiness," that continence is not only possible but healthy also; and above all you must teach them to fill their imaginations with some other interest besides sex. Make them stop whining and complaining. If they have not much manhood, then at least show them what a self-sacrificing, self-denying creature a woman can be. If they *must* imitate women, for God's sake let them imitate female virtues, womanly restraint, instead of imitating female vices. If they must feel and act like women, let them act like high-hearted, self-controlled women, and not like prostitutes. Such men can be helped. But what they need most is the discipline of the Christian life; not merely the ritual and the ceremonial that looks pretty but means little and costs still less. If, by way of the sacraments, you can introduce this element of self-discipline into their lives, you will have helped them indeed.

There are, nevertheless, many homoerotics of this type, who are neither self-indulgent nor self-centred, men who live their whole lives in constant terror lest their secret be discovered. And for all members of this class, the pastor as well as the social worker must have an abiding pity. For, among all types of homoerotic men, this effeminate type is the most despised, the most tormented, the most persecuted. Among certain groups of self-righteous heteroerotic youth, it is considered a meritorious act to "beat up a fairy."[28] And the "fairy" has no real redress. I have found in the cells of some station-house men of this type who had been beaten into insensibility, then picked up by some policeman on his rounds and tossed into a cell, until the "damn fairy" can pull himself together and slink off, amidst the jeers of the officials. He knows that it is no use to complain. If he does, the magistrate will imagine that he has been trying to "seduce some pure youth" and that he has only got what he deserved.

No, this type is not attractive. But neither is some unfortunate mongrel-puppy attractive, a puppy that has been tormented and chased with his tail between his legs, until he snaps at every hand held out to feed him. You may not admire the dog's looks. But you can't help being sorry for him. And although he may never take a first prize in a dog show, he might, if properly cared for and broken of his bad habits of eating from swill-pails and of rolling himself in decayed matter, become a faithful watch-dog and a not unpleasant companion. You will, I hope, forgive this plea for the under-dog. One of my most persistent faults is a tendency to always take sides with the man or with the animal who has been kicked and mauled into sullenness and rebellion.

I have already told you, in discussing the heteroerotics, how to evaluate any sexual relationship. There is not much to be said for the heteroerotic relationship that is purely animal, and that never rises above that animal plane of physical satisfaction. There is much to be said for any sexual relationship in which the dominant motive is what we call love: constructive love; a love that is unselfish, that is more interested in giving than in taking, more interested in the loved one than in the

---

[28]For some obscure reason the effeminate homoerotic is known as a "fairy," just as the boy or youth who has a masculine homoerotic partner is called a "punk."

lover. When that element is present, even in a slight degree, there is hope for that relationship. It may be made into something higher, better, more useful. As long as the sexual satisfaction is a secondary reaction, so long the relationship has possibilities of constructive development.

Judge homoerotic relationships in the same way. If you are disturbed by gossip about some man in your parish, or in your social group, about his influence on the older boys, examine a little his influence on the boy in whom he seems most interested. If he is really interested in this boy's welfare, if he is willing to sacrifice his own ease, to go without small luxuries in order to help the boy; if, in a word, the boy can say, "I am really better off for knowing him," then, I think you will do no harm if you permit that relationship and others like it to continue. On the other hand, I should be inclined to interfere if the older man were merely showering a boy with presents that cost him nothing, merely paying him, in the form of gifts, the price that every prostitute or demi-virgin demands.[24]

And so, when some father comes to you in distress about his adolescent son, a son who has no interest in girls, who is always hanging around with some younger man or boy, or who has "come under the evil influence of some older man," go into the matter carefully. Get the son's early history. You may find

[24] I do not think that many men can attain to the objective judgment of a man of my acquaintance. This man had a son who was rather delicate, shy, backward, not athletic. He sent him to a well-known school. Here the boy came under the influence of one of the younger masters. He improved greatly, physically and mentally. While the boy was still at school, there was a "scandal" about this younger master. The headmaster investigated. It was found that the young man had had sexual relations with two or three of the older boys. Knowing that my friend's son had been intimate with the young master, the headmaster sent for my friend and told him of the master's "scandalous behavior." My friend said, "I think, Sir, that you'll make a mistake if you lose that young man from your staff. I don't know what the fathers of the other boys, with whom he has behaved scandalously, would say, but I should like to say this. When my boy came to this school, he was a good deal of a sissy, he couldn't swim, or play games. He was shy, and introspective. During the two years of Mr. X's influence over him, my boy has be-

homoerotic symptoms there; you may not. But at any rate do reassure the father. Make him understand that the boy is not perverse or decadent or rotten. Send for the boy. Tell him plainly just what homoerotism is. Get the father and son together in your office. Then if you have made up your mind that the son is really a homoerotic, explain to father and son that the boy is not responsible for his desires; that he has been born with a certain type of sexual reaction. Let him, if he likes, look upon it as a kind of handicap. But don't let him be *afraid* of it. Make him accept it; make his father accept it. And then show him how he can make his particular type of love as ideal, and as fine as the love of Jonathan for David. Give him continence as an ideal. But tell him not to despair if he cannot always live up to it. Establish between the father and the son a feeling of mutual confidence and understanding. Make the father realize that he has no reason for despising his son. He can at least be sure of one thing. Whatever difficulties his son may meet with in life, he will never get into trouble with women. And help the son to talk openly with his father; make him willing to ask his father's help if he ever does get into trouble in connection with his sexual life. For all homoerotics, especially the males, are exposed to danger from the lowest of all criminals, the blackmailer. A young heteroerotic man, who has had a liaison with some woman, has very little to fear from her in the way of public disgrace. But if the young man be

come a different person. He has learned to swim, to play games. He can hold up his own end among other boys. He has become more of a man. You say that Mr. X has probably had with him what you call scandalous relations. Very well. You may think me strange, but I don't mind. Mr. X is a clean, good-looking, well-developed young fellow. My boy must meet sexual experiences in one way or another. And I had rather that he had his first sexual experiences in the arms of a decent fellow like Mr. X, than in the lap of some diseased chamber-maid or the skirts of a neighbor's sexually starved daughter. What my boy has gained, in manhood, from Mr. X has been, I consider, very cheaply bought." The headmaster nearly had a fit. The young master disappeared, although my friend tried to get into touch with him before he left the city. I do not know what has become of that young man. But my friend's son is a fine fellow.

homoerotic, if he has had some physical relationship with another man—one of those parasites that fatten on the sexual mistakes of others—he may be blackmailed and bled white. The gravest danger that arises from the present attitude of our laws toward homoerotism is the frequency with which these legal taboos furnish opportunities for the blackmailer. Especially for the male prostitute or semi-prostitute.

People forget that prostitution is not entirely a feminine form of social activity. There is a whole class of self-indulgent, lazy young men—some homoerotic themselves, others of the usual heteroerotic type—who live on the favors of older homoerotic males. They are indirect, graceful blackmailers. If such a man happens to spend the night with a homoerotic acquaintance, and if there has been even the slightest suggestion of homoerotic intercourse, then, if the guest walks off with his host's watch or pocket book, the host has no redress. He dare not go to the police. And if he demands back his property from his guest of a night, this same guest will retaliate with veiled threats that make the renewal of such demands an impossibility.

Still lower down in the scale is the young, good-looking man, who hangs about older women, who travels around with them as "secretary." Sometimes I cannot help feeling sorry for such men when I see the type of ancient harridan, jealous, dominating, insistent in her demands, on whom the youth is dependent for the luxurious life of the big hotels, for his pocket money, for even his clothes and his tobacco. It must be a bitter slavery. You may meet him during some hours of rebellion. But he seldom succeeds in getting free. For he has forgotten what regular work is like. He is really fit for nothing in the world of active men. After a few spasmodic efforts, he relapses into his old servitude, hoping that, if he sticks it out long enough, his "belle amie"—aged seventy-five—may die and leave him something in her will. When she does die, her money usually goes to her family, or to a home for stray dogs.

She has not been ashamed to flaunt her "secretary" in the face of society while she was alive. But she does not intend to leave behind her any excuse for scandal by providing for him in her last will and testament.

Before closing this chapter, there are three other subjects that must be considered, two of them closely associated with the sexual life, the other correlated with it.[25] There are two extreme forms of sexual activity that are called by the names of two men—men who represented in themselves extreme cases of these same sexual reactions. At the beginning of the nineteenth century there lived in Austria a young nobleman, named Sascher-Masoch. He wrote a number of books, the best known of which is *Die Venus in Peltz*. These books all deal with sex experiences, but it is a peculiar form of sexuality. The masochists, as we call such men or women, get their sexual satisfaction, not directly from the sexual act itself, but from the infliction on themselves of physical pain, of humiliation. In almost all the important houses of prostitution, there is a special room for the masochist; it is filled with various instruments of torture, especially with whips and scourges; for the masochist gets intense sexual satisfaction from flagellation, from being chained up and beaten up, and utterly dominated by some stronger personality.[26] The self-tormentor belongs in this category. Boys or girls who love to cut themselves, to keep little wounds open; who in their childish games always want to be the victim that is burned at the stake or the prisoner that is to be executed, are displaying masochistic symptoms. The masochistic man wants to be dominated by some strong, cruel woman. He wants her to maltreat him, to put her booted foot on his neck, to hold him in absolute subjection. Many so-called "hen-pecked" husbands are of this type. They are hen-pecked

[25]In the Clinical Material of this chapter, cases of sadism, masochism and of the inferiority complex will be found, which will give more detailed descriptions of such reactions than is possible in the chapter itself.

[26]Flagellants who developed so widely in Europe during the Middle Ages were probably masochists.

because they like it. So also the woman who longs for a "cave man" companion who will stun her and carry her off; or for a mysterious "sheik" who will ravish her away on the back of his Arab charger.

Inasmuch as the woman's rôle in sexual intercourse is normally a passive one, therefore there is a masochistic element in all women. The clinging-vine type who looks up at the man saying, "Ah, you are so much stronger than I," is longing for a dominating personality that will satisfy her masochistic desires. In males, when the masochism is pronounced, we get a type that stands out more prominently because the rôle of submission and subjection is not normally the rôle of the male animal. However, masochists do little harm except to themselves. They do not disturb society, they are not socially dangerous.

Quite different from masochism is the type of sex reaction that is named from the Marquis de Sade.[27] De Sade also wrote books in which his type of sexual reactions is described. But he also practiced what he preached. Sadism, as it is called, is the type of sexual satisfaction that comes from the inflicting of physical suffering upon others. And the sign over the door is blood—red blood—blood lust. Every war lets loose all sadistic individuals. They revel in killing, in the infliction of pain. The sight of blood makes them drunk.[28] During every war one hears about the "atrocities" committed by the enemy. Of course, such atrocities do occur. But there are really just as many English and American atrocities as there are German or

[27]Among de Sade's most important works are *Justine ou les malheurs de la vertu,* imprimé en Hollande chez les Libraires Associés, 1791, 2 Vols.; and *La nouvelle Justine en Hollande,* same printers, 1797. See *L'Enfer de la Bibliothêque Nationale,* nouvelle edition, Paris, 1919, *Bibliotheque des curieux.* Nos. 94, 106, 500–538, 802, 803, 804, 807, 808–813.

[28]I have never forgotten an experience at a big Spanish bullfight. I was sitting next to a little Spanish woman and her ten-year-old boy. The bull had already gored two horses that had dragged themselves around the arena with their entrails trailing on the ground. But two horses were not enough for the audience. It wanted more blood. And I remember the little boy in his excitement standing up and shouting in Spanish, "More blood, more blood." There is a sadistic element in us all.

French atrocities. For there are sadists in every nation. And no one nation has a monopoly of them.

I am often asked if I believe in "demoniacal possession." I usually answer or try to answer from my own experience with sadistic cases. For, in some such cases, there is such a suggestion of evil—of evil for its own sake—such a joy in the infliction of pain, that it seems as if the patient were really obsessed by some evil power. This is especially noticeable when such a patient recognizes his tendencies and is afraid of them, realizing himself that he is sometimes forced to do certain things that he hates, impelled by a force that he cannot resist. Of all the appalling things with which the psychiatrist, the pastor or the social worker has to deal, I think that sadism is the worst, the most appalling. There is only one way to deal with such people, only one way so far as I know, to help them. And they need help badly enough, God knows. It is the old way that I have already insisted upon so often.

In the first place, keep out of your voice, out of your whole mental atmosphere, any suggestion of horror, of condemnation. Do not let your patient see that you shrink from him. Remember again Our Lord's words, "Judge not." If you are brought into contact with a boy who has been torturing animals in some hideous way; if you are asked for help by a man who is a dirty fighter, who loves to attack and to smash up any unsuspecting person that crosses his path, a man who loves the sight of blood, who goes to prize-fights, not because he rejoices in clever boxing, but because he gets intense excitement from seeing two men battering one another into bloody pulp —don't scold, don't hold up your hands in horror. Explain to the boy or the man just what is wrong with him. Show him his mental handicap. It is a very serious one. Make him accept it. And try your best to take away his fear of it. If he fears it and tries to run away from it, it will overtake him sooner or later. But if he can try to understand it; if he will recognize it as something that is to be overcome by understanding it; then you will have some chance of teaching him how to control its activities.

Sadism, in its grosser manifestations, is, as a usual thing, more frequent among men than among women. But there are plenty of sadistic women in the world, nevertheless. Women who rejoice in making others unhappy, who are strangely enlivened when they hear of some neighbor's misfortune, who are always nagging and tormenting those whom they pretend to love. Occasionally, one sees the two elements of masochism and of sadism illustrated in some married couple. The man who comes home a little drunk and who loves to beat up his wife, to inflict pain somehow, is reacting sadistically. His wife, who rather likes to be beaten up and who almost will kill any third person trying to protect her, is functioning in a masochistic way. In sexual relationships the man as the aggressor, the pain-giver, has the sadistic rôle; the woman, as the passive partner, the pain-bearer, is masochistic. Such reactions, like homoerotism, like depression and elation, are common to all men. Every one of us is sometimes depressed or elated; every one of us has homoerotic tendencies; every one of us has sadistic and masochistic elements in our personalities. The pathology of these tendencies begins when they are developed to excess; the mental sickness, the maladjustments lie in the extremes. The psychiatrist is often tempted to return for his philosophy to Aristotle and to his doctrine of the Golden Mean, in which lie health and proper adjustment to life and its duties.

All these sexual reactions are supposed to be governed and restrained by what ethical philosophers call "sanctions." Thus, the sanction of human life, its inviolability, should prevent the sadist from indulging his blood-lust. But sanctions vary in strength with different individuals; they are matters of mental habit. My own mental habits, the products of my life-environment and experience, may automatically protect me from stealing. I could not steal if I wanted to. For it is easier for me not to steal than to steal. On the other hand, my sanction against fornication may be worn thin by past habits of sexual indulgence. It is so much easier for me to yield to this temptation than not to yield to it, that it becomes almost impossible for me to make any lasting resistance. But there is scarcely any sanction that cannot be swept away by some powerful emotion. And the wise man is he who learns, by dint of habit, to control or to limit his emotional reactions. Some of us are, by our very nature, apparently more emotionally stable than others. But all of us ought to aim at some sort of emotional control. And the man or the woman who has no ideal of this control, and who has what is commonly called a "temper" is gradually losing his or her hold on a very important element in human happiness and achievement. A "temper" is an emotional discharge, that takes place usually as the result of some utterly inadequate stimulus. A man has been annoyed and depressed all day by his business affairs. He comes home in the evening and at table one of the children upsets a glass of milk over his father's trousers. The result is like the turning of a wooden handle that sends an electric spark into a mass of nitroglycerine. The man "blows up." And, while blowing up, he does things and he says things that may be of far-reaching consequences, things that he would never have done or have said had he not had a "bad temper." I need not remind you of the evils that a quick-tempered woman may bring down on the heads of her family or of her friends. People are much too easy-going about this whole question of "temper." When some emotionally unstable man gets into a difficult situation as a result of his "temper," so many of us shrug our shoulders and murmur, "Well, you know his temper has always been so uncontrolled." From my own experience, I think I may justly say that I have known no form of mental maladjustment that is more fraught with the possibilities of tragedy than this same disregard of emotional control that we look upon merely as a harmless personal peculiarity. A "bad temper" is a dangerous companion. The man who harbors one and who makes no effort to dominate it, is going through life with a dynamite cartridge in his insides that may be exploded by any chance spark and that may scatter to the winds of heaven his own happiness and the happiness of his family.

Finally, I must say something about one other form of mental maladjustment that is very difficult to deal with, and that is often responsible for many unnecessary failures. We call it "a sense of inferiority," or an inferiority complex. Not long ago, a psychiatrist had an opportunity of examining a large number of undergraduates at an American university. He blocked out a group of these men whose development was impeded by various kinds of mental difficulties. And among this maladjusted group he found that more than 50 per cent were hampered and inhibited by this same sense of inferiority. It is a very subtle thing. It apparently begins to develop in early childhood. The first baby monopolizes the attention of the family. Then the second baby comes. The first child's "nose is out of joint." The normal child soon adjusts himself or herself to the idea of a baby brother or sister. But if the parents allow themselves to make comparisons, if the elder child hears its mother saying, "The baby is so much cleverer than Johnny was at its age," or "Johnny was never half as good-looking a baby as this last one"—then Johnny, if he be shy and introspective and easily hurt, begins to make comparisons for himself. He accepts it as an undisputed fact that the baby *is* cleverer and better looking than himself. What is the use of his struggling? He is evidently an inferior type of child. And then, if the younger brother or sister grows up and outstrips Johnny at school, if he or she is more popular than Johnny is, more athletic, more able to win prizes, then Johnny's sense of inferiority deepens. So all through life he finds himself comparing himself unfavorably with others. He may make a brave attempt to show people that he is *not* inferior; and he may succeed to a reasonable extent. But if his attempt meets with any

unexpected difficulty, if he has to pass through a period of discouragement or failure, he gives up at once. What is the use of
trying? He can never do what other boys do. He was born
inferior.

From such thoughts it is only a short step to mild ideas of
persecution, to self-pity. The young man who has acquired a
sense of inferiority assumes that he has never had a fair
chance. Nature gave him no good looks, he is little and skinny
and has a receding, weak chin, and he never had an opportunity for any real education. He forgets that he would not go
to college because he was sure he couldn't pass the examinations. So it goes on in later life. His partners in business have
double-crossed him, and there is no use to struggle. He is fore-
doomed to failure.

Unless you are familiar with the complexities of undergraduate life, or with the lives of young men between eighteen
and twenty-four, you will not realize how tormenting, how
obsessing such a sense of inferiority can be. It robs a young
man of all automatic happy living. He is always self-conscious,
self-critical, self-tormenting. He imagines that so-and-so does
not like him, when so-and-so does not give him even a passing
thought. He is on the look-out for imaginary slights. And he
does not react to them courageously, he does not try to find
out the reason for them, he simply accepts them as part of his
accursed heritage of inferiority. Unless this inferiority sense can
be, at least partially, eradicated during a young man's early
life, it will torment him and hamper him all his days. It is a
mental habit, often so ingrained, that it defies the most expert
psychiatrist. To any one among my readers who will show me
how to deal with it successfully, I shall be everlastingly grateful.

We have now, I hope, touched upon all the more important
elements in the varying reactions of human sexual relationships. I know that I have only skimmed the surface of the subject. For the sex life of human beings is still more or less of

an unexplored country. We legislate about it, we preach about it, we even, as now, try to write about it. But its reactions are often so complicated, they interweave themselves so closely with the other reactions of our lives, they color our thoughts so deeply, that they contain always, even after the most complex analysis, a remnant of mystery that puzzles and that sometimes frightens us.

But we must not be afraid of them. Above all, we must remember that we human beings, hampered by our physical bodies, are trying to express with these same bodies the supreme emotion of love: the highest, the most Godlike thing in the universe. Love that is God Himself. What wonder, then, if with these same imperfect bodies of ours, we often go astray in our clumsy attempts to translate love into terms of human life and activity. But so long as it is "love" and not "lust" that we are trying to express, so long and no longer may we feel safe; so surely may our imperfect expressions find their complement and their fulfillment in the everlasting love of Almighty God.

CLINICAL MATERIAL

A. Heteroerotic Cases.

The modern books on the physical technique of marital or promiscuous sexual intercourse could never have been published twenty years ago. As an example of them, I suggest that you look at *Ideal Marriage* (see above, p. 228, footnote) translated from the German. In the course of the last chapter I have already referred to other books of the same kind. Perhaps they do some good. At any rate, they furnish for the young a new type of printed excitement and they have taken the place of the old "Molly Bawn" books, that were once the delight of our bawdy-minded Victorian ancestors. The Molly Bawn type of book was purely pornographic and merely a source of sexual stimulation. Our modern sex books have at least no direct pornographic aim. But it is curious how, in our age, we worship anything that goes under the name of "science." If a book is "scientific" or "written from the standpoint of the scientist," then it may be safely printed and almost as safely circulated. One cannot help remembering the bitter persecution of the really valuable works of Havelock Ellis when they first appeared thirty years ago. We have come a long way since them. Books like *Ideal Marriage* always make me think of the following experience.

(1) Many years ago I was in India, at Benares. I had just visited a famous Jain temple. On the outside of this temple there were ancient bas-reliefs in stone, each relief depicting some method of heteroerotic intercourse. There must have been thirty of them, all told. Coming out of the temple, I was led by my guide to the banks of the Ganges. On one part of the shore sat a holy man, a sparsely clothed ascetic, wrapped in meditation. I asked my guide about him. "That," said my guide, "is a very, very holy man. For the past forty years he has sat here, day after day, wrapped in meditation." "And what," I asked, "does he meditate about?" My guide dropped his voice to a reverent tone. "I cannot tell exactly," he answered, "but people say that he is connected with that Jain temple where you saw those ancient bas-reliefs. And I am told that, during his long years of meditation, he has thought out eleven new sexual postures, quite different from those depicted by the sculptor." To a man who looks upon sexual intercourse as a divine mysterious process, in which the creating of new life is involved, such meditations might well be possible. Fortunately, or unfortunately, our western minds do not work in this way. Who is right? The Indian holy man who finds food for meditation in something that is to us repulsive; or we, who connect thoughts of evil with almost every manifestation of our physical sex needs? Perhaps some modern Aristotle will, in matters of sex, finally hit upon the Golden Mean—the safe middle-ground between these two extremes.

(2) Coitus Interruptus: Francis Childs, one of your vestrymen and a devoted churchman, has four children, and a very delicate wife. He has been told that another pregnancy will endanger her life. He is bitterly opposed to the usual machinery of preventing conception, but he is a man highly sexed himself, who fears the possibility of temptation if he tries to live in absolute continence. He has, therefore, practiced for several years what is called "in-

terrupted coitus." Before each seminal emission, he withdraws, and this prevents pregnancy. Of late he finds that he is becoming rather irritable, a little fearful and depressed. He comes to you to ask your advice. Is his habit of interrupted intercourse harmful? Many psychiatrists hold that this form of intercourse is always dangerous in the long run. The danger, however, does not lie in any physical impairment. The dangers are all mental; but they are none the less dangers for all that. Marital intercourse ought to involve a complete relaxation of mind and body, what the German writers call a "detumescence"—a loosening of tension and a release of all the stimulated physical and mental functions. It should bring with it a sense of complete satisfaction, of refreshment, of rest. But, in the interrupted coitus, the man is bringing into intercourse an element of fear. When his mind ought to be lying fallow, when he should be mentally relaxed, he is kept mentally tense and alert because he has to keep one idea always before him. He must watch the sexual process; he must withdraw in time. He is like a man having sexual intercourse, who knows that he may be interrupted at any moment by the unexpected appearance of some third person. Hence, he never gets from his marital intercourse the complete relaxation and satisfaction which the act should give. And, because of this, his sexual desires are not really satisfied. He feels tired out, tense, irritable. These are the dangers of coitus interruptus. It is a very unsatisfactory method of contraception. Unsatisfactory, because it gives the man no real release; because the woman is always afraid of becoming pregnant; and because frequently it does not work and the wife becomes pregnant after all, for the spermatozoa of the seminal fluid are persistent little animals. They have a way of getting to their goal in the uterus; of creeping up into it in some mysterious way, that defies the most careful interruptor. I should advise my parishioners against this method of birth control.

(3) Sexual Psychoneuroses:[29]

(a) A sensitive, neurasthenic man of forty, intellectual and

[29]I take the following cases from the valuable article of Dr. W. R. Reynell, already mentioned above. The author and The Royal Society of Medicine have graciously given permission for their use in this book.

artistic, had been married five years to a woman of thirty-five whose sexual trend was mainly towards her own sex. He had never been able to consummate his marriage, although his feelings were at times strong and always heterosexual. He felt sure that he could have been potent with a woman of inferior social position, such as a certain housemaid or a prostitute, but moral scruples would not have allowed him to put this to a test. He had always suffered from a strong sense of inferiority; his wife was his superior in size, strength, social standing and will-power. The psychological difficulties were too great for him to be considered a favorable case, he was an instance of "marital misfit."

(b) The same condition gives rise to another common sexual neurosis, namely, "ejaculatio praecox." The treatment of these conditions becomes obvious when the cause is understood. Spontaneous ejaculation with no sexual stimulus is not uncommon as an anxiety symptom. A few months ago I saw a remarkable case. The patient was a powerful man aged forty-eight, weighing fourteen stone. He had been a considerable athlete and had nothing in common with the typical neurasthenic. His profession was the pursuit of criminals in a lawless tract of country and his life had been one of dangerous adventure. He was fearless in his work and had reached the top rank of his profession. The symptom he complained of was spontaneous ejaculation, and he estimated that he had an average of more than one a day for the last ten years. They would occur if he was spoken to suddenly or with any sudden emotion. He had often consulted doctors but had come to the conclusion that his condition was incurable. I found evidence of an irritable condition of his whole nervous system, exaggerated knee-jerks, hyperacusis and hyperasthesia. I advised him to be teetotal, to reduce his weight, and I gave him a bromide mixture. Within a month's time he had reduced his weight by a stone and a half, was completely cured and able to discontinue his bromide. I saw him two months later and there had been no relapse. The above is an extreme case, but most of us can remember cases in which occasional spontaneous ejaculations were complained of in situations which tended to cause anxiety, for example, travelling by train or motor car, or any circumstance causing a sudden rise of emotional tension. A doctor recently gave me an instance of his experience and the only one he had had. His wife had gone on a motor journey and the next day he was handed a telegram. He suddenly felt a pang of fear that his wife had met with an accident and he had an ejaculation. He thought his experience unique, but I can recall many similar cases.

(c) Dr. Reynell has noticed cases in which there had been fixation at an infantile stage, and he stresses the importance of "mother-fixation" in this connection. Two or three years ago he saw a man, between thirty and forty, who was of a literary turn. He came because of symptoms due to a condition like Graves' disease. On his (the physician's) inquiring about sexual matters, the patient became excited and said, "You must accept as a primary fact in my life the perpetual virginity of my wife." He married in 1913, his mother having died in 1911. The physician did not pursue the subject at the moment, but later asked, "Does your wife resemble your mother?" "The very image," he said. Here the wife was simply the mother-substitute, and this had become a necessary part of his existence. Other physicians have pointed out that the ordinary weaning away of the attitude of mother-fixation went through various members of the family, and in one case finished with an attraction, amounting even to a feeling of love, towards a girl cousin. It would be agreed that in many of these cases of mother-fixation the only possible happy marriage would be to a maternal cousin. In others, mother-fixation took the form of incapacity for sexual intercourse with any one for whom they entertained respect or with whom they were in love, but they were potent when associating with women of a lower social class. He has seen a marked instance of that in a man of great ability and culture. Early in life he recognized that he had a very strong mother-fixation, and he told the physician that he could not conceive of intercourse with a woman he loved, but he frequented the company of prostitutes of a low order on many occasions. He married, but marital relations ceased after he had several children; he said he was practically impotent, except during a sadistic outburst.

(d) Much unhappiness results from marital misfits, as in a case Dr. Reynell saw not long ago—a woman who was nursing during the war. An officer for a long time pursued her with attentions. She was not very anxious to marry him, but gave way owing to his persistency. Shortly after the war, after one futile attempt at intercourse, he made no further attempts. She had a very strong maternal impulse but as she was now aged forty-two the chance of bearing a child was slender. She was now developing a series of tremendous phobias, particularly associated with thunderstorms, probably linked up with air raids, which occurred while she was nursing this officer. Dr. Reynell did not think this husband was alive to the seriousness of the situation.

B. Homoerotic Cases and Notes:

(1) When you have had some experience in dealing with homoerotic men of the masculine type, you will come to recognize them fairly easily. The next time that you are invited to some big demonstration of a boys' organization, I suggest that you make an experiment that I have myself tried several times with some success. At one part of the demonstration, all the squads with their more mature leaders will march past a reviewing post. Take your stand there and watch these leaders. You will not make any grave miscalculation, if you take it for granted that at least half of these men are more or less homoerotic types. Try to pick out those that strike you as homoerotic types. Write their names on a bit of paper. Later on, during the evening, get a chance to talk to the "Head Devil" of the whole show, whatever he is called. Ask him, as a favor to you, to give you or to write down for you the names of his best leaders. Then compare his list with yours. You will find, I am sure, that almost all the men whom you recognize as homoerotic types are classed as the most successful leaders of the entire organization. Of course, you will make about 25 per cent mistakes. But you will get at the principle of the thing. Finally, if you can, ask the major-domo *why* these men that he has picked out are the best leaders. He will say: "I can't tell you exactly why. But they take more interest in the boys, they are willing to sacrifice their own ease and comfort to the welfare of their squads. They are all busy men, and yet they give at least one whole evening every week to boys' work. And that evening is Friday evening, the one evening in the week when they are probably tired out with the week's work and would like to go to the theatre or to

some kind of amusement. Moreover, the boys look up to them, admire them, want to imitate them. *The boys will do things for them that they will not do for other leaders.* And yet, many of them are not particularly able or well-educated men. I like this work myself, but I get terribly tired of boys after a while. These fellows love to be with them and the boys like to have them around. They seem to understand the kids somehow. And there is nothing that they won't do to help them." If you should know this same individual fairly well, you might ask a further question. "Isn't it possible for men to be too interested in adolescents? I mean, don't you have an occasional scandal? You know what I mean." He knows very well what you mean. If he is a man of experience he will probably say: "Well, yes, occasionally. But very seldom with one of my really valuable men. You see these men, whose names I have given you, are so popular with their boys, that if any one member of the squad did begin to raise a scandal, as you call it, the others would nearly kill him. Boys are rather sensible animals; and they are, for the most part, intensely loyal. If something should happen between them and their leader, something that they did not like or did not approve of, well they'd try to forget it as soon as possible, and pretend that it never happened. They remember all the things that this same man has done for them, and they don't think it too great a return to, well, to keep their mouths shut. I should not, however, want you to imagine for an instant that, among my squads there is any unusual amount of the things that lead to what you have called scandals. My lads are normal, healthy boys, my leaders, or most of them, are normal healthy men. And whatever does go on is, I am sure, normal and healthy too. Good evening."[80]

(2) Repression of the homoerotic trend. Now and again we are shocked by the story of some homoerotic tragedy. A man who for years had been beloved and respected is abruptly plunged into dis-

---

[80]In connection with boys' work I can speak from some small measure of personal experience. For two years—my first two years in Baltimore—I had a boys' troop. I learned what a sacrifice it involves for an older man to give up at least one evening in every week to go a long distance to the basement of some church or parish house and to spend two or three hours with a group of boys of varying ages and varying abilities. I have known also a good many prominent and successful leaders. Just how many of them are

grace. He has been caught *flagrante delicto,* has been perhaps arrested, and the whole unfortunate story has got into the newspapers. The man's friends are aghast. He must be out of his mind. Their first idea is to clap him into a mental hospital. Many such tragedies might have been avoided if the man had been taught how to accept and to make constructive his homoerotic conditioning. But he has always been afraid of it. During early manhood he has had enough power of restraint to bridle his desires, and so he makes the fundamental mistake of pretending that these desires do not exist at 'all. He forces them into the back of his mind, he submerges them, but he does not assimilate them. He reaches middle-age perhaps and has attained rather a prominent place in the community. Then, he may overwork, he may have a serious illness, he may have to pass through a period of mental strain and stress. All this wears thin his old habits of resistance; all this weakens the wall that he has built up between his public life and his intimate sexual desires. Then, all of a sudden, the repressed thoughts rush back into his mind. He is overwhelmed by them. He realizes that there is something in him that is clamoring for satisfaction, for expression. It wears him down. It begins to break through, first into thought and desire, finally into action. But, because in the past he has never had any homoerotic experience, because he does not know how to find some source of satisfaction without endangering himself, because, in a word, he has always lived a continent life, he makes some hideous blunder, a blunder that would never have been made by a man with any past sexual experience, a blunder that turns upon him the sudden light of publicity, of arrest, of disgrace. And once the disgrace has come, the man throws all restraints to the winds. He defies all criticism, he gives the lie to all his past life. He has been, he says, a slave hitherto. Now at last, he is free. He can do as he pleases. He can at last satisfy those desires that tormented him all his life. Alas, he is not free at all. He has only plunged himself into a new kind of

homoerotic types I do not want to know. But I do know that I respect them for the work they are doing; and I envy every adolescent who is lucky enough to arouse their interest. For no boy could possibly come under their influence without being the better for it, without becoming more of a man. I soon grew tired of the work. I did not have an adequate motive to keep me interested.

slavery; the slavery to one part of his nature that does not deserve to be the primal power of his existence. And once he has satisfied these same desires, once his sexually starved soul has feasted itself on the good things that it has so often longed for, these same good things turn to ashes in his mouth. He is eating husks —and with the swine. For these same desires are soon satisfied. And then he realizes that in filling himself with the husks, he is still bitterly hungry, hungry for the things that once made life worth living, the things that he has thrown away. And the pity of it all is that it might have been avoided. Had the man only learned how to deal sensibly with his own temperament, had he not been afraid of it, he might have used even the things that he once looked upon with horror to the benefit of his own soul and for the greater glory of the God whom he has now lost.

(3) Less dangerous, but not very constructive, is the manner of dealing with homoerotic desires as if they were wild beasts that were kept in a cage, but that had to be fed occasionally. This is the purely physical level of homoerotic reaction. A man of this kind accepts, indeed, his homoerotic conditioning. But he puts it out of his mind temporarily. He knows that for safety's sake no one in his immediate entourage must suspect the secret of his homoerotism. So, to speak in modern slang, "he puts up an heteroerotic front." He is prominent at teas, he takes girls out to dances, he tells smutty heteroerotic stories in his club. But, once or twice a year, he goes off for a "week-end holiday." He goes to some large city, registers under an assumed name in some small hotel. He makes no mistakes, he has done the thing so often. He knows just where to go, just whom to speak to, just the right words to say. He is not particular as to the companion that he finally selects. What he wants is to get the thing over with as soon as possible. So he gets it done. And then he slinks off home. If he has money, he can go to Europe, where he need have no fear of the law. A week in Paris or Berlin will give him enough sexual activity to last him a year or more. After that he comes back to his home, puts on his usual mask, starts going again to teas and to dances. And all the old ladies wonder why Mister so-and-so, who is such a delightful young man and so popular with the girls, does not get married. There are some rather peculiar people in a certain

big city, some other people in Paris or Berlin who could answer that question satisfactorily. Luckily the old ladies do not know them socially. For a man who lives on such a sexual level, there is little to be said. And often he does not escape retribution. For some of his casual "friends" in the distant big city may wander by chance to his home town; they may find out his name; they may suddenly present themselves, smiling, mysteriously, at his office, at his home, yes—I am sorry to say it—at the door of his church. And now he has to begin paying for his former "week-ends." If he is wise, he will come to you for help. And you can, at least, protect him. You can make him bring his blackmailing friend to see you, and when you have heard this blackmailing friend's story, you can tell him exactly where "he gets off." You might even have a detective, in plain clothes, waiting outside the door, so that he can overhear enough of the conversation to assure himself that here is a man demanding money under threats of exposure. The detective will not be at all interested in what the exposure consists of. He will be very interested in informing the blackmailer how he may leave town, and in advising him never to return. And perhaps, when you have protected this terrified homoerotic parishioner of yours, you may be able to give him an entirely new conception of how to deal with his sexual difficulties.

(4) Feminine Homoerotics. I have told you before that there is *one* kind of advice that you must never, *never* give to the homoerotic man or woman who seeks you out and asks for help. *Never* advise him or her to get married. Matrimony is not a cure for homoerotism. Of course, if you have a man who is bi-erotic, who is attracted to both men and women, then you may safely advise him to try marriage. Or, if a homoerotic man wanted to marry a homoerotic woman—supposing such a thing to be possible—one might consent to the suggestion. The pair would probably not be able to consummate the marriage. But they might be happy together on a brother and sister basis. But the biologically conditioned homoerotic is a misfit in Holy matrimony. From such misfits tragedies develop often enough. And inasmuch as the female rôle in sexual matters is the passive one, a homoerotic woman *can* marry—and can bear children. But once married, she is seldom happy.

Mrs. Jones has been married for ten years and has borne her husband three children. You have never noticed anything unusual about her, except perhaps that she is never very affectionate with her husband, never expressive. She never takes his arm, or pats the back of his hand, or touches his shoulder. One day Mr. Jones comes to you in a panic. His wife has left him. He can't understand it. He thought she was perfectly happy. If she had fallen in love with another man, he would have allowed her to get a divorce. But *there is no man in the case*. That is what makes it so puzzling. Yet there must be a man in the background somewhere. You ask, "Where is your wife?" "Oh, she is staying with a woman friend in a distant town." "Who is this woman—a relation —a friend of long standing?" Poor Mr. Jones is still more puzzled. "No," he says, "no relation. And my wife never met her until six months ago. She came to stay with us for a week, and since then Mary has been very cold to me. She was never very affectionate. But I thought she did love me, in her way. But since this friend's first visit, Mary has insisted on giving up our old double bed. She has wanted a bedroom of her own. She said that I snored and disturbed her. But she never minded that before. I think, Father, that her mind must be going. Or else she is having a change of life." Ah, that useful "change of life." It has been made responsible for so many things that people could not exactly explain. But it will not explain Mrs. Jones' case. If I were you, I should see Mrs. Jones, yourself. If she won't come to you, go to her. She will probably tell you that all her life she has been more attracted to women than men; but she had never understood what was wrong with her. She had once consulted her general practitioner and he had told her to get married and all would be well. So she had married. Marital intercourse had been an utter abomination. Her husband's physical presence, the odor of his male body made her almost cry out in agony. But she had gritted her teeth and had stood it somehow. She had borne him two sons. If they had been daughters— But boys! The male animal disgusts her. Yet she had expected to stick it out till she died, when, six months ago, a new, a real love, the only love of her life had come. She had followed it without hesitation. What was her husband to her? What were her two sons? This woman, with whom she is now living, gives her something that neither husband nor children could give. Let her husband get a divorce—on any grounds. She doesn't want his money. She and her friend are going into business together. Her own life—her own happiness is just beginning She is sorry for her husband. But she cannot help herself. You will have a hard time explaining this situation to Mr. Jones. Probably all his life he will imagine that there was always some "man" in the background. But he will never get his wife back, I am afraid. And you as his parish priest can do nothing to make her come back. Here is a case in which you can accomplish nothing except make Mr. Jones understand, so that he may not blame himself, nor blame his wife over much. But make him keep his blame for the general practitioner who advised a homoerotic woman to enter the Holy state of matrimony.

C. Other peculiar reactions of the sexual life: Masochism and Sadism.

(1) The attraction to heteroerotic men of the immature female must be noted here. The courts are familiar with the cases of apparently normal young men who are repeatedly arrested for "assaults upon minors." In this class is the older man who has perhaps lost his potency, and who likes to fondle the exposed bodies of little girls or of adolescents. But I have known younger men, in the very flush of their sexual life, who were utterly impotent with mature women. One of them told me, "Mature women have a horrid smell. And I can't stand hair on a body." Such young men are attracted by the smooth bodies of young girls from ten years up to puberty. They seldom make a definite sexual assault. At the worst, they press their own bodies against the girl's exposed skin, and so secure satisfaction. Perhaps such sexual habits are the results of some early unpleasant sexual experience that has disgusted the young man with ordinary sexual intercourse. In this class belong, alas, those fathers who happen to have young daughters of eight or ten, while they themselves are on the borderland of old age, at fifty or sixty. Many a child has been introduced in her early years to sexual stimulation at the hands of her own father, who "loves her so much" that he is always "dandling her upon his knee," or fondling her. Such cases are the exception, but you

will come across them. The child, as a matter of fact, sustains no serious physical injury. Her injury is mental. For she will never forget what her father, or her uncle, has done. That memory will poison her relationship with them. It may become the foundation of an intolerable domestic situation.

(2) Masochism.—I may illustrate masochistic reactions by an actual case. A well-educated man of middle-age was accustomed to secure his sexual satisfaction in the following manner. He would make certain arrangements each month with a prostitute, picking out a stern older dominating type of woman. He would give her a pair of handcuffs. Then, late in the evening, after dark, he would start out on the streets alone. He would slink along, attempting to escape observation as if he were a criminal escaping justice. In the deep entrance hall of some shop, he would stop, slink back into a far corner and wait there with trembling limbs. Suddenly, in the entrance to this hall the prostitute would appear. She would utter no word. She would go up to the cringing man, would take him by the throat and shake him a little, she would slap his face, then she would take out the handcuffs and slip them on his wrists. "And now," she would say, "you are in my power, completely in my power at last." She would twist the handcuffs so that they bit into the skin of the man's wrists, and she would lead him, thus manacled, out into the street. His hands would be covered by her dress; no one would notice that he was chained to her. Thus they would start for the prostitute's home. On the way, the sense of complete powerlessness would result in a seminal emission. The man's sexual tension would be relieved. He would look up at the woman, she would take off the handcuffs, he would pay her and they would separate. This act, this little sexual drama was performed about once a month, and it gave this middle-aged masochist complete satisfaction. Such a means of satisfaction is harmless enough. It does not endanger any one and there is not very much that any of us can do about it, except try to understand it.

(3) Sadism—the desire to inflict pain on others and to get sexual satisfaction from the process.

(a) A young man of twenty-one, with normal body and only one unusual characteristic in childhood—cruelty to animals—first

came under my observation during a rat-hunt. In one of our university buildings there were a number of rats. One day, while
several young men were loitering in the central court, a large rat
ran out of the bushes and tried to cross the enclosure. The men
began to chase him in a good-natured way. But one of them became strangely excited; his eyes began to gleam, his face to flush.
He finally cornered the rat in an open space between two of the
walls. The other men had sticks, but he had none. He jumped
upon the cornered animal, and stamped it to death with his feet.
Long after the animal was dead, he continued to stamp, until his
shoes were covered with blood and entrails. The other men stood
staring at him. Slowly he seemed to come to himself. He looked
around in a shame-faced way, muttered something and went off
by himself, leaving behind him in the minds of his fellows an uneasy sense of fear, a sort of horror. Later on, that same week, he
came to see me. He was tremendously inhibited, but fortunately
I knew what he wanted to tell me. From childhood he had always
been fascinated by the mere idea of blood. To see blood actually
flowing gave him a sense of intoxication, a kind of exalted happiness, that he could scarcely describe. As a little boy, he had been
frequently punished for tormenting dogs and cats. Later, during
adolescence, he developed no autoerotic habits, but he found a
source of vicarious sexual satisfaction in a procedure of his own.
He would catch mice, or buy those that other boys caught. Then,
he would take off his shoes and stockings, he would let the mice
loose in some small room where they could not escape and then,
in a frenzy of excitement, he would stamp them to death with
his bare feet. To feel the blood well up between his bare toes, to
see his feet spattered with blood, this was to him complete satisfaction and relief. As he grew older and developed autoerotic habits, all his sexual imaginations connected with these autoerotic
acts were imaginations of torments and of tortures. He had a
hidden library, just as the ordinary young man has a copy of
Rabelais or of the *Decameron* or of Molly Bawn. But his library
consisted of histories of the Inquisition, the *History of Torture*
(this last in German, but he learned German so as to be able to
read it), and other similar publications. Like the average boy, who
has his collection of "smutty pictures," photographs of actresses

in tights or of naked women, this boy had a series of pictures of Chinese tortures, his most treasured possession. But, although he would yield every now and then to an orgy of sadistic imagination that usually ended in some autoerotic act, he had begun to be afraid of himself, for he had noticed that his sadistic impulses were getting beyond his control. In his relationships with other men, he was becoming quarrelsome, anxious to pick a fight, he was becoming known as a "hard-boiled guy," a "dirty scrapper." Fighting tempted him as alcohol tempts the drunkard. He would pick a quarrel, get into a fight, always try to make his opponent's nose bleed, and then he would lose all self-control. He would try to gouge out the other's eye, to kick him below the belt, to throttle him. After one or two such experiences, the other men began to avoid him. They were afraid of him. Yet he was a good student. He was hungry for the approbation of others. He liked girls. But when he danced with them and became at all sexually stimulated, he held them so tight, he was so fiercely intolerant of any interference from another man who wanted to dance with the same girl, that the women also began to avoid and to fear him. Just before the episode of the rat-hunt, he had got into trouble with the police. He and two other men had been in town, at a speak-easy. They had not been drinking very heavily. The other two were merely pleasantly happy, and perfectly masters of themselves. They were driving home in the car of the sadistic undergraduate. As they came around a corner, a child crossed the street. The child saw the car coming and stopped to let it pass. To the horror of his companions, the driver swerved and drove straight at the helpless child, stepping on the gas and making the car plunge forward. One of his companions yelled, the child jumped and the front of the car just grazed the child's body. But a policeman had seen what had happened. He thought that the young man had lost control of his car, and he made him stop. The sadistic young man got out to speak with the policeman, while the other two men remained in the car. To their utter surprise, their companion waited until the officer had bent down to get the license number and then picking up a heavy spanner from the bottom of the car, was about to bring it crashing down on the back of the policeman's head. One of his companions reached out and just caught his arm. But the blow fell aslant, and without much power, knocking off the policeman's helmet. Naturally, all three young men were arrested for being drunk and disorderly. The policeman, being a kind-hearted soul, did not mention the attack on himself, indeed he did not realize how close he had come to serious injury. "One of the boys knocked off my helmet," he said. So the real details of this affair were never known. Only, the young man's two friends never went out with him again. All this I pieced together slowly. The young man himself, when he came to see me at last, was in despair. What was the matter with him? When one saw him in his quiet moments, he seemed normal enough. But the moment he became excited, his eyes had a look in them that one sees only in the eyes of excited sadists. We all know that it is foolishness to talk about the "crazy look" in the eyes of mentally disturbed patients. Nevertheless, something looks out of the eyes of the sadist that sometimes stirs the most experienced psychiatrist. It is like a glimpse of some evil presence, something that is at war with the world, something inherently evil, and cruel and malignant. The patient often feels as if he were really "possessed." As if some evil entity took possession of him at times and made him do things that he would shudder at when the attack was passed. Of course the emotional urge towards sadistic acts comes from the sexual material of a man or woman's individuality. If the sexual life can be satisfactorily adjusted, then often the sadistic acts cease. If such a man, as I have described, can find a wholesome outlet for his sexual desires in marriage with a well-balanced, normal woman, the sadistic elements will sometimes tend to disappear. But neckings and huggings and the "near-beer" of sexual intercourse are tremendously dangerous. They stimulate such a man—rouse all his sadistic tendencies, but do not satisfy his sexual cravings. In dealing with such cases, you must make the young man understand himself and his handicaps. As I have so often said, if he can understand, and not fear himself, he has started on the right road to a solution of his difficulties. Sadism is a very difficult subject. Sadistic tendencies crop up in all kinds of human relationships. You must be on the look-out for them.

(b) Repressed Sadism in marriage. The following case was

given to me by a colleague. I have known others like it. Mrs. Samuel Sanders was apparently happily married. She had no children, although she and her husband had been married for fifteen years. This husband was a hard-working clerk in a bank, not very robust in body, and with a quiescent tuberculosis, that gave him no trouble if he took reasonable care of himself. The wife began to develop symptoms of heart trouble. She would not go to a doctor, for she felt that this was an unnecessary expense. Her heart attacks would come on, usually in the night, after she had been asleep for an hour or two. Then she would begin to feel "smothered"; she would wake her husband, and he would get up, give her bicarbonate of soda or a hot-water bottle. She always felt better if he would hold her in his arms, and sometimes she would go to sleep in his arms at about four o'clock. The husband would sit up in bed, afraid to move for fear of waking her. She had such attacks, at first, about once a week. Of course, when she had an attack, her husband got no sleep. She would awaken at midnight, and he would fuss over her or hold her in his arms until day broke. Then the attacks began to become more frequent. Twice a week, then three times, then every other night. When the case finally came to the notice of my colleague, the woman was gradually breaking her husband. For five nights of every week, he would not get more than two hours' sleep; he would go to his bank tired out, sleepy, liable to make mistakes, inefficient, frightened, and beginning to cough and to have occasional night sweats again. Still the wife refused medical aid. Finally the husband confided in a colleague of mine, telling him that his wife was a Christian Scientist, that she abhorred doctors, but that he felt that she ought to get some help. Would my colleague come and see her, without letting her know that he was a physician? So my colleague went. He could see no evident cardiac symptoms in the wife's general appearance. He was much more worried about the husband, who was gradually breaking for want of sleep, and stirring up his former tuberculous condition. My colleague, being something of a social detective as well as a medical man, became interested. From the neighbors he soon learned that Mrs. Samuel Sanders, as soon as her husband was safely off to the bank, would get herself some breakfast, and would then sleep until the early afternoon. Neighboring women had wandered in to see her and knew how much and how soundly she slept. There was also a whisper—just a whisper of scandal. In the early afternoons, while the husband was still at the bank, Mrs. Sanders sometimes received visitors, or rather a visitor. This visitor was a rather good-looking man, somewhat younger than Mrs. Sanders, who worked on a night shift in the railroad shops. When my colleague was in possession of these facts, he went to the Sanders' house one day at noon. It took him some time to get in as Mrs. Sanders was fast asleep. My friend, pretending that he was looking for her husband, got into the house at last. Then, he and Mrs. Sanders had a heart-to-heart talk. He said, "I have a great respect for Christian Science and those who really believe in it. I have discovered from the authorities of your church that you became a member of it only a year ago, that you do not go much to the church itself, that, in a word, you are not really a Christian Scientist at all. You are merely using it so as to avoid consulting a physician. For if you did consult one, you would be told that there was nothing the matter with your heart at all. Just how conscious you are of what you are doing, I cannot tell. But this I *can* tell you. You hate your present husband. You want to get rid of him. You want him to die. And you are doing your very best to kill him, because you want another man, a decent sort of fellow who will not break up another man's home by having an affair with his wife, but who might, if that man should die, marry his widow. If I am wrong, then let me examine your heart. I am a physician." The woman broke down. I do not believe that she clearly realized what she was doing and what her real motives had been. But once she had faced the facts of the case, once she had been able to talk over the situation with her husband, to tell him that she had no love for him and that she cared for another man, her heart attacks began to disappear. Very soon, her husband was getting adequate sleep. What happened eventually I do not know. Perhaps the young mechanic removed himself from the picture, perhaps the wife got a divorce from her husband and married this young man. But at any rate, my colleague lost track of the case because the little bank clerk, Mr. Sanders, would not speak to him any more. He insisted that my colleague was to blame for all the domestic difficulties, that he had put "crazy ideas" into his wife's head and made her dissatisfied. "What!" he exclaimed, "my wife hate me and want to kill me! Utterly ridiculous." Sometimes it is difficult to save a man from the foes of his own household.

Cases of these types might be endlessly multiplied. For human nature and its reactions are so diverse, often so unpredictable, that no collection of cases can ever cover all possibilities of mental friction or of imperfect adjustment. I hope, however, that the clinical material that I have given will be sufficient to illustrate at least the general outlines of those reaction-types with which you will most frequently be brought into contact. The best way for a pastor, seminarian or social worker to get his clinical material would be to spend a few months in some large mental hospital, either as an orderly or as an observer. I believe that, in the future, such an experience will be made possible for seminarians and divinity students. Valuable also would it be for you, if somehow you might be allowed to spend some hours every week in those penetralia of mental hospitals, called "The Case History Rooms." Here are the complete records of thousands of mental cases. Here is the clinical material, indeed, that can never find its way into print. If, on one day you could study ten case-records of depressive psychoses, ten others of schizophrenias on the day following, and so on through all the psychoses and psychoneuroses, at the end of a month or two you would know so much that you would have no need at all for these ABC chapters of mine.

Chapter VIII

RELIGIOUS FAITH AND PRACTICE

THE LONELINESS OF THE MENTALLY ILL. THE THERAPEUTIC EFFECT
OF "DOING." PREVENTIVE MENTAL MEDICINE. OUR LORD THE GREAT
PHYSICIAN OF THE SOUL. "DIX MINUTES À DIEU." CONCLUSION

In this last chapter I wish to discuss certain general proposi-
tions; matters that should affect your general attitude and your
technique in dealing with psychoses and mental difficulties.
Had there been time, I should have liked to give an entire
chapter to the consideration of certain definite classes of individuals and to those members of them who are liable to give
you the most trouble, to ask for the most help. I wished to discuss your dealings with that blessed class, the Poor. With that
class of lonely, difficult individuals, whom we call the Aged—
a class to which no man or woman willingly claims admission
until circumstances force him or her into it. With another
classification of individuals who go under the name of criminals, delinquents, prisoners. And finally, I should have desired
to say a word about modern social service, about its present
ideals, its so-called scientific practice. But I must pass over these
things. Perhaps it is just as well. For I feel sure that there are
among my readers a number of "social servicers" whose good-
will I covet, but whose friendship I might lose if I had the chance
to say some of the things that must—perhaps fortunately for
me—be crowded out. Moreover, when one is lecturing or writing on a general subject such as ours, it is well to steer clear
of those subdivisions of it, to which the lecturer or the writer
tends to react emotionally—in the discussion of which he is
inclined to take sides, to allow his judgment to be colored by
his personal feelings, to talk or to write, not as he thinks, but

283

as he feels, and so to make part of his audience and his readers angry and to make a fool of himself.

Some years ago, a priest, who had ministered for many years to the inmates of a great mental hospital, wanted to write a book about his experiences. He intended to call his book, "God and the Lunatic." I do not know whether or not the book was ever published, but the title was most suggestive. As a usual thing, there is not a very close connection between the "lunatic" and God. Think of one of our great mental hospitals, with many thousand odd patients, men and women in various stages of mental clouding and decay. In times past, the parson was not welcomed by the hospital superintendents. Or if he was allowed occasionally to hold a service, he was told that he must "say nothing to excite the patients." Superintendents, even to-day, still have an idea that religious services are something "said." And a lot of "said words," full of emotional content, do excite mental patients and are undoubtedly bad for them. But the Catholic religion is not merely a "something said"; it is the "something done." Not, "say this in remembrance of *Me*," but *do* this. What might it not mean to those starved, clouded souls to be able to watch the quiet ceremonial of the mass. To "hear that blessed murmur" could not excite them. To *see* "God made and eaten" as Browning's bishop says; to watch—to take part in the Holy Sacrifice—to *make* their communions—surely this would not "up-set" them; it might "set them up," set them up on a rock, and bring them some source of new strength, some glimpse of the light eternal that would surely find some cranny of thought by which to enter the darkened room of their twisted and tormented minds. It has never, so far as I know, been tried. Psychiatrists, nowadays, are quite tolerant of the Catholic faith as a sort of pleasant self-hypnosis, a kind of diluted Eleusinian mystery, that might have some sort of therapeutic effect like occupational therapy. Why not introduce into the occupational therapy that has become such a wonderful agent in our mental hospitals, a little occupation with the Christian Religion and the Sacraments? Surely, if a mental hospital can find money for a book-bindery and a rug-weaving room and a carpenter-shop, it might find money enough for a chapel, for an altar, for a tabernacle. At any rate, I commend the idea to your attention.

Every large mental hospital ought to have a priest—a chaplain—not some broken-down cleric who cannot get on with sane people and is therefore supposed to be able to get on with crazy ones—but a priest who knows something about psychiatry, who has not only book learning but the learning of experience, and who is prepared for this particular type of work. So far as religion is concerned, our prisoners get very little of the right kind; but our mental patients, as a usual thing, get nothing at all. I hope that the day is coming when priests who are interested in mental illness will be able and willing to devote their lives to bringing to the inmates of mental hospitals and clinics, not sermons and things said, but sacraments and things done.[1]

And how much the parish priest or the social worker can do in the way of preventive mental medicine! As I have said, the pastor comes into early contact with the development of faulty mental habits; he, much more than the psychiatrist, holds the key to a patient's confidence; he, in a much deeper sense than can ever be applied to the physician, is a physician of the soul. He stands, as it were, like a watcher at the gate, the gate that leads to the mental hospital. He can, if he will, turn back hundreds, who, but for him, will have to pass through that same gate; many unfortunate men and women who will

[1] I am glad to know that at the College of Preachers in Washington one of the new fellowships has been given to a priest who is especially interested in psychiatry and who has been for some years attached as chaplain to a large mental hospital. In Washington this priest will have a whole year's release from parochial work in order to continue his psychiatric studies, to visit mental hospitals and to get personal training and direction from distinguished psychiatrists themselves.

not be able to get out of it again until they have indeed "paid the uttermost farthing" in mental torment and despair. He can show to the man or the woman, who comes to him in mental illness or difficulty, sources of help that the cleverest psychiatrist cannot give. The priest may not be able to offer his parishioner a course of psychoanalytic treatment, but he may offer him the Sacrament of Penance and the Sacrament of the Altar. He may establish the renowned "transference" of the psychoanalyst, not to himself, but to Our Lord and Savior Jesus Christ. He can show his parishioner, through the Sacrament of Penance, a "catharsis" that is infinitely more powerful than any emotional cleansing of the most enlightened mental sanitarium. He may not be able to teach his mental patient to make baskets or to bind books, but he can teach him to pray. What do we know about the real value of prayer—of mental relaxation in the presence of God—when applied to mental cases? Very little. But here again it is a type of occupational therapy that is worth trying.

For, above all else, the mental patient needs first a human, outstretched hand; secondly, a patient understanding and appreciation of his difficulties; and thirdly, a source of strength and help to which that human hand and that sympathetic understanding can lead him. Teach him to find God—after, and because, he has found you. For he is very lonely. That is the torment of most mental illness. It seems to cut the patient off from contact with the friendly, familiar, normal world. He is often horribly alone.

> "Oh Wedding Guest, this soul hath been
> Alone on a wide, wide sea;
> So lonely 'twas, that even God
> Scarce seemèd there to be."

Into this loneliness your help and understanding may come like light in a very dark place. But, you will soon tire of trying to help, and of trying to understand, unless you love human souls—unless you are afire with such a desire to help, that you cannot help helping. One is tempted to change a little the two familiar lines and to make them read:

"He *helpeth* best who loveth best,
All things both great and small."

But your physician-hood of souls depends for its power and its efficiency upon the great Physician of Souls Himself. He, if I may say it reverently, is the Great Psychiatrist. If you will take your Greek Testament and will read through the Gospels, or if you have forgotten your Greek, if you will get a text with the Greek on one side of the page and the English on the other—anyhow, if you will read through the Gospels, pretending to yourself that you are a Greek or a Roman of the second century into whose hands these new books have just fallen, you will get away from the too-great familiarity with the English words, you will understand just why the reader of the second century read and re-read these books over and over again. Nowadays I sometimes hear one of my psychiatric colleagues proclaiming some new truth in connection with mental illness or mental therapeutics. And somehow the new doctrine seems to have a familiar sound. And when I trace this familiarity to its source, I find myself, not in the last book by Freud or Adler or Morton Prince, but in the Greek of the Gospels. Many general principles that Our Lord laid down have been rediscovered and proclaimed from the house-tops as something new.

There were clever physicians all over the Roman empire when the Gospels first passed from hand to hand;—medical men who knew a lot about mental illness. And as they read these short Greek narratives of a Mark or a Luke—himself a physician—they must have thought: "This man, of whom they write, was indeed a great physician; not only of the body, but also of the mind."

Let me take only three examples from Our Lord's psychiatric teaching. Let me show you how "modern" they are. How —God save the mark—how scientific.

In the Parable of the Empty House [2] we are told about a mental patient who, after a long mental illness, has recovered. The "unclean spirit" of depression, or of excitement, of lust or of sadistic desire, has "gone out." The patient is convalescent. Meanwhile, the spirit wanders about until he thinks of returning to his former domicile. In other words, there is danger of a recurrence of the psychosis. The psychosis, in Our Lord's Parable, returns to the cured patient; it makes another attack upon the citadel of the patient's mind, and it gets in. Moreover, it comes in ever greater strength than before. This new recurrent attack is even stronger—"seven devils worse than the first," more dangerous than the last. But how does the psychosis gain a foothold in the patient's personality? The house—the mind of the patient—had indeed been "swept" by the psychiatrists of a mental hospital; it had been "garnished" by the kind ladies who gave occupational therapy; but nevertheless, that mind is empty. Modern psychiatrists are never tired of pointing out to their convalescent patients the dangers of the Empty House. Such a house invites the return of its previous occupant. In our psychiatric jargon, the convalescent mind, after an attack of mental illness, must be readjusted to life, but above all it must be prepared against the possibility of a recurrence of the original psychosis. It must be filled not only with new and healthy interests; it must be filled so full that there shall be no open cranny of anxiety by which the seven new devils may find an entrance. We tell such patients that if they want to protect themselves thoroughly, they must develop "outside interests." They must acquire interests beyond the daily duties of their routine lives. Patients often despise such suggestions. They don't want "hobbies." But "hobbies" are valuable things; they are often protective mecha-

[2] St. Matthew XII, 44, St. Luke XI, 25.

nisms. They fill the house, and in filling it, they defend it. Or, rather, they fill the bare spaces in it—the places that are not filled by the patient's business or household activities. And it is exactly these interstitial bare places that are the spots of lowered mental resistance—the *loci minoris resistentiae*—in which the first seeds of a mental illness may be planted and may flourish until they choke out the good air and poison everything else in the room. Above all else such a convalescent patient must get what we call "insight," must see just where the bare, empty spaces are, must be able to fill these with healthy mental habits and activities. And he must remember that the devil who has "gone out" may try to come back again. He must not be afraid of him. And he need not be afraid, if the house of his life is so completely filled and protected that no mode of entrance is possible any longer.

Among all useful "hobbies," among all powerful "outside interests," I know of no more useful hobby, no more powerful "outside interest" than the practice of the Christian Religion, than growth in the spiritual life of Catholic faith and practice. One does not find it frequently recommended by modern psychiatrists. Nor is a training in it included in our diversified occupational therapy. But you may take it from me—and I speak from some experience—that it is more helpful than psychoanalytic treatment—more protective than book binding or basket weaving—for, by means of it, the patient taps a reservoir of strength and of peace that not even the best mental hospital, not even the cleverest occupational therapist can give. Happy are they that find it. And helpful may you he, helpful beyond words, if you can get set the feet of your mental patients on that straight and narrow road.

In all four of the Gospels, we find a certain rather mysterious saying of Our Lord's—one that He must have repeated many times in somewhat varying forms. "He that loveth his life, shall lose it."[3] "He that loseth his life shall find it." Strange,

[3]St. Matthew X, 39; XVI, 25; St. Mark VIII, 35; St. Luke IX, 24; XVII, 33; St. John XII, 25.

apparently contradictory aphorisms. And yet they contain the essence of so much of modern psychiatric advice. Our Lord told his followers the very same thing that modern psychiatrists are telling their patients to-day, and in the telling are imagining that they are proclaiming some new therapeutic principle.

"He that loveth his life." The man who loves life too much, who fears death and sickness and invalidism, who is afraid of cancer or tuberculosis, who worries over possible business losses, or frets petulantly over his children, whose "own life" is the centre of all his interests—such a man soon finds that his mind is so concentrated on himself that he has lost the old power of happy automatic function—lost the power to forget himself altogether—and that, in thus lowering his level of consciousness, he is becoming aware of all sorts of disquieting physical sensations and is growing gradually so poisoned by fear that, as he himself will tell you, "life is not worth living." He has "lost his life," lost everything that makes that life of any value, of any help to others or to himself. Of so many, many patients, I have felt that I could diagnose their entire complex cases in those few words of Our Lord's: "He loved his life; and so he has lost it."

But "He that loseth his life shall find it." Our Lord is never satisfied by merely doing what we physicians call "establishing a diagnosis." He always suggests a remedy. He is the great master of mental healing. How shall the man, who has lost his life through loving it, regain it again? In order to find it, he must accept the possibilities of illness and loss and disappointment; he must turn his eyes so completely away from himself that he loses himself entirely. As I have so often said, true mental and physical happiness lies in automatic functioning that is unconscious of itself. To lose oneself utterly in one's work is to find in that work not only work well done, but work happily done also. And if a man can recover his happiness, his power to function without friction, by losing himself in his daily work, in his domestic activities, in his "external interests," surely he can find still greater power, still greater peace by losing himself in the service of Almighty God. Surely, if there is any moment or any one place in this whole world of ours, in which the human mind loses itself in complete surrender, in complete happiness, that moment is the moment of a devout Communion—and that place is the Altar.

He that loseth his life—*for my sake*—shall find it. The words are as true to-day as they were when they were first spoken. Try it. Believe me, it is not only a mentally harassed, depressed patient that needs to "lose his or her life" in order to find it again. In this hurrying, unstable, unhappy world of ours we are more and more forced by circumstances, by competition, by personal ambition, to make ourselves the centres of our daily thoughts; tempted—almost impelled to measure ourselves by comparison with other men and women so that we never have time to measure ourselves by the standards and the ideals of Jesus Christ, until gradually our lives become egocentric; until gradually we become more and more self-conscious; until the one thing that we love so much that we are constantly anxious about it, is our own life. And so, loving our lives, we lose them. The world is cluttered up to-day with the remnants of such lost lives.

People feel their loss. They ascribe it to all sorts of causes except the right one; they hasten, panting after all kinds of false remedies—all the patent medicines of a false Humanism, of excitement, of sports, of social interests. They crowd the meeting-places of any new sect that will give them a new sensation so that, for a moment, they may forget themselves. And they are all going the wrong way. They do not like the plain truth of Our Lord's words. They do not want to "lose their lives." And yet, as even the psychiatrist knows, the losing of their egocentric attitude—of their life—is the only means by which they may ever find that same life again.

I could, I think, write a whole book on Our Lord's psychiatric teaching; on his attitude to mental patients, on his divine method of diagnosis and of advice. But I must content myself with one more example. "Judge not, and ye shall not be judged." And the implied converse of the statement, "If you do judge, judged you shall also be." This is hard advice to follow. But the advice—the warning—is based on a marvellous knowledge of the human mind.

Modern psychiatrists will tell you that if a man reacts with emotions of intense horror or disgust to any one definite act of his fellowmen, he is producing what is called a "protective mental mechanism," for the action that he so bitterly condemns in others is the very thing that he would like to do himself. He may not be conscious of this, he may have repressed these desires so deeply that they lie below the level of consciousness. But, at one time in his life, he was himself tempted along these same lines, he may be tempted in this way still. And his reaction of disgust or of intolerance is merely a kind of self-assurance that he will never do anything of the kind himself. It is patting himself on the back; a kind of whistling to keep up his own courage while walking in the dark. Therefore, be careful how you judge the failings of human beings, especially if there is a psychiatrist lurking anywhere near.

You will hear some man say: "I am broad-minded. I can put up with a lot of things. I don't mind if a man drinks too much on occasions, or if he runs after women. But there is one thing that I cannot forgive—dishonesty. If a man is dishonest, if he takes money that does not belong to him, then I have no further use for him. That I can't forgive."

What is such a man doing? He is "judging." And what happens? Often his "judging" results in his "being judged" with the very same judgment that he once meted out to one particular kind of sin. Not once or twice have I heard men of this type denouncing or "judging" dishonesty. And after some years I have not been surprised to hear that they themselves had been arrested for falsification of accounts, for peculations of various kinds; that they, who had so harshly judged, had been judged themselves indeed.[4]

So I should always be very cautious with a man who reacts with emotions of intense disgust to any definite type of sexual activity. His disgust is a mere cover-up reaction for his interest in these matters; a sort of protective mental mechanism. Probably he would be outraged if you suggested that the things he abhors are exactly the things that he has once done or that he still wants to do. But if he is really truthful with himself, if he will take the trouble to trace the source of his disgust, of his "judgment," he will find that you are not far from the truth.

Keep your eye also on the older boy or the young man, or even the middle-aged man who is bitterly opposed to all forms of autoerotism; who is always suspecting younger boys of having "bad habits"; who is on the look-out for pimply faces and for blue lines under young eyes; who likes to have "heart to heart talks" with younger people, and to lead them to autoerotic confessions, so that he can warn them against

[4] I shall never forget one case of this kind. A young man, a sort of social reformer, had "prostitution" on the brain. He could talk of nothing else. He could put up with all kinds of human sins, but impurity—promiscuous sexual intercourse—sins of the flesh, he denounced—these he persecuted. He enlisted much public sympathy for his "Crusade against Commercialized Vice." He broke up the Red Light district and scattered diseased prostitutes through the tenements and the homes of the poor and of the middle-class. He made a great effort at reclaiming "fallen women." He was deeply interested in them, and for about two years, he worked against "vice" in a large city. Then, suddenly he disappeared. Those of us who knew him soon discovered what had happened. The police had made an unexpected raid on a house of prostitution, a very low type of house, that contained only negro prostitutes. And in one of the rooms—with one of these negro prostitutes—half undressed—the young reformer was discovered. He had "judged." And by the same judgment that he had meted out to others, he was judged himself. Most men laughed at the young reformer as a hypocrite. He was not a hypocrite at all. But he did not know himself. He did not realize that his attitude towards prostitution, towards fallen women was merely the protective mechanism with which he tried to protect—from himself—his own half-conscious sexual desires. One night these suppressed desires broke through into action.

the "solitary sin" and help them to "keep pure." Such a
man's interest in this one type of reaction is a "judging" that
often brings with it a judgment that may, in the end, result in
some homoerotic scandal. Of course, the man may not be
clearly conscious of his motive. But you may be sure that his
interest in these sexual matters is a sort of camouflage for
his own homoerotic desires or a reaction to his own struggle
against autoerotic habits.[5]

What we must all strive for is Our Lord's ideal of "not
judging." There must be no human action, however hideous
and vile it may seem to you, from which you shrink away
with emotions of absolute condemnation. It is bitterly hard
sometimes to keep from your face every expression of emotional distress. But unless you can do so, you will not be
able to give much help to the unhappy person who comes to
you, asking for aid against these same actions that horrify
you, but that are habitual to him. For it is very difficult to
disassociate the sin from the sinner. The sin only comes into
existence, it only becomes understandable, apparent to us,
through the physical means of the sinner's body, through his
behavior. And no matter what he or she had done, no matter

[5]A man of this type once visited an American university, and was asked
by an undergraduate friend to meet a number of other undergraduates in
the friend's room. While the others were talking, the man sat down beside a
cheerful young sophomore to whom he had just been introduced. Perhaps the
sophomore's cheek disclosed a few pimples; perhaps there were blue lines
under his eyes. At any rate, the man, after a few moments of desultory conversation, laid his hand on the sophomore's knee, and asked in a deep whisper, "George—tell me—do you—do you abuse yourself?" The sophomore
carefully removed the man's hand from his knee, looked up at him, grinned,
and said, "Of course, I do, Mister X, isn't it fun?" This was a just rebuke.
Another reformer of the same type was well known in undergraduate circles
as a hunter of homoerotism, only he called it by other names. He was especially bitter in his denunciation of all homoerotic relationships between the
adolescents and the older men in the gymnasium classes. One hot summer
afternoon, he was caught *in flagrante delicto* with an eighteen-year-old member of a gymnasium class. His campaign against vice came to a sudden end.
He was not a hypocrite either. Only a man who did not know himself, who
judged and who was judged.

how horrified or disgusted we may be, it is a *human soul* that has expressed itself, wrongly and sinfully perhaps, in these same actions. And you and I are, or we ought to be, lovers and physicians of human souls. The physician does not shrink from the most hideous pathological conditions in the bodies of his patients. So we should get the better of our emotions of disgust in dealing with our penitent's soul.

Moreover, it is a good thing to remember that, if you ao catch yourself reacting with horror or disgust to some human action, this same emotional reaction may be like the words over the Temple at Delphi—*gnothi seauton*—an exhortation to self-knowledge and self-examination.

"Judge not; and ye shall not be judged." It is only the man or woman who can look upon *all* human activity from the standpoint of understanding, of pity, of eagerness to help, who is free from the "danger of the judgment." The old French tag is applicable here, *tout dire, pour tout comprendre, et tout guérir.*

I cannot end this book in any better way than by bringing you through our long discussion of mental diseases, of mental maladjustments and of sexual and emotional difficulties— bringing you through all this complex mass of mankind's mental suffering—all this foggy, often muddy country—out into the light that beats so clearly, so cleanly upon the figure of the Divine Psychiatrist—the one Great Physician of the soul. I want to leave you, not with memories of psychoses, of phobias, of obsessions, of erotic reactions, but with Him. And if you and I could continue with Him, walk with Him in our daily lives, live through Him and with Him, then we could put all these chapters of mine into the fire and might throw in with them all the books on moral theology, all the books on marriage and birth control, all the machinery of prohibition, of condemnation, of regulation, that have come down to us from the Ten Commandments and the Jewish Law. If people lived up to the ideals of the Sermon on the Mount, there would be no need for the Ten Commandments. If you and I made full use of the power of our religion; if we grew, year by year, in the development of our spiritual lives; if we practiced the Catholic faith, day in day out—then there would be no need for discussions about sexual continence, no need for understanding the lower physical sexual reactions, no necessity for trying to make the world realize the surpassing and permanent value of the Christian Religion. We, *by our lives,* would solve all these problems. And the world, beholding us, would come hastening to us, in order to ask what the strange power might be that has solved all our difficulties, that has smoothed the most dangerous of our paths, that has given us a mysterious source of strength and of peace. If we, Catholic Christians, were only what we might be!

And with that "if" I leave you. I wish that it might stir up in all your hearts, not merely a desire to know a little more about mental illness, but a desire to know a great deal more about God. Not simply a determination to deepen your experience of human nature in order that you may be able to help, but a determination to develop your own experience of Our Lord Jesus Christ in your daily prayers, in your confessions, in the Blessed Sacrament of the Altar. So many people think that they are leading satisfactory Christian lives if they say their prayers, go to mass on Sundays, make their confessions and their communions, and, so far as in them lies, live in charity with all men. But that is a very low level of spiritual development. It corresponds to the low level of mere physical satisfaction in sexual relationships. Friend, go up higher. Ask yourself one question. Are you really making a definite progress in your spiritual life? Can you truthfully say that you are closer to God, more fully in contact with the unseen world, than you were a year ago to-day? I know that I cannot say it of myself. The realization of this state of luke-warmness, of smug self-satisfaction at being able to go through the habitual motions of my spiritual life—this condition of mind that we all slip into so easily—the realization of it is one of the things that terrifies me.

All our knowledge, all the works on moral theology, and all books like this one of mine, will not help us much to help others, unless our own spiritual growth shines out more brightly, unless the people around us are forced by our very lives to take notice that "we have been with Jesus."

In the first chapter, I referred you to an important list of books given in the Appendix (see page 301). Among the many titles listed there, is one, a recent publication, which I call to your especial attention. *Les voies ordinaires de la vie spirituelle*. The Ordinary Ways of the Spiritual Life, by Monseigneor Farges. Take this book as a means of orientation. In it are described merely the "ordinary," the every-day ways of the spiritual life. Test your own lives by it. Have you already attained to these ordinary ways? It would be better to learn how to walk in them before you are ready to congratulate yourself on being good Christians—faithful Catholics—"not as other men are."

I know what busy active lives most people lead to-day. No one understands better than I how hard it is to find time for adequate prayer, for meditation, for proper preparation for confession and communion. For sometimes I feel that I am even more hard-pressed by the rush of daily life than even an Anglican bishop. So I do not speak from any lofty perch of personal achievement. I am down in the valley with most of you. But, strangely enough, this book, especially the preparation for writing it, has forced upon me the realization of the lowness of my own spiritual valley. The writing of these chapters has made me more anxious than ever to get out.

I am coming more and more to believe that the real solution for many of the difficulties that you and I have been studying in these chapters is to be found in one type of mental and physical activity alone: in the Christian faith and in Catholic practice. And I am realizing more and more that no man and no woman can really be of constructive help to the confused, unhappy people of this unbelieving world, unless they themselves are dynamic Christians; not static forms of energy that have reached a certain level and that remain there; but forms that are intensely activated, that go on and on developing and diversifying their spiritual reactions, until they set up in the world so much radiant heat, and so much light, that the darkness begins to grow thin at its deepest edges and the earth to become full of the knowledge of God as the waters cover the sea.

Make "time for God" then in your lives. A strange expression, to "make time." Perhaps it would be more accurate to say that God makes time for us, and that we must "find" time for Him. To find a thing one must really look for it. But sometimes one stumbles on a precious object. Let me give you one that I stumbled on. My last gift to you at the end of this chapter.

Not long ago I was in the house of a friend of my sister. This friend is a devout Roman Catholic, head of a family, a woman of many duties, of many obligations. She has an old Irish maid. I had come to her cottage unannounced. It was about ten o'clock in the morning. Mrs. X—my sister's friend —was lying on her sofa. The maid has just brought her the morning post, a tea tray, and some books. I heard the maid say, as she put down her tray:

"There now, I think you've got everything you need. Here's the tea and the newspaper. There's your household account books. And the new novel. And here—here's your *Ten Minutes for God.*"

I tiptoed out of the front door. I did not want to interrupt that ten minutes for God.

But what was it? It was a small book of Meditations on the Gospels—a little book that you can slip into your pocket or carry in your handbag. "Dix Minutes à Dieu."[6] Each medita-

[6]By Y. D'Isne. *Courtes meditations sur l'Evangile.* 18th to 22nd thousand (Paris (VI): L. Lethellieux, 10 Rue Casette, 1916).

tion is so simply arranged, so full of useful happy suggestions and you need "find" no more time than ten minutes for God, and for your soul.

If my sister's friend had had this little book lying on her "prie-Dieu" in the recesses of her bed-room, I should not have been so impressed by it. But the book was brought to her, with the morning post, with the newspaper, with her account books. It was a part of her every day's morning activity. Her *Ten Minutes for God* was as definitely a mode of her mental reactions as the reading of the paper, or the addition of the figures in her account books. And that is what I should like to urge upon you all. Take your ten minutes for God—whenever and wherever you can find them. I know that you have your regular hours with Him; your hours of daily prayer; your hours at the Holy Sacrifice; the hours or half hours of your meditations, your spiritual reading. But, believe me, "the ten minutes" are important also. If you can make such occasional "ten minutes" a kind of spiritual salt, with which to season the whole twenty-four hours of each day of your lives, you will have found the right antidote to all the hurry and rush, to all the anxieties and fears and obsessions, to all the temptations of the sexual or the domestic life that have formed the subject matter of this book.

A life that gets its pervading savor from such "ten minutes for God" soon makes itself felt in the saltless lives that surround it. It will give tone and taste to the most insipid environment. And, physiologists will tell you, that without the presence of salt—as a chemical entity—there can be no life. For all life comes originally from the sea. Salt is as necessary in the blood of our bodies as it is everywhere else. "Ye are the salt of the earth." Unless you can keep your mental and spiritual lives seasoned and vivified by frequent contact with the source of all life, of all growth, you will indeed soon lose your savor and be good for nothing.

To be able to interpenetrate with the salt of the spiritual life the whole mass of human reactions—the daily duties of your own life and the lives of others—that is what I have really been trying to teach you. Whether I have succeeded or not, must rest, not with me, but with you.

Finito libro sit laus et gloria Christo.
Qui scripsit scribat semper, cum Domino vivat.

A DESCRIPTIVE LIST OF BOOKS ON MORALS, MORAL THEOLOGY, AND PSYCHIATRY, ETC.

TO BE REFERRED TO IN CONNECTION WITH CHAPTER I

A DESCRIPTIVE LIST OF BOOKS ON MORALS, MORAL THEOLOGY, AND PSYCHIATRY, ETC.

I. The Roman Catholic Authorities on Moral Theology.
Some of these are in Latin, others in English.
A. Standard authors. Of earlier date.

1. *Summa theologiae moralis,* scholarum usui accommodavit H. Noldin, S.J. 5 Vols., editio quinta, oeniponte, Innsbruck, Felicien Rauch, 1905 (a new edition appeared about 1925). "De principiis, de sexto, de poenis," etc. Concise, but without case material.

2. *Theologia moralis,* auctore Augustino Lehmkuhl, S.J. 2 Vols., editio duodecima, Friburgi Brisgoviae, B. Herder, 1914.

3. *Synopsis theologiae moralis et pastoralis ad mentem S. Thomae et S. Alphonsi hodiernis moribus accommodata.* 4 Vols. Vol. I., *De poenitentia et matrimonio et ordine,* Ad. Tanquerey. Baltimore, St. Mary's Seminary, S. S. Tornaci (Belgiae), 1902.

4. *Theologia moralis per modum conferentiarum,* autore clarissimo P. Benjamin Elbel, O.S.F., novis curis edidit P. F. Irenaeus Bierbaum, O.S.F. Editio secunda, 3 Vols., Paderbornae, J. W. Schroeder, 1894. One of the best of the older books, with compendious case material.

Then of quite supreme value, because of their detailed discussions of modern moral problems and their marvelous bibliographies, are:

B. More modern works, 1920 and later.

1. In Latin.

a) *Compendium theologiae moralis,* 2 Vols., 14th ed. by P. Ioanne B. Ferreres, S.J. Barcelona, 1928. See especially the Index scriptorum and Catalogus operum in Vol. I, pp. xx–li. In Vol. II see the section on Holy Matrimony (pp. 507–645) with a discussion of Birth Control (pp. 635–644), giving the actual decisions of the Roman Holy Office (Nos. 1160–1165, pp. 643–645).

b) *Theologiae moralis principia, responsa, concilia,* by Arthurus Vermeersch, S.J. 5 Vols., editio altera, Bruges, 1926–1930. See especially, Vol. IV, "De castitate et vitiis oppositis cum parte moralii de sponsalibus et matrimonio," with a very modern bibliography on pp. 113–143.

c) *Tractatus theologico-canonicus de sponsalibus et matrimonio,* by Al. de Smet, S.T.D. 4 ed. Bruges, 1927. Best modern Roman treatise on matrimony and allied questions. Valuable for bibliography, pp. xxiii–xxiv; the section on sources, "de fontibus," pp. xvii-xxii; the decisions on birth control (onanismus), secs. 240–248.

2. In English.

a) Roman authors.

(1) *Moral Theology: A Complete Course Based on St. Thomas Aquinas and the Best Modern Authorities,* by John A. McHugh, O.P. and Charles J. Callan, O.P. 2 Vols., New York, J. F. Wagner, 1929.

(2) *Readings on Fundamental Moral Theology,* by the Rt. Rev. Louis J. Nau. New York, Pustet, 1926. Useful for fundamentals.

(3) *A Manual of Moral Theology for English-speaking Countries.* 6th ed. by Thomas Slater, S.J. 2 Vols., New York, Benziger, 1928. A very useful book. See especially, "A Short History of Moral Theology," in Vol. II, pp. 305–337. Still more valuable, although now out of print, is the same author's *Cases of Conscience: Arranged for English-speaking countries,"* 2 Vols. I advise every student to read at least parts of these volumes if he can find them. They contain the best case histories I know; they show also the worst, most legalistic side of Roman casuistry.

b) Anglican authors.

(1) *Moral Theology,* by Francis J. Hall and Frank H. Hallock. New York, Longmans, 1924.

(2) The Series *Studies in Moral Theology* by Kenneth E. Kirk. New York, Longmans. *Ignorance, Faith*

and Conformity, 1925. *Conscience and its Problems:
An Introduction to Casuistry,* 1927. *Some Principles
of Moral Theology and their Application,* 1930.
Three important volumes. Kirk is the only Anglican
who writes on Moral Theology with the authority
of one who knows the entire field.

All these books except the first three (Noldin, Lehmkuhl and
Tanquerey) are modern works; all up to date, all very much worth
while. No one would expect you to wade through the whole five
volumes of Vermeersch, but you should at least know what they
look like inside the cover. All the titles mentioned, except Kirk's,
deal with moral theology from what one may call the traditional
legalistic or schematic point of view. Human behavior is considered as consisting of efforts to attain the three theological virtues; as offenses against each one of the ten commandments; as a
falling short of each of the three Christian duties; as imperfect or
sinful reactions to the various ecclesiastical laws that govern the
reception of each of the seven sacraments. In a word, these books
look more like law books than theological treatises, and they are,
in the best sense, statements of the Christian laws of behavior.
Some of the old books (like Elbel) have a certain amount of casu-
istic material; that is, imaginary case histories. But most of them
(except the out of print volumes of Slater) deal with antiquated
conditions and difficulties.

In the next group of books there is much less system, and more
case histories, and more insistence on what the writer believes than
on what the Church teaches. The titles of these volumes are legion.
Only a few of them are written by men who have any faith in
supernatural motives or ends. But the fact that such books are
constantly appearing bears witness to the revival of interest in
problems of behavior and in the mental states that make certain
types of behavior possible to understand. I do not mention these
books in order of merit; but simply as they come to hand.

II. ENGLISH BOOKS ON PSYCHIATRY, MENTAL THERAPEUTICS AND
   MENTAL DIFFICULTIES IN GENERAL.
   A. Books primarily for laymen.
      1. *Psychology in the Service of the Soul,* by L. D. Weather-

head. New York, Macmillan, 1930. The author is a well-known Methodist minister of Leeds, England, who has taken the trouble to inform himself as thoroughly as he can on the whole subject of mental therapeutics. One of the few books on the subject that is not written from a purely materialistic point of view.

2. *Body, Mind and Spirit,* by Doctor Elwood Worcester and Canon Samuel McComb. Boston, Marshall Jones, 1931. Valuable chiefly for the case histories it contains; the records of Doctor Worcester's personal experiences in dealing with certain types of mental difficulties.

Of much greater and of permanent value are the three following books:

B. Books on Psychiatry intended primarily for the physician, but useful to laymen also.

1. *The Human Mind,* by Doctor Karl Menninger. New York, Knopf, 1930. A very useful presentation of the facts of modern psychiatry.

2. *Outlines of Psychiatry,* by Doctor William A. White. 11th ed. Washington, D. C., Nervous and Mental Disease Pub. Co., 1926. Difficult for the non-medical reader, but useful as a reference book for the symptoms of various types of mental illness.

   Introduction to the Study of the Mind, by Doctor William A. White. *Nervous and Mental Disease Monograph Series. No. 38.* Washington, D. C., Nervous and Mental Disease Pub. Co., 1924.

3. *Factors in the Sex Life of Twenty-two Hundred Women,* by Doctor Katherine Bement Davis. New York, Harpers, 1929. Contains a mass of valuable and often surprising facts.

There is another group of books of a somewhat different type. They deal with human behavior from the standpoint of the pastor, and may be classified under the head of Pastoral Theology or Pastoral Medicine. I shall limit ourselves to a few titles:

III. PASTORAL THEOLOGY, PASTORAL MEDICINE AND BOOKS OF SPIRITUAL DIRECTION.

A. Pastoral Theology.

1. *Pastoral Theology,* by James M. Hoppin. 7th ed., New York, Funk and Wagnalls, No date. A Protestant book that contains little useful material for the priest, but even Catholic pastors might read with profit sec. 22, pp. 387–402 on "Qualifications for the Cure of Souls."

2. *Pastoral Theology,* by the Rt. Rev. Wm. Stang, D.D. Revised according to the New Code of Canon Law. New York, Benziger Bros., 1921. A Roman book with chapters on Preaching, Catechizing, the Sacraments, and Pastoral Direction. Valuable is the sense of historical continuity in the exercise of the pastoral office, which the writer maintains by constant useful quotations from St. Gregory Nazianzen, St. Ambrose, St. Gregory the Great, from decisions of the Sacred Congregations and Provincial Councils. Worth reading carefully is the section on "The Ministry of Reconciliation," pp. 159–189. But one hopes that it will not be necessary to tell Anglican priests never to wet "the finger or thumb in turning the pages of the Missal" and "never to spit on the altar" (p. 145).

B. Pastoral Medicine. There are useful books of this type in German. Those in English are few. The best I know is:

1. *Pastoral Medicine: A Handbook for the Catholic Clergy,* by Alexander E. Sanford, M.D. New edition revised and enlarged by the Rev. Walter M. Drum, S.J. New York, J. F. Wagner, 1905. Although somewhat out of date, this is a useful handbook. Under Hygiene, there is a section on Death, Signs of Death, Burial. Another useful section on First Aid to the Injured, pp. 175–219. Also the discussion of Abortion, p. 88, and of Celibacy, p. 101. The section on Mental Diseases, pp. 124–149, is rather antiquated, but is the only attempt that I know of to put into pastors' hands some knowledge of these important matters. The really important contribution is in the appendix, pp. 266–320, "Neurasthenia in its Pastoral Psychiatric Aspects," although the word neurasthenia is improperly used in

this connection. Psychoneuroses of compulsion, obsession and inhibition are described, and actual cases are cited in the form of complete psychiatric case histories.

C. Modern Books on Spiritual Direction. These are books of direction for the priest as confessor and spiritual guide. Of these—and they are many—two modern works are important.

1. *Epitome morale-asceticum de sacramenti poenitentiae ministerio,* by Sac. Sebastianus Uccello. Taurini-Roma, Libraria Marietti, 1930. Written in easy Latin in compact form. This is the best and most helpful of all the Guides for Confessors and Directors that I know. It ought to take the place of Doctor Pusey's translation of Gaume's *Neoconfessarius* and of Doctor Webb's *Cure of Souls* that is long out of print.

2. *Les voies ordinaires de la vie spirituelle: Traité de théologia ascétique,* par Mgr. Albert Farges. Paris, Librairie St. Paul, 1924. This book has been done into English as *The Ordinary Ways of the Spiritual Life* and is easily obtainable. But those who read French should have it in the original. The best, most helpful guide that I know for a priest who is trying to develop his own spiritual life and the spiritual lives of his people.

3. *Vademecum theologiae moralis in usum examinandorum et confessarium* auctore Dominico M. Pruemer, O.P. Friburgi Brisgoviae, Herder et Cie., 1921.

Let me set down also the titles of two books just published. They have nothing at all to do with religion, or with moral theology or even with ethics. But they offer us valuable material.

IV. MODERN BOOKS ON SUBJECTS ALLIED TO PSYCHIATRY.

A. *The Emotions of Men,* by Frederick H. Lund. New York, McGraw-Hill Book Co., 1930. "Man," says the author, "is not a rational being. It is emotion, not reason, that governs most of his actions." I commend chapter II, "How Emotions Shape Man's Beliefs," pp. 19–59, with the section, p. 25, on "The Conflict between Religion and Science," also

"The Physical Basis of the Emotions," pp. 109–130, and "Emotional Differences in the Sexes," pp. 192–225.

B. *The Physical Basis of Personality*, by Charles R. Stockard, Professor of Anatomy in Cornell Med. College. New York, W. W. Norton & Co., Inc., 1931. This is an objective statement of morphological experiment, full of interesting facts and suggestions. See especially, "Developmental or Embryonic Personality," pp. 152–167, "Postnatal Development and Periodic Changes in Personality," pp. 199–217, and "Personality and Structural Types among Normal Individuals," pp. 275–300.

Last of all for your general reading and in order to get some historical idea of the development of Christian morals and of moral theology let me recommend to you most warmly a series that is being published in France: *Les Moralistes Chrétiens*. Here are volumes on the early Fathers, Tertullian, St. Cyprian, St. Basil, etc. Mediæval moral teaching is represented by a volume on St. Thomas Aquinas. More modern tradition by St. François de Sales, Bourdaloue, etc. Each volume contains a translation of the Greek or Latin text of the early authors with an historical introduction and a bibliography. The selections from each man's writings are arranged according to the usual divisions of moral theology: principles, the Christian virtues, the methods of attaining to them, etc. The volumes are small—can slip easily into a pocket —and they are inexpensive.

V. Christian Morality from an Historical Standpoint.

Les Moralistes Chrétiens: Textes et Commentaires. Paris, Librairie Lecoffre, Rue Buonaparte 90, 1924 to 1931. The complete list is as follows:

Bourdaloue, par R. Daeschler.
Clément d'Alexandrie, par L'Abbé Gustave Bardy.
Malebranche, par Henri Gouhier.
Pierre Nicole, par Emile Thouverez.
Pascal, par Jacques Chevalier. 2 Vols.
Les Pères du désert, par Jean Brémond. 2 Vols.
Saint Basile, par L'Abbé Jean Rivière.

Saint François de Sales, par Paul Archambault.
Saint Jean Chrysostome, par Ph. E. LeGrand.
Saint Thomas d'Aquin, par Etienne Gilson.
Tertullien et Saint Cyprien, par le Chanoine L. Bayard.
(Other volumes in preparation.)

A BIBLIOGRAPHY OF PASTORAL PSYCHIATRY

I

MORAL AND PASTORAL THEOLOGY

Briscoe, J. F. *The Priest in the Confessional.* Being papers read
at the Priests' Convention, May, 1931. Edited by Rev. J. F.
Briscoe. London, the Faith Press, 1931.

Dewar, Lindsay, and Hudson, Cyril E. *A Manual of Pastoral
Psychology.* London, Philip Allan, 1932.

Elbel, P. Benjamin, O.S.F. *Theologia moralis per modum conferentiarum,* autore clarissimo P. Benjamin Elbel, O.S.F.,
novis curis edidit P. F. Irenæus Bierbaum, O.S.F. Editio
secunda, 3 Vols., Paderbornae, J. W. Schroeder, 1894. One
of the best of the older books, with compendious case material.

Ferreres, P. Ioanne B., S.J. *Compendium theologiae moralis ad
morman codicis canonici,* 2 Vols. Editio decima quarta, sep-
tima post codicem. Barcelona, Eugenius Subirana, 1928.

Hall, Francis J., and Hallock, Frank H. *Moral Theology.* London and New York, Longmans, 1924.

Hoppin, James M. *Pastoral Theology.* 7th ed., New York,
Funk and Wagnalls, no date.

Kirk, Kenneth E. *Some Principles of Moral Theology and their
Application (Studies in Moral Theology,* I). London and
New York, Longmans, 1930.

—— *Ignorance, Faith and Conformity (Studies in Moral Theology,* II). London and New York, Longmans, 1925.

—— *Conscience and its Problems: An Introduction to Casuistry
(Studies in Moral Theology,* III). London and New York,
Longmans, 1927.

Lehmkuhl, Augustinus, S.J. *Theologia moralis,* auctore Augustino Lehmkuhl, S.J. 2 Vols, editio duodecima, Friburgi Brisgoviae, B. Herder, 1914.

Les Moralistes Chretiens: Textes et Commentaires. Paris, Librairie
Lecoffre.

(1) *Les Pères du desert,* par Jean Brémond. Introduction par
Henri Brémond. Deuxième éd. 2 Vols.

(2) *Pascal: Pensées sur la vérité de la religion chrétienne,* par Jacques Chevalier. Troisieme ed. revue. 2 Vols., 1927.

(3) Pierre Nicole, par Emile Thouverez, 1926.

(4) *Malebranche,* par Henri Gouhier, 1929.

(5) *Clément d'Alexandrie,* par L'Abbé Gustave Bardy, 1926.

(6) *Bourdaloue,* par R. Daeschler, 1929.

(7) *Saint Thomas d'Aquin,* par Etienne Gilson. Cinquième ed. revue et corrigée, 1930.

(8) *Saint Jean Chrysostome,* par Ph. E. LeGrand. Deuxième ed., 1924.

(9) *Tertullien et Saint Cyprien,* par le Chanoine L. Bayard, 1930.

(10) *Saint François de Sales,* par Paul Archambault, 1930.

(11) *Saint Basile: Évêque de Cesarée,* par L'Abbé Jean Rivière, 1925.

McHugh, John A., O.P., and Callan, Charles J., O.P. *Moral Theology: A Complete Course Based on St. Thomas Aquinas and the Best Modern Authorities,* 2 Vols. New York, J. F. Wagner, 1929.

Nau, Louis J. *Readings on Fundamental Moral Theology.* New York, Pustet, 1926.

Noldin, H., S.J. *Summa theologiae moralis,* scholarum usui accommodavit H. Noldin, S.J. 5 Vols., editio quinta oeniponte, Innsbruck, Felicien Rauch, 1905 (a new edition appeared about 1925). "De principiis, de sexto, de poenis," etc. Concise, but without case material.

Preston, John Hyde. "D.D. versus M.D." See *Magazine Article Readings,* edited by Ernest Brennecke and D. L. Clark, pp. 523–531. New York, Macmillan, 1931.

Pruemer, Dominico M., O.P. *Vademecum theologiae moralis in usum examinandorum et confessarium.* Friburgi Brisgoviae, B. Herder, 1921.

de San, Ludovico, S.J. *Tractatus de poenitentia,* auctore Ludovico de San, S.J. Bragis, apud Carolum Beyaert, 1900. Universa theologia scholastica quam in collegio Lovaniensi tradebant XL. de San, G. Lahousse et A. Vermeersch.

Sanford, Alexander E. *Pastoral Medicine: A Handbook for the*

Catholic Clergy. New ed. revised and enlarged by the Rev. Walter M. Drum, S.J. New York, J. F. Wagner, 1905.

Slater, Thomas, S.J. *A Manual of Moral Theology for English-speaking Countries.* 2 Vols., 6th and revised ed. New York, Benziger, 1928.

Stang, William. *Pastoral Theology.* Revised according to the New Code of Canon Law. New York, Benziger, 1921.

Tanquerey, Ad., S.S. *Synopsis theologiae moralis et pastoralis ad mentem S. Thomae et S. Alphonsi hodiernis moribus accommodata.* 4 Vols. Vol. I., *De poenitentia et matrimonio et ordine.* Baltimore, St. Mary's Seminary, S. S. Tornaci (Belgiae), 1902.

Vermeersch, Arthurus, S.J. *Theologiae moralis principia, responsa, concilia,* by Arthurus Vermeersch, S.J., doctor iuris et scientiarum politicarum theologiae moralis professor in pontificia universitate Gregoriana. 5 Vols. See especially Vol. IV., "De castitate et vitiis oppositis cum parte moralii de sponsalibus et matrimonio." Altera editio, auctior et emendato. Bruges, Charles Beyaert, 1926–30. (Paris, Charles Beyaert.)

II

BIOLOGY, MEDICINE, AND PSYCHIATRY

Alexander, Dr. Franz. "The Present Status of Psychoanalysis as a Psychologic and Therapeutic System." *Archives of Neurology and Psychiatry,* Nov., 1931, Vol. 26, No. 5, pp. 1108–1112. Chicago, American Medical Association.

Association for Research in Nervous and Mental Disease. *Proceedings of the Association for Research in Nervous and Mental Disease: A Series of Investigations and Reports.* "Heredity and Mental Disease," Vol. III. New York, Hoeber, 1923. Also "Epilepsy and the Convulsive States; An Investigation of the Most Recent Advances," Vol. VII, Baltimore, Williams and Wilkins, 1931. "Schizophrenia," Vols. V and X. "Manic Depressive Psychoses," Vol. XI.

Bleuler, M. "A Contribution to the Problem of Heredity Among Schizophrenics." *Journal of Nervous and Mental Disease,*

Vol. 74, No. 4, Oct., 1931. New York, Dr. S. E. Jelliffe, editor and publisher.

Bowman, Karl M., and Raymond, Alice F. "A Statistical Study of Delusions in Manic Depressive Psychoses." *The American Journal of Psychiatry*, Vol. XI (old series Vol. LXXXIII), No. 1, pp. 111ff. Baltimore, Johns Hopkins Press, 1931.

Ebaugh, F. C. "Some Present Day Trends in the Teaching of Psychiatry." *Journal of Nervous and Mental Disease*, Vol. 73, p. 384. April, 1931. New York, Dr. S. E. Jelliffe, editor and publisher.

Fliess, Wilhelm. *Der Ablauf des Lebens: Grundlegung zur Exakten Biologie.* Leipzig und Wien, Deuticke, 1906.

Freeman, Walter. "Psychochemistry: Some Psychochemical Factors in Mental Disorders." *Journal of the American Medical Association*, Vol. 97, No. 5, Aug. 1, 1931, pp. 293 ff. Chicago. Interesting new aspects of physical causes of mental illness.

Henry, George W. "Gastrointestinal Functions in Manic Depressive Psychoses." *The American Journal of Psychiatry*, Vol. XI (old series Vol. LXXXVIII), No. 1, pp. 19 ff. Baltimore, Johns Hopkins Press, 1931.

Hinsie, Leland E., and Katz, Siegfried E. "Treatment of Manic Depressive Psychoses: A Survey of the Literature." *The American Journal of Psychiatry*, Vol. XI (old series Vol. LXXXVIII), No. 1, pp. 131 ff. Baltimore, Johns Hopkins Press, 1931.

Hoffman, Frederick L. *The Suicide Record of 1930.* Reprinted from the London *Spectator*, May 14, 1931.

Jewett, Harold A. *A Report of Recent Evidence of Telepathy in Hypnosis.* Fredonia, New York, 1930.

Kempf, Edward J. *Psychopathology.* St. Louis, Bosby, 1920.

Kretschmer, Ernst. *Physique and Character: An Investigation of the Nature of Constitution and of the Theory of Temperament.* Translated from the second revised and enlarged edition by W. J. H. Sprott. London, Kegan Paul, 1925. German edition: *Koerperbau und Charakter: Untersuchungen zum Konstitutions-Problem und sur Lehre von den Temperamenten.* Berlin, Julius Springer, 1921.

—— *The Psychology of Men of Genius*. Translated from the German by R. B. Cattell. London, Kegan Paul, 1931.

Lambert, Helen C. *A General Survey of Psychical Phenomena*. Foreword by Stanley De Brath. New York, Knickerbocker Press, 1928.

Lund, Frederick H. *Emotions of Men*. New York, McGraw-Hill, 1930.

Menninger, Karl A. *The Human Mind*. New York, Knopf, 1930.

Ordway, Thomas, M.D. "The Similarity between the Aims and Ideals of Physicians Today and Those of Seventy-five or More Years Ago with Particular Reference to Conservative Therapeutics." *The Clifton Medical Bulletin*, Vol. 17, No. 2, Apr., 1931, pp. 77–85. Clifton Springs Sanitarium and Clinic, Clifton Springs, N. Y.

Prince, Morton, and Drs. Ferrish, Putnam, Taylor, Sidis, Waterman, Donley, Jones, and T. Williams. *Psychotherapeutics: A Symposium*. Boston and Toronto, Badger, Gorham Press, 1910.

Reynell, W. R. "Sexual Neurosis." Royal Society of Medicine, *Proceedings*, May, 1931. (Section of Urology, pp. 27–36.) London and New York, Longmans.

Steckel, Wilhelm. *Peculiarities of Behavior: Wandering Minds, Dipsomania, Cleptomania, Pyromania and Allied Impulsive States*. Authorized Eng. ed., translated by S. Van Tesslaar, 2 Vols. New York, Boni and Liveright, 1924.

Stockard, Charles R. *The Physical Basis of Personality*. New York, W. W. Norton, 1931.

Weatherhead, Leslie D. *Psychology in the Service of the Soul*. New York, Macmillan, 1930.

White, William A. *An Introduction to the Study of the Mind*. (*Nervous and Mental Disease Monograph Series. No. 38.*) Washington, D. C., Nervous and Mental Disease Pub. Co., 1924.

—— *Outlines of Psychiatry*. 11th ed., Washington, D. C., Nervous and Mental Disease Pub. Co., 1926.

Zilboorg, Gregory. "Depressive Reactions Related to Parenthood." Reprinted from *The American Journal of Psychiatry,*

Vol. X, No. 6, May, 1931, pp. 927–962. Baltimore, Johns Hopkins Press.

III

MENTAL HYGIENE

American Foundation for Mental Hygiene. *Twenty Years of Mental Hygiene.* New York, published by the American Foundation for Mental Hygiene, Inc., 1930.

Bumke, Oswald. *Die Grenzen der Geistigen Gesundheit.* Rede gehalten beim Stiftungsfest der Universitaet Muenchen am 22. Juni 1929 von Oswald Bumke. Muenchen, Max Hueber Verlag, 1929.

Coster, Geraldine. "Religious Training of Children." The London *Spectator,* Mar. 21, 1931, pp. 446–7. (Psychology and Religion.)

University of Notre Dame. *Official Bulletin,* Vol. 25, No. 1. Report of the Prefect of Religion with Supplementary Documents. Notre Dame, Indiana, 1930.

Wilbur, R. L. "Mental Health as a National Problem." *Journal of American Medical Association,* Vol. 96, p. 994, Mar. 28, 1931. Chicago.

Ziegler, Lloyd H. "Mental Hygiene and Its Relationship to the Medical Profession." Read before the Section on Nervous and Mental Diseases at the 82nd Annual Session of the American Medical Association, Philadelphia, June 10, 1931. Printed in *The Journal of the American Medical Association,* Vol. 97, No. 16, Oct. 17, 1931, pp. 1119–1122. Chicago.

IV

SEXUAL PROBLEMS

(1) Married Life: Heteroerotic Reactions.
(2) Contraceptive Methods and Birth Control.
(3) Homoerotism.

Bloch, Iwan. *The Sexual Life of Our Time. Complete Encyclopedia of the Sexual Sciences,* by Iwan Bloch, translated from the German. New York, Eugenics Pub. Co., 1931.

(1) Married Life: Heteroerotic Reactions.

Brosnahan, Timothy, S.J. *The Heart of a Holy Woman.* New York, America Press, 1927.

Connell, Francis J., C.SS.R. *The Catholic Doctrine of Matrimony.* New York, America Press, 1929.

Courtship and Marriage. *Practical Instructions by Priests of the Society of Jesus.* Associate editors of *America.* New York, America Press, 1928.

Dickenson, Robert D., and Beam, Laura. *A Thousand Marriages.* Opposed to former figures: 56 per cent healthy, 27 per cent below par, 17 per cent ill. Baltimore, Williams and Wilkins, 1932.

Dennett, Mary Ware. The Sex Side of Life: An Explanation for Young People. Published by the author, 1928.

Deming, Julia. "Problems Presented by Children of Parents Forced to Marry." *The American Journal of Orthopsychiatry,* Vol. II, No. 1, pp. 70–82. Menasha, Wis., George Banta Pub. Co.

Fliess, Wilhelm. *Die Beziehungen zwischen Nase und weiblichen Geschlechtsorganen in ihrer biologischen Bedeutung dargestellt.* Leipzig, 1897. Also *Der Ablauf des Lebens.* Leipzig, Deuticke, 1906.

Husslein, Joseph, S.J. *The Wedding Ring.* New York, America Press, 1929.

Kittredge, George Lyman. *Witchcraft in Old and New England.* Cambridge, Mass., Harvard Univ. Press, 1928.

Le Buffe, Francis P., S.J. *Broken Homes.* New York, America Press, 1925.

Lonergan, William I., S.J. *Eugenics.* (Problems of Sex.) New York, America Press, 1927.

Marriage and Divorce. *Bulletin of Sanctity of Marriage Association,* No. 14. New York, Jan., 1930.

Meisel-Hess, Grete. *A Sexual Crisis: A Critique of Our Sex Life.* Authorized translation by Eden and Cedar Paul, with an introduction by W. J. Robinson. 3rd ed. New York, Critic and Guide Co., 1923.

Modern Morality-Wreckers. Reprinted from the *Catholic Mind.* New York, America Press.

Phelps, William Lyon. *Love.* New York, Dutton, 1928.

Placzek, S. *Das Geschlechtsleben der Hysterischen: Eine medizinische, soziologische und forensische Studie.* 2 auflage, Bonn, Marcus und Weber's Verlag, 1922.

Power, Albert, S.J. *The Tangle of Marriage.* New York, America Press, 1925.

Robinson, William J. *Sexual Truths Versus Sexual Lies, Misconceptions and Exaggerations.* Hoboken, N. J., American Biological Society, 1919.

—— *Married Life and Happiness: The Menopause or Change of Life.* New York, Eugenics Pub. Co., 1931.

de Smet, Al. *Theologia Brugensis: Tractatus theologico-canonicus de sponsalibus et matrimonio.* Editio Quarta, Bruges, Charles Beyaert, 1927.

Stetson, Caleb R. *Civil and Religious Marriage,* by Caleb R. Stetson, Rector of the Parish of Trinity Church in the City of New York.

—— *Proposed Canon on Marriage. Birth Control. Opposition to the Remarriage of Divorced Persons by a Priest of this Church.* Year Book and Register of the Parish of Trinity Church in the City of New York, 1930. Published by authority. See pp. XXI and XXIII.

Stopes, Marie Carmichael. *Married Love: Or Love in Marriage,* edited by W. J. Robinson. New York, Eugenics Pub. Co., 1927, and Putnam.

Tierney, Richard H. *The Church and the Sex Problem.* Catholic Sociology. Riordan, M. J., *Agenics.* New York, America Press, 1929.

Weiniger, Otto. *Geschlecht und Charakter: Eine prinzipielle untersuchung.* Fünfte unveränderte auflage. Wien und Leipzig, Wilhelm Braumüller, 1905. Authorized English translation from the 6th German edition, under title *Sex and Character.* New York, Putnam, 1906.

Zilboorg, Gregory. "Side Lights in Parent-Child Antagonism." *American Journal of Orthopsychiatry,* Vol. II, No. 1, pp. 35–43. Menasha, Wis., George Banta Pub. Co., 1932.

(2) Contraceptive Methods and Birth Control.

Bureau for Contraceptive Advice. *Third Report,* 1931. 1028 N. Broadway, Baltimore, Md.

de Guchteneere, Raoul. *Judgment on Birth Control: A Human Document on Human Life.* New York, Macmillan, 1932. A very valuable new book. The author, a well-known physician, holds that birth control is not only immoral but unsound.

Dowling, M. P., S.J. *Race-Suicide.*
Blakely, Paul L., S.J.: "Conscious Birth-Restriction."
Ryan, John A.: "Birth control: An Open Letter."
Blakely, Paul L., S.J.: "The Absurdity of Large Families."
Wiltbye, John: "Four-fifths of a Child."
New York, America Press, 1925.

Himes, Norman E.
(1) *Charles Knowlton's Revolutionary Influence on the English Birth-rate.* Reprinted from *The New England Journal of Medicine,* Vol. 199, No. 10, pp. 461–465, Sept. 6, 1928. Mass. Medical Society, Boston.
(2) British Birth Control Clinics: Some Results and Eugenic Aspects of their Work. *Eugenics Review.*

Himes, Norman E., and Verna C.
(3) *Birth Control for the British Working Classes: A Study of the First Thousand Cases to Visit an English Birth Control Clinic.* Reprinted from *Hospital Social Service,* XIX, 1929, pp. 578–617.

Himes, Norman E.
(4) *Contraceptive Methods:* The Types Recommended by Nine British Birth Control Clinics. Reprinted from *The New England Journal of Medicine,* Vol. 202, No. 18, pp. 866–873, May 1, 1930. Mass. Medical Society, Boston.
(5) *A Critical Review of Medical Aspects of Contraception.* Reprinted from *The New England Journal of Medicine,* Vol. 200, No. 1, pp. 13–17, Jan. 3, 1929. Mass. Medical Society, Boston.
(6) *Eugenic Thought in the American Birth Control Movement 100 Years Ago.* Reprint from *Eugenics,* Vol. II, No.

5, May, 1929. Published by *Eugenical News,* Cold Spring Harbor, N. Y.

(7) *John Stuart Mills' Attitude Toward Neo-Malthusianism.* Reprinted from *The Economic Journal* (Supplement), Jan., 1929. New York, Macmillan, 1929.

(8) *McCulloch's Relation to the Neo-Malthusian Propaganda of His Time: An Episode in the History of English Neo-Malthusianism.* Reprinted from *The Journal of Political Economy,* Vol. XXXVII, No. 1, Feb., 1929. Chicago, Univ. of Chicago Press.

(9) *Robert Dale Owen, the Pioneer of American Neo-Malthusianism.* Reprinted from *The American Journal of Sociology,* Vol. XXXV, No. 4, Jan., 1930. Chicago, Univ. of Chicago Press.

McDowall, S. A.
"Problems of the Christian Conscience," III. "Marriage and Sex." The London *Spectator,* Oct. 24, 1931, pp. 519–520.

Pariogen Tablets. "Chloramine for 'Feminine Hygiene'." *Journal of American Medical Association,* Feb. 7, 1931, pp. 458–459. Chicago.

Robinson, William J. *Practical Prevention or the Technique of Birth Control.* Hoboken, N. J., American Biological Society, 1931.

Sanger, Margaret. *My Fight for Birth Control.* New York, Freethought Press Association, 1931.

Waddington, Joseph E. G. "Rational Birth Control: Its Hygienic, Social, Moral and Economic Implications." *Clinical Medicine and Surgery,* Vol. 38, No. 1, pp. 553–558. Chicago, American Journal of Clinical Medicine, Inc., Publishers.

(3) Homoerotism.

Ellis, Havelock. *Studies in the Psychology of Sex,* 6 Vols. Vol. II. *Sexual Inversion.* London, The University Press, 1900. German edition: *Das Konträre Geschlechtsgefühl.* Havelock Ellis and J. A. Symonds. Übersetzt von Dr. Hans Kurella, Leipzig, Max Spohr, 1896.

Hirschfeld, Magnus. *Jahrbuch für sexuelle Zwischenstufen—unter besonderer Berücksichtigung der Homosexualität,* 10 or more Vols. Editor, Dr. M. Hirschfeld. Leipzig, Max Spohr, 1898–1908. Containing an imposing amount of literary historical and legal material.

—— *Vierteljahrsberichte des Wissenschaftlich-humanitären Komitees.* Editor, Dr. Magnus Hirschfeld. Leipzig, Max Spohr, 1908–12. Valuable bibliographies, medico-legal discussions, clinical material.

The Invert: and his Social Adjustment by Anomaly (pseud.). Introduction by R. H. Thouless. Baltimore, Williams and Wilkins, 1930.

Symonds, John Addington. *A Problem in Greek Ethics: Being an Inquiry into the Phenomenon of Sexual Inversion. Addressed especially to Medical Psychologists and Jurists.* London, privately printed, 1901.

Willy, Collette.
    Claudine à l'Ecole.
    Claudine à Paris.
    Claudine en Menage.
    Claudine *s'en va.*
    New ed. Paris, Albin Michel, 1930.

V

THE INTERIOR LIFE

Bennett, Charles A. *A Philosophical Study of Mysticism: An Essay.* Reprinted with a preface by Rufus M. Jones. New Haven, Yale Univ. Press, 1931.

Farges, Mgr. Albert. *Les voies ordinaires de la vie spirituelle: Traité de théologie ascétique.* Paris, Librairie Saint-Paul, 1924.

Grant, Frederick C. *New Horizons of the Christian Faith.* Milwaukee, Morehouse, 1929. The Hale Lectures, 1927–28.

Herzfeld, K. F. "Science and Prayer." *Pastoral and Homiletic Review,* 1930, July.

Northcott, Rev. Father, C.R. *Ascetic Theology or the Science of*

Soul-training. London, Association for Promoting Retreats, 1928.

Shaw, Gilbert. *Introductory Notes to the Study of Devotional Literature.* Compiled by Gilbert Shaw. London, Association for Promoting Retreats, 1928.

—— *For Times of Recreation: Notes for Use during Private and Corporate Silent Times.* No. 1, *The Love of God.* London, Association for Promoting Retreats.

Uccello, Sac. Sebastianus. *Epitome morale-asceticum de sacramenti poenitentiae ministerio.* Taurini-Roma, Libraria Marietti, 1930.

Y. D'Isne. *Dix Minutes à Dieu: Courtes Meditations sur l'Evangile.* Paris, L. Lethellieux, 1916.

VI

MISCELLANEOUS

Hooker, Elizabeth R. *Hinterlands of the Church.* New York, Institute of Social and Religious Research, 1931.

Stiles, Henry Reed. *Bundling: Its Origin, Progress and Decline in America.* Privately issued for subscribers only, no date.

THE HALE LECTURES

The Rt. Rev. Charles Reuben Hale, D.D., LL.D., Bishop of Cairo, Bishop Coadjutor of Springfield, was born in 1837, consecrated Bishop in 1892, and died on Christmas Day in the year 1900.

In his will he bequeathed to Western Theological Seminary, now of Evanston, Ill., a fund to be held in trust "for the general purpose of promoting the Catholic Faith, in its purity and integrity, as taught in Holy Scripture, held by the Primitive Church, summed up in the Creeds, and affirmed by the undisputed General Councils, and, in particular, to be used only and exclusively for the establishment, endowment, printing, and due circulation of a yearly Sermon . . . and . . of Courses of Lectures."

The following lecture courses have thus far been delivered upon this Foundation:

Church Hymns and Church Music. By Peter C. Lutkin, Mus.D., A.G.O. Dean of the School of Music, Northwestern University. 1908.

The National Church of Sweden. By the Rt. Rev. John Wordsworth, D.D., LL.D., Bishop of Salisbury. 1910.

Biographical Studies in Scottish Church History. By the Rt. Rev. Anthony Mitchell, D.D., Bishop of Aberdeen and Orkney. 1913.

The Ethiopic Liturgy: Its Sources, Development, and Present Form. By the Rev. Samuel A. B. Mercer, D.D., Ph.D., Professor of Semitics, University of Toronto. 1915.

Some Aspects of Contemporary Greek Orthodox Thought. By the Rev. Frank Gavin, M.A., Ph.D., Th.D., Professor of Church History, General Theological Seminary. 1921.

New Horizons of the Christian Faith. By the Rev. Frederick C. Grant, D.D., S.T.D., Dean of Western Theological Seminary. 1928.

Christ in the Gospels. By the Rev. Burton Scott Easton, S.T.D., Ph.D., Professor of the Literature and Interpretation of the New Testament, General Theological Seminary. 1930.

Pastoral Psychiatry and Mental Health. By the Rev. John Rathbone Oliver, M.D., Ph.D., Associate in the History of Medicine at the Johns Hopkins University, Baltimore. 1932.

INDEX

Adler, Alfred, 287.
Age of consent, *see* Minors.
Agoraphobia, 141.
Alcoholism, its classification, 32; delirium tremens, 107, 112; strength of habit, 108; causes of, 109–111; cure of, 110–113; use of religion in combating, 112 f.; more toxic today, 114, 126–131; amnesia in, 114; cases of, 126–131.
Amnesia, in alcoholism, 114; in hysteria, 140.
Asthenic type, 60.
Autoerotism, definition of, 186; reaction on individual, 188–194, 199 f., 293 f.; universality of, 190; cases of, 190–194, 217–220; priest's part in dealing with, 191, 195–197; "purity talk," 192; harmful in excess, 195; as mortal or venial sin, 197 f.; its loveless character, 201.
Autonomous nervous system, 59.

Bad temper, 261.
Behaviorism, 2 f., 22.
Bi-erotics, *see* Homoerotism.
Binet and Simon, 123.
Birth control, *see* Contraceptive methods.
Blessed Sacrament, 17, 113, 152, 162, 171–173, 284–286, 291, 296 f.
Borderland and episodic states, *see* Psychoneurosis.
"Bundling," 206 f.

Cæsarius of Heisterbach, 198.
Causation of mental illness, *see* Mental illness.
Childless families, *see* Sterility.
Children, sexual life of, 180.
Christian Science, 10.
Cirkulaeres irresein, *see* Manic-depressive psychosis.
Claustrophobia, 142, 157.
Cocaine, 115.
Coitus interruptus, case of, 265 f.
"Collar and tie," 240.

Companionate marriage, 208.
Confessional, Protestant leaning toward, 13; as place for mental consultation, 14; difficulties in connection with, 15; *see also* Sacrament of Penance, Spiritual counsel.
Contraceptive methods, 208–213; their social result, 208 f.; attitudes of Anglican and Roman communions to, 209, 211 f.; prevalence among Roman Catholics, 210; "feminine hygiene," 210, 213; similarity to autoerotism, 211 f.; cases requiring, 212 f.
Convulsions, in epilepsy, 79; in paresis, 94.
Cushing, Dr. Harvey, 18.

Davis, Dr. Katherine Bement, 189 *n.*, 190.
Decameron, 228, 277.
Delirium tremens, *see* Alcoholism.
Delusions, definition of, 30; of persecution in schizophrenia, 54 f.; of persecution in paranoia, 77.
Dementia præcox, *see* Schizophrenia.
Demoniacal possession, 33; in sadism, 259.
Detumescence, 266.
Diagnosis, mental factor in, 11 f.
D'Isne, Y., 298.
Divorce, *see* Home.
Domestic Relations Courts, 226.
Drug addiction, 115–118; types of, 115; use of veronal, 117; mental habit in, 117 f.; connection with crime, 121; case of, 131–133.

Emotional immaturity, 231.
Esquinol, 33.
Euphoria, in manic-depressive psychosis, 40.

"Fairy," definition of, 253.
Farges, Mgr. Albert, 297.
Fear of impotence, 199 f.
Fear of physicians, 5.

CPSIA information can be obtained
at www.ICGtesting.com
Printed in the USA
LVHW041909151222
735317LV00004B/189